Death Ethics

DEATH ETHICS

*Religious and Cultural Values
in Prolonging and Ending Life*

Kenneth L. Vaux

Trinity Press International
Philadelphia

Trinity Press International
3725 Chestnut Street
Philadelphia, PA 19104

Cover design by Jim Gerhard.

Library of Congress Cataloging-in-Publication Data

Vaux, Kenneth L., 1939-
    Death ethics : religious and cultural values in prolonging and
ending life / Kenneth Vaux.
        p.   cm.
    Includes bibliographical references and index.
    ISBN 1-56338-045-5 (alk. paper)
    1. Euthanasia—Moral and ethical aspects.   2. Physician-assisted
suicide—Moral and ethical aspects.   3. Suicide—Moral and ethical
aspects.   4. Homicide—Moral and ethical aspects.   I. Title.
R726.V38   1992
179'.7—dc20   92-24701
                                                                    CIP

This book is printed on acid-free paper.

Printed in the United States of America.

92 93 94 95 96 97   6 5 4 3 2 1

Contents

Introduction

> I would gladly have my Life;
> but if that may not be,
> I have the next best thing to it
> which is death.[1]

Fairfax, in "Yeoman of the Guard"
Gilbert and Sullivan

In a previous book, *Birth Ethics*,[2] I attempted a broader way of conceiving ethics, one more receptive to the breadth and subtlety of the issues involved and responsive to a richer sense of good and evil. Taking many threads—ecological, biological, psychological, through theological and eschatological—we wove a tapestry of normative value regarding the inception of life. That tapestry sought to depict the moral color and depth of that particular realm of issues and that set of ethical principles. In that book, we lifted out one dimension of human-life ethics, the sphere of natality, and then displayed that zone of life into a set of moral issues including population control, genetics, abortion, decisions regarding imperiled newborns, and societal care for children. In this sequel volume, we turn from the initial to the terminal threshold of life. Now issues like suicide and euthanasia will be considered to further test the adequacy of the same multiphasic ethical scheme. I also hope to show the connections among death issues and the relationship of those with birth issues. Not only is geriatric triage, what Daniel Callahan calls "setting limits," inextricably associated with euthanasia, but euthanasia is related to eugenics as a society forms its biomedical vision. Similarly, the norms that nature gives, society generates, and God commands all intertwine to form an evaluative matrix. Complexity in ethics is a necessity.

This book is about prolonging and ending life, dying and killing. Unpleasant subjects, yes—but unavoidable. No set of issues so vex and perplex people who seek both to honor the being of others and to have mercy on the suffering. We will start with the most controversial issue of death ethics in our time: that of physician-assisted suicide and euthanasia. All over the world, but especially in societies where people die in hospitals surrounded by life-sustaining technologies, the agony of such decisions is being faced. In Missouri, a young woman lay in deep, irreversible coma for twelve years after an auto accident. The courts finally accepted her parents' wish to withdraw the feeding equipment.[3] In Minnesota, the hospital and physicians caring for an eighty-seven-year-old comatose woman asked the courts for permission to discontinue life support against the wishes of the family.[4] Across the ocean in Holland, a physician eases a patient with terminal lung cancer into the sleep of death, prescriptive law turning its head and allowing the practice. In the state of Washington, a political referendum tests whether the citizenry will accept active euthanasia. As the thread of this question weaves its way through the book, we will consider other death dealings: ecocide, nuclear winter, genocide, feticide, infanticide, and various species of homicide and suicide. Our central purpose, however, is not to develop a theoretical treatise on killing per se. I wish, rather, to examine the ethical challenges we all face in the experience of growing old, becoming infirm, and facing death.

The purpose of the book is to examine in a comprehensive and systematic way the human art of defying and delivering death. Along the way we will turn to the various ethical parameters of philosophy, theology, and history as these come into our experience and help us see what we must do and not do.

In the end, I hope to establish that it is morally legitimate in selected cases for doctors, families, and perhaps even parishes to aid in the death of persons who are irretrievably sick and in great suffering. I will contend that this "ethics of exception" is in keeping with our concerted moral tradition. More generally, I will contend that there is benign and malign killing, and that the distinction is of profound consequence. Beneath it all I hope to convince the reader that loving

and honoring our own life and that of another person is fully compat-
ible with the choice to accept even death in due season.

I contend that the boundaries of actual life situations—surfaces as
diverse as ecology and history—pose for us both possibilities and limitations, *imperativa* of freedom and *prohibitiva* of transgression. The
human moral capacity—call it reason or conscience—is stimulated to
ethical response by these forces. For example, the response of wonder
and dread is activated in the moral soul by ecological vastness and
splendor, the glory of creation evoking the negative and positive acts
of protection and stewardship of the environment. History, or the
weight of cumulative human experience, does the same as it activates
conviction in the anamnestic part of our soul called memory. Many
voices without and within call us to righteousness. This book hopes to
widen our perceptive range so that we hear more contributing instruments of that grand symphony.

I wish to make three substantive ethical claims. The first has
already been mentioned. Just as moral situations are infinitely complex, the moral reality—that normative bedrock that yields knowledge
of right and wrong—is also polyfactoral. I have arbitrarily designated
nine dimensions of reality (our experience of objective reality) that
convey moral truth. They fall into three groups:

Naturalistic:	ecologic, biologic
Rationalistic:	psychologic, politic, philosophic, historic
Theistic:	theologic, apocalyptic, eschatologic

Each sphere of moral direction and received insight has an integrity of
its own, is not superior or inferior to any other, and phases into its
cognate zone behind and beyond. For example, love for another
prompts us to moral commitments to protect and sustain that person.
Love is a phenomenon that arises from the emotive or psychic dimension of our being. It resides, therefore, in the psychic dimension of
ethics. Love is rooted in certain biological instincts, and it verges
toward reason and faith in expressions the Greeks called philia and
agape. Love sinks and soars into the richer atmosphere of the good.
Our first assumption in this book is the integrity, indispensability, and
complementarity of the myriad spheres of ethics.

A second assumption grows out of the first. Put simply as a thesis: naturalistic ethics pertain unless superseded by humanistic (rationalistic) values. Humanistic ethics pertain unless superseded by theistic values. Rather than elaborate this point here (it will be elucidated throughout the book), suffice it to say that I believe that the good is that which comes naturally unless that good is contradicted by the even finer reaches of our reason and conscience. Beyond rationality, extraordinary experiences, and transcending imperatives arise from the reality of God known to our moral mind and will. These imperatives supervene that which is natural, even rational. In death, for example, we confront the unknown and mysterious, touching *sacramentum*, the divine in our midst. Our decisions must reflect this "deep calling to deep."

A final assumption also has theological grounding. Redemption is the primal moral reality in nature, history, and existence. The paradigm of suffering, death, and transfiguration interprets the ethical significance of all that is and all that happens. Doing the good is an act of participation in that redemption and of facilitating that liberation.

Time and place always shape a book more than author or reader realize. As I write, I wish the reader to know the assumptions and the influences that bear on these reflections. I think this knowledge will enhance the critical understanding and reception of the work. A sabbatical leave in Oxford, England, has allowed a short time away from my regular work at the University of Illinois College of Medicine and its hospitals in Chicago. Sitting in a study on Banbury Road, overlooking the stately Victorian red brick homes of nineteenth-century England, one can see the memorable stone of fourteenth-century New College or Magdalene, or the market where Nicholas Ridley and Hugh Latimer were burned at the stake in the sixteenth century. Such an atmosphere steeps one in an outlook deeply cognizant of history and heritage. William Shakespeare, John Locke, Thomas Sydenham, Robert Boyle, John Donne, John Henry Newman, and countless others who walked these streets are close companions whose influence, if not direct words, you will find in this book.

It is the discontented winter and spring of 1991 as I sit down to write. Sandstorms of war hang over the lands of Iraq, Kuwait, and Saudi Arabia. All of the nations of the world are somehow enveloped in this crisis, including Great Britain, France, and Germany; indeed, the entire fledgling European community, east and west. Again my own nation, America, is at the eye of the storm. I knew two years ago when I projected and outlined this work that the question of human death accelerated by high-dose morphine to gain release from agonal cancer dying had somehow to be related to questions of war and nuclear holocaust. But current events have brought those cosmic and geopolitical dimensions of mortality into urgent and compelling focus. Throughout the work I will share my daily reflection on these events.

In this same winter, my wife's parents, our dear Grandma and Grandpa Anson, lie in the hospital section of a Methodist retirement home in Indiana. At eighty-seven and eighty-three years of age, bearing the hard toll of aged minds and bodies, with Parkinson's disease, dementia, and other ills, their experience—of leaving home, of failing health, of costs that liquidate life savings in a matter of months—bears on our experience and is reflected in my thoughts.

I begin by setting forth the recent provocative dilemma of physician-assisted suicide and euthanasia. The moral debate on this issue is framed by a theological con tradition and a philosophical pro tradition. The former perspective tends to animate a conservative legal and professional posture on the question. The latter resonates with a natural and biological wisdom and an ethos of care for dying patients found among country doctors in provincial settings the world over. Starting a conversation on the question raised by the case of Janet Adkins and Jack Kevorkian, M.D., in Michigan sets us forth on a path where we can examine all relevant moral perspectives and all cognate issues of mortality.

A Composite Case

We begin our exploration together with a case that sets forth the nature of the ethical quandary. The composite case (the assisted suicides of Janet Adkins and Virginia Harper) involves the tension between affirming one's life and sustaining it in another, on one hand, and, on the other hand, wishing to die and assisting someone in that final act. Sometimes a physician ends the life of a patient who is sick and dying. Sometimes she assists a miserable patient in committing suicide. As the decade of the 1990s dawned, the discussion in the United States has focused on two cases in Michigan: Kevorkian/Adkins and Harper.

Jack Kevorkian is an M.D. pathologist who has long been a renegade in medical practice. A career-long advocate of physician-assisted suicide and euthanasia, he has recently turned his attention to contriving machines called thanatrons. With these devices, patients who wished to commit suicide could do so in a way less gruesome and violent than is customarily the case. The Michigan courts, which issued an injunction on further use of the machines and eventually a first-degree murder indictment against Kevorkian (which was subsequently dropped), have now become the arena for national debates and moral adjudication of this critical issue. The states of Washington and California have now made euthanasia a matter of political referendum.

In the case in question, the thanatron functioned after Dr. Kevorkian inserted an intravenous drip into the arm of Janet Adkins, releasing a harmless saline solution. When she pressed a button, Adkins released thiopental into her own bloodstream. This strong barbiturate caused sleep and then unconsciousness. After a minute, the machine itself switched the drip solution to potassium chloride, which stopped the heart and brought death within minutes.

Janet Adkins was a fifty-four-year-old teacher from Portland, Oregon. Suffering from Alzheimer's disease, she had been in contact with Kevorkian for nearly a year after she learned of the device. She had been an associate of the Hemlock Society, an organization that advocates the right of persons, especially of those who are gravely ill, to commit suicide. Her husband, two adult sons, and several friends were taken into confidence in the decision. While there was disagreement over her decision (she was alert and active, still playing tennis), they supported her wish that had been resolute from the moment of diagnosis of Alzheimer's disease a year earlier. Her final words to Kevorkian were "Thank you, thank you, thank you."

Watching the national media coverage of Kevorkian/Adkins were Bertram and Virginia Harper, also from the West Coast, making their home in Loomis, California. The sixty-nine-year-old woman, who suffered from late-stage cancer in the breast and liver, had come to Michigan with her husband, believing, because of Adkins' experience, that assisted suicide was legally possible in this state, which has no statute in the matter. Resting with her husband in a Detroit motel, Virginia Harper swallowed about a dozen pills in a coffee liqueur, then pulled a plastic bag over her head. Afraid that this crude procedure would not work, her husband tied the bag shut around her head. Here also several friends and relatives were party to the act.

Nineteen ninety-one witnessed several new developments. In Michigan Dr. Kevorkian assisted two other women to commit "medicide."[5] The state moved closer to prosecution despite the absence of any family initiative. Legislation to condemn assisted suicide was in the works. Being the graveyard for the U.S. auto industry it seems was enough thanato tropism for Gerald Ford's Michigan. The Washington initiative was defeated, though not even as convincingly as George Bush defeated Pat Buchanan in the 1992 presidential primaries. As the election year unfolded, more and more political rhetoric argued that a good way to pare thirty percent from the 800 billion dollars health-care budget would be to take three measures:

- eliminate malpractice suits (10 percent)
- prevent the diseases caused by neglect, e.g., low birthweight babies (10 percent)
- forgo the last two weeks of high-tech life-prolongation (10 percent)

It is at last becoming evident that questions of person's dying in the health-care system have ramifications ranging from economic and political to scientific and technical—indeed the whole range of parameters that we will explore in this book. If we tie "right-to-die" practice to economic cost-cutting, a most mischievous expediency will have displaced ethics—further justification of the present text.

I thank my family on both sides for all they have taught me about life and death. I also thank my friends at Chicago, Second Presbyterian Church, and Fay Dickerson, our archivist, who prepared the index for this volume. Sara Anson Vaux helped throughout with content and form and Becky Veatch masterfully prepared the manuscript.

1
The Philosophical Ethics of Suicide

Frag nicht warum Ich gehe . . .

Marlene Dietrich

Janet Adkins's suicide has raised anew perennial questions that go back to ancient Greece. Should one who is very sick and without much chance of recovery take one's life or ask assistance in that difficult act? Can a society tolerate such acts? Should such acts be forbidden and prosecuted under the general rules of murder and manslaughter? Should physicians, whom patients entrust with their living and dying, participate in such actions? And what of spouses, children, parents, friends? Should they resist, concur, or remain neutral?

The case is grist for the ethics mill because goods and harms gather around both the choice to allow it, even aid it, and to thwart it. The moral imperative of preserving, protecting, and sustaining other persons' lives is called into question. It takes commitment and cost to care enough for others to safeguard their life, provide for their well-being, and protect them from harm. But what if one you love, or who is under your care, asks to be relieved of unbearable suffering? The impulse of care and mercy may now prompt us to help that person find relief. Such a plight may tempt us as physicians to help our patients find a peaceful end. Or as friends and loved ones, we may be inclined to aid and abet the sufferer's suicide. When asked to endorse such decisions and offer support through the difficult process, why are our moral responses ambivalent, even polar and paradoxical? The impulse within us to resist giving up and to encourage a dear one through to an agonizing end, as well as the impulse to ease one out of misery, is fully human. The social policy to condemn without punishment and allow the practice without

1

condoning it is also fully human and appropriate. As I thought about the Adkins and Harper cases at the invitation of *CBS News*, I came to feel that there were two highly charged moral traditions shaping personal choice, family decisions, and public policy on such matters. These traditions were now coming into open conflict.

Initially and simplistically, there is the divergence of our two archaic, radical, and constitutive moral traditions on the matter of suicide. The theological tradition says no! "Life is a gift—not ours to give or take." God, who is life, is alone the giver and receiver of life. Suffering, though unfathomable in its agony and excruciating pain, is related to the crucifixion at the heart of reality. It is therefore a cross that we can bear. Suffering and death are a destiny appointed to us in the will of God. Hebraic prolongation of life and proscription of murder are added to a Hippocratic holism and purism that sees the medical profession as the guardian of holiness by abstaining from the mischief of abortion or euthanasia. Both convictions are then baptized by Christian care and commitment to give and sustain life, creating a formidable view of life's sacredness and a reticence even to deal with death.

Philosophy says yes! Nearly all great thinkers from Plato through the Stoics (Seneca and Cicero) to David Hume, Albert Camus, and Sidney Hook deal with suicide as the defensible moral act of an autonomous agent. Theological reason says no, but with serious qualifications (think of John Donne's apology in *Biathanatos*). Secular reason gives allowance, but with great variation in positions of advocacy. (Think of Immanuel Kant's opposition to suicide.) In some philosophers, suicide is an expression of noble necessity, even heroism. Tracing the outlines of the philosophical ethics of suicide through ancient and modern history can help us see the virtue of this parameter of ethics or this particular theme of morality. It also helps us assess the strengths and weaknesses of philosophic ethics per se.

Ancient Philosophy on Suicide and Euthanasia

Moral truth in philosophy is found in that which is rational, coherent, consistent, and affirmative of the self and its well-being. Philosophy also maintains the validity of societal claims on personal freedom. Depending on the libertarian, egalitarian, or contractarian leaning of the system, individual or communal imperatives are stressed. Plato may be regarded as the first important philosopher to see the collective reflected in the rightly ordered individual soul and the state as simply the individual writ large.

In a much discussed passage in *The Republic*, Plato defends what apparently was a widespread assumption of pagan (non-Pythagorean, nonholiness) medical doctors in ancient Greece. Even in Hippocratic medicine, we find the residue of a Platonic conviction that the incurably ill should not be treated but abandoned to their deaths (III, 405a–410a). The passage even argues that this giving over (*paradokein*) to death may be involuntary, even resisted by the patient. Not only will the burden of being an incapacitated invalid diminish the activity and vitality of that person, it will consume the energies of others in the preoccupying support required. As with severely deformed infants, those who in midlife become seriously debilitated should not be patched up and stabilized in grievous condition but be allowed to pass on.

Socrates argues that in the ideal society the ancient Asclepian medical ethic will obtain, and the good of other people will be the paramount consideration in a person's aging, becoming sick, and confronting life-threatening illness.

> His [Socrates] objection to [intensive] treatment . . . is that it requires the patient to give himself over substantially and permanently to the management of his disease and so, in large measure, to give up the normal productive pursuits that characterize his prior life. Such a person, he says (407e12, 408b12), would benefit [*lusitelein*] neither himself not other people by his mode of life; the treatment would lengthen his life but also make it a very bad one (cf 407d6–7), and it is an abuse of the art of medicine to use it for that end. He should be allowed to die a natural death, untreated.[1]

This idea is all the more striking when we consider the more general Pythagorean, holiness, and idealist tenor of the Platonic corpus. Here on the issue of suicide, for example, we find the note purportedly derived from the Pythagorean mystics, that one should not abandon one's "post" in the world by opting out and committing suicide. The gods do not give and snatch back life, as we find in more oriental and Semitic texts, but rather place us each one providentially in some station of opportunity and responsibility; they have us in their charge. They dismiss us when they are ready.[2]

For Plato and Socrates, the important thing in life was to live justly, with some prudent concern for one's own pleasures and functions, and with serious consideration for the needs and resources of others who would be called to attend and sustain you.

Some years ago, when I was working in the Texas Medical Center in Houston, I met a family that was experiencing severe stress because of the exhausting experience of attending a mother who was suffering from a chronic terminal disease. The son and daughter came to the hospital every evening after work, leaving their children at home. Tired and weary, they kept up a facade of good cheer and encouragement for the mother. Yet the resentment was eating away at them, and the mother was picking up on their stress and experiencing great stress herself for being such trouble and burden to them. Finally, at my prodding, they both blurted out their frustration. "Mom, this is becoming torture to us. Our children are neglected. We're at wit's end." Mother replied, "It makes me mad that you feel this duty to be here all the time cheering me up. I know you hate it. Let's ease off from both sides." From this confession and candid sharing, a new sensitivity emerged for each of them, and the pain was considerably relieved. The family discovered freedom in the suffering that was allowed to have redemptive purpose.

This reality of suffering seasonal bonder and imposed caring bonder on others was what the Greeks responded to in their early ethic of chronic and terminal disability and the obligation to offer medical treatment. The notion of giving up and abandoning the person to her fate was to be transformed into living on and caring through desperate situations only when a different philosophy of suffering and burden-bearing was introduced in the *caritas diaconate* of primitive Christianity. Passive euthanasia, refraining from curative and stabilizing measures when deep and chronic disease and debility had set in, was well established in ancient Greek ethics with assent from the Platonic, Aristotelian, and Stoic schools.

On suicide itself, the early Greeks were ambivalent. What we mean today by suicide—desperation, hopelessness, biological or behavioral depression—was not the primary concern of the Greeks. They reflected more on the rational choice to depart a sadly diseased and debilitated body. In the *Phaedo*, Socrates comments on the suicide of Philolaus, an important brother of the Pythagorean community in the fifth century. Apparently in oral and perhaps written teaching, this early Pythagorean taught that human beings live stationed at a particular "guardpost" (*phroura*). Placed there by the gods, we are not to release ourselves from this service (captivity?). Socrates dissents in part from this teaching. He drank the hemlock rather than running away, as was offered, because he held a different interpretation of the notion of the "post." Socrates refused to accept the full-blown mystic and dualist idea that this body and this station was a prison. For him there was nothing to fear in death. The gods were not capricious slave-masters of people. In justice, one could die in the full confidence of immortality. Suicide is shortsighted and foolish because the gods, under whose charge we serve, are benevolent and provident, and we may assume that they will care well for their charges. At the end of antiquity, Plotinus and the other neoplatonists, like the early Pythagoreans, denounce suicide. Three concerns rooted in pragmatic reason, however, provide the fertile soil that will later allow the philosophical doctrine of morally licit suicide to grow. These are: (1) to do right to yourself is to follow the prudent and rational course, and not to be subject to extraneous authority; (2) to live in justice for the good of others often means subjugating personal desires and needs; and (3) this body and this world are fleeting, perhaps figmentary realities. Rest your trust in reality beyond. The true philosopher welcomes death just as the fragmentary yields to the whole, the erroneous to the truth.

Before we leave the Greeks, we should not neglect a most thoughtful and serene scholarly notion, one that was to deeply impress Western thought by virtue of its influence in the Roman Empire: Stoicism. As far back as Zeno, we find a moving and forceful defense of "rational" suicide[3] when incurable illness, relentless pain, even extreme poverty have so diminished life that it has lost its delight and has become a burden to self and others.

For the Stoics, especially Seneca and Cicero, the good life is realized in the fulfillment of one's rational nature and in the achievement of contentment and purpose. Living one's life well, tutoring one's impulses; bringing up all of one's gifts and energies into pursuit of self-control and salutary purpose is the goal of our being. Taking hold and giving direction to our lives is a Stoic doctrine that compares to the modern notions of self-governance and autonomy. Not to be overwhelmed by anything or to be at the mercy of life's vicissitudes is to find the good life. The application of this underlying life view to the question of suicide is summarized by Cicero:

> When a man's circumstances contain a preponderance of things in accordance with nature, it is appropriate for him to remain alive; when he possesses or sees in prospect a majority of the contrary things, it is appropriate for him to depart from life. . . . [T]he primary things of nature, whether favorable or the reverse, fall under the judgment and choice of the Wise Man, and form so to speak the subject-matter, the given material which wisdom deals. Therefore the reasons both for remaining in life and for departing from it are to be measured entirely by the primary things of nature aforesaid. For the virtuous man is not necessarily retained in life by virtue, and also those who are devoid of virtue need not necessarily seek death. . . . Even for the foolish, who are also miserable, it is appropriate to remain alive if they possess a predominance of those things which are pronounced to be in accordance with nature.[4]

Second, we note in the Stoics a very early articulation of what might be called a completely pragmatic and utility-based calculus of what makes sense in the decisions we make about our lives: "Weigh it up and see if it is worth going on." When all the philosophical and theological theories of the moral life are set aside, it becomes clear that common folk in common circumstances think through life's choices in this crude and rudimentary fashion: Is the cost required for this benefit going to be worth it? Though philosophy in the existential tradition, as in Camus, extols suicide as forcefully as it repudiates it in the theistic philosophy of Augustine, in the end, as with the Stoics, philosophy finds suicide acceptable and rational behavior if it is in keeping with a true reading of life's circumstances and the pattern of our existence. To act in accord with nature will emerge as a central theme of ethics in this study.

Be it nature (*physé*) in the sense of the physical world or in this gentle doctrine of the Stoics where "nature" refers to what we might call providence, to honor nature's way with us is to live well and at peace.

In the Christianized Roman Empire, a new kind of sanctified (some would say Byzantine) moral reasoning comes to control the philosophy and jurisprudence of all forms of killing, including euthanasia and suicide. As we will note in the next chapter on theological ethics, a practice on these matters quite different from official thought also continues. But in Augustine, and to a lesser degree Thomas Aquinas, one finds a censure of the classical and even early Christian practice of suicide and the forceful formulation of a new holiness doctrine stressing the sacredness of human life and the purity (from complicity in killing) of the healing profession. Though Christian philosophy was the dominant philosophy of these ages, it would more properly be called a theological perspective and will be treated in that chapter.

In the Age of Reason and in the modern age, philosophy continues the spirit of Stoicism in the emphasis on the primacy of the autonomous self and the validity of suicide under compelling circumstances. Although David Hume is in constant contention with the Calvinist clergy, and in that dialogue in tension with the entire medieval and Reformation thought on the subject, he articulates a doctrine of moral freedom and allowance of suicide that was quite in keeping with classical thought as expressed by the Stoics.

Hume's arguments justifying suicide are founded in the two foundational principles of philosophy identified earlier: (1) the primacy of the autonomous individual person to follow the leading of his or her reason uncensored by any heteronomous (theonomous) authority; and (2) utility assessment about what course of action would best serve the general good. Like the more general common-sense philosophy of Scotland and France in the late eighteenth and early nineteenth centuries, Hume simply takes a sharp and discerning look at the human condition and concludes that suicide is certainly justifiable, even reasonable, when one has become brutalized with unbearable suffering and when one's obligations to others have been adequately dispatched.

That freedom is the keystone of Hume's thought even prior to these common-sense concerns is clear:

> Let us endeavor to restore men to their native liberty, by examining all the common arguments against suicide, and showing that action may be free from every imputation of

guilt or blame. . . . If suicide be criminal [immoral], it must
be a transgression of our duty either to God, our neighbor,
or ourselves.[5]

Refuting arguments from both the Thomistic and Calvinistic traditions,
Hume contends that suicide offends none of the three Blackstonian
parties.[6] Indeed, suicide may serve the good, at least of our self and of
our neighbor. Release from the unpleasantness—even unbearable
pain—of our existence and sparing the family and community the dis-
traction of sympathy and consuming nursing was, from the perspective
of calculating reason, surely a good.

Immanuel Kant, in less anticlerical and more pietistic tones than
Hume, defends the Christian opposition to suicide. He does so on the
basis of universal and transcendental moral law, which must therefore
also be seen primarily as a theological argument. Hume speaks for the
historic position of natural reason, sustaining the heritage that one may
dispatch oneself in good conscience when the course of one's life has
become an excessive burden to oneself and others. As far as we know,
Hume did not entertain the question of physician- or family-aided,
sickness-induced suicide. This is what we would expect from philosophy, which focuses on personal liberty, courage, and decisional
authority.

During the universal conflagration of the Second World War,
Albert Camus wrote *The Myth of Sisyphus*, a long essay in which he
explored the provocative opening words, "There is only one serious
philosophical problem and that is suicide."[7] In this existential confession, strikingly similar in genre to Augustine's *Confessions* though
diametrically opposite in conclusion, Camus asks, as did Augustine,
"What is the meaning of life?" "What makes life worthwhile?" The
question itself betrays the fact that some new and frightening theme
has entered human consciousness since Hume and Kant. Hinted at in
Mill, Schopenhauer, and Nietzsche, a new consciousness was now
full-blown in the searching intrapersonal reflection of the mid-
twentieth century existentialists. If the human question in Augustine
and Aquinas was "Who, by God am I meant to be?" now the question has become "Who shall I make myself to be?"

In his moving lyric, Camus speaks not of Isaac Newton's grand
design and order but of the "denseness and strangeness of the world"

that is the absurd. The experience of death in others—in the numbing absurdity of murder and war and in the nihilistic anticipation of our own end—is a focal point of a personal philosophy that can only begin with the contemplation of suicide. As with Martin Heidegger,[8] for Camus death is the starting point of philosophy. As we ponder the fact that we are dying, relentlessly, albeit in increments of time, we ask, "Is one to die voluntarily or to hope in spite of everything?" Do we, as Sisyphus and any pyramid builder, push the boulder up to the top of the mountain only to see it tumble down so that we must start again? Or do we, with the Judaic secret known to Einstein, carry on when we have accomplished this mountain knowing we need never climb it again, even though one greater now lies on the horizon? Though Camus ultimately decides against suicide, he restates the fundamental philosophical premise that allows voluntary death in particular circumstances. Requisite conditions are the candid probing of the actual circumstances affecting the self and the affirmation of the self as the only authentic arbiter over life and death. One must choose to live amid all the pain, anguish, and absurdity of life or enter the silent sleep of annihilation.

CASE STUDY: Philosophic Ethics, Anesthesia, and Euthanasia

The stark and somber mortality ethic of Camus draws us back into our central concern of ethical choices about human life and death. Through the experience of war that shaped his reflection and the more horrible and gruesome inhumanity of the Holocaust, which that war masked, we are led again to that bioethical question. Ever since Auschwitz, the entire civilized human family has been morally opposed to gassing or drugging persons to sleep and death. We take offense at Kevorkian's thanatron and at the bag over Virginia Harper's head in part because we remember the retarded children who were drugged into coma and death in Germany in the early 1930s or the victims who were suffocated by Cold War water experimentation late in the decade.

One of the strongest reasons for the moral assertion of personal freedom has been the human destruction of malevolent and even benevolent paternalism. During the recent Gulf war we felt that horror writ large as Saddam Hussein threatened to use the biological and chemical weapons that he learned about in the United States and that were supplied to him by West Germany. These gruesome actions had already been inflicted on the gassed bodies of the Kurds found during the Iran-Iraq war. These acts were outlawed by Nuremberg and Geneva conventions as were the biomedical acts of terminal anesthesia of the Nazis. Today, in events considered more innocuous by some and more ominous by others, anesthesiologists and oncologists put their patients to permanent sleep in Holland, a small country noted for its courageous resistance to the Third Reich and its adherence to the Nuremberg code of medical ethics. In an apparent polar antipathy to that practice, a new rule of medical practice has evolved in the United States whereby surgeons will not allow persons to die while asleep under anesthesia even if the patient had previously authorized DNR (do not resuscitate) orders. Examining the apparent inconsistency and conflict between these two practices will help us sort through this aspect of euthanasia and physician-assisted suicide and characterize further the philosophic vector of ethics.

Medical ethics in the United States has been deeply shaped by reminiscences of the Holocaust and by the atrocities of Nazi medicine. One of the reasons for the power of this memory in our medical ethics is the generation of medical statesmen and women (including some philosophers), who as Jewish émigré scientist-physicians fled the Third Reich. The names of Paul Heller, Max Samter, Alex Tulsky (to mention a few of Chicago's medical leaders), and Jay Katz and Hans Jonas, among others, come to mind. Indeed, if one scans the list of Nobel prize-winning biomedical scientists in recent decades, one will see the extraordinary influence of this community.

Holland, on the other hand, though deeply offended by the Nazi atrocities, has not enjoyed a sizable Jewish medical community and has reflected in its euthanasia policy the liberal and permissive spirit of secularized Protestantism, renewal Catholicism, and humanism. In my view the United States has overreacted to the same danger that Holland has slighted. Let us place the euthanasia practice where terminally ill and suffering patients are placed in barbiturate coma and then eased into death through infusion of a muscle-relaxer alongside the present practice of surgery where all DNR and advance "let-me-die" directives are temporarily vacated while the patient is in the "interoperative window" and under induced chemical sleep. This contrast will enable us to line out the subtleties of health-care ethics. Public law and professional practice say that we must never put another person to death, even at their pleading. In the extreme position, somewhat reflected in our surgical policy, even allowing one to die through passive inaction is wrong. The presenting cause is very different in the Dutch and American situations, however, limiting the force of the contrast. In Holland a terminally ill person in great suffering asks to be assisted in death. We might assume that the patient undergoing surgery hopes to survive. The concern in Holland is whether active euthanasia can be administered when one is incurable and in intractable pain. In the United States the concern is that the health team not induce or even allow death under the status of asphyxia (Baby Linares), anesthesia, or in those poignantly vulnerable moments when one is asleep under the watchful care of anesthesiologists, surgeons, or nurses. Persons must not expire, it is said, while asleep under our care. More noble, it seems, is to die alert and standing with one's boots on.

Some years ago I was involved in an ethics committee's evaluation of the protocol of a clinical study that sought to study biological patterns during sleep that might forewarn of an impending heart attack. A major cause of death in older adults and tragically in infants is sudden coronary death (SIDS—sudden infant death syndrome in children). When I asked whether it might be a merciful thing in some cases for a person to die suddenly in his sleep, my scientist-clinician friends agreed, as human beings and family members, but rigorously objected to my reservation by reason of their commitments to clinical vigilance. Indeed the whole mandatory hospital resuscitation policy and emergency medical team apparatus (squads available within minutes armed with CPR [cardiopulmonary resuscitation] technology) is based on the conviction that one should not be allowed to lapse into the sleep of death under medical attention—and one should never be beyond medical attention. If medical attention is to assume such hegemony and power over a person's departure, new attentiveness to personal good beyond rules and necessities will be required.

The contradiction and comparison not only shows the difference in ethical perspectives in two cultures, it also points up the distinction between philosophical and theological ethics and their derivatives. The moral power of religious observance and historic remembrance (ethical vectors to be subsequently explored) is clearly evidenced in traditions of politics and professional practice that abhor active complicity in a person's dying. These imperatives are at variance, however, with those of philosophy that focus on rights, principles, and case rules (casuistry) imbedded in secular human reason. The exaggerated death aversion of the one discipline and the too easy accession to autonomy of the other will come under scrutiny in this book.

Indeed, connection is now found in the emerging fields of pastoral theology and clinical philosophy or ethics. The historic, theologic, and politic vectors of ethics are predominantly conservative, prohibitive, and protective. Precepts out of this persuasion include *non nocere* (do no harm) and "preserve life." The ethics of rights are predominantly creative and affirmative. They are the ethics of allowance, freedom, and noninterference. "I have a right over my own body." "I have a right to die." These schools of thought clash in cases such as Dutch euthanasia and U.S. surgical ethics. The moral position I wish to defend is that the self-chosen or divinely appointed moment of death should be allowed to occur, even if it takes place in one of the new intensive settings of medical practice: the ICU, CCU, NICU, SICU, or surgical theater. Philosophical ethics concur here with theological in conferring this right to critically ill persons. While this right should be honored, we should also be sensitive to the feelings of others: physicians, surgeons, nurses, and family members who may find it unconscionable to aid death in any way. Sensitivity to the environment (household) of all those affected by our life may prompt us on occasion to suspend our rights and wishes so as not to offend another.

Life *in Extremis* and the Sleep of Death

Taking oneself into chemical coma (Adkins) or being taken into that sleep of death (Holland) confronts us with a frightful specter. Be it the gas chamber of Treblinka, the capital punishment by lethal injection of the Texas prisoner, or the young woman rushed to hospital with a barbiturate overdose—all such ordeals conjure up the terrifying visage of paralysis, loss of control, consciousness, and the dread judgment or nothingness of death. The power of which we speak, even in its most modest form as hypnosis, is no light matter. We do not go gently into that good (or evil) night. We rage and kick because of the sheer delight of vitality and consciousness and the primitive awe by which we stand back in honor and respect, safeguarding the grace of life in one another. The primal attention, what Albert Schweitzer called *achten* or reverence, is the basis of all law, ethics, and the life-sustaining impulse of medicine.

Holland

As we view the recent experience of Holland, we see the working out of a tendency that has been with us now for over a century. Indeed, since the rise of the Enlightenment in Europe and its association of human-rights philosophy with technological prowess, a course was set bringing us to where we are today. Building on the Hemlock Society and other suicide traditions in Greece and Rome, nineteenth-century England and Germany witnessed many zealous movements to legitimize medical suicide or euthanasia. The twentieth century brought forth numerous initiatives to legalize mercy killing. Through the studies of Robert J. Lifton[9] and others, we now know that nineteenth-century propensities toward euthanasia combined with the biological and racist theories of the period served to elicit practices where sick and disabled children, and physically and mentally disabled adults were put to final sleep. Now after forty years of moral counterreaction to these early modern tendencies, propelled by a formidable array of life-prolonging techniques and procedures, Holland has begun a quasi-legal practice of conceding to the wish that the life be ended of those persons who are incurable and suffering.

The custom is quasi-legal in that, although the laws proscribe medical killing, offenders are not prosecuted if the following conditions, set forth by the Dutch medical and judicial systems are met:

A. that there be explicit and repeated request by the patient that leaves no doubt concerning his or her desire to die;
B. that the mental or physical suffering of the patient be very severe with no prospect of relief;
C. that the patient's decision be well-informed and free and enduring;
D. that all options for other care have been exhausted or refused by the patient; and
E. that the doctors consult another physician (in addition he or she may consult nurses and pastors).[10]

The above criteria go to the heart of the body of assumptions of modern philosophical ethics and the derivative jurisprudence of the Western "right of man" tradition. Any act is ethically valid if it emerges from the uncoerced mind and will of a person and does not harm anyone else. This ethic, however, conflicts with the "choose life" ethic.

Operating Room Ethics in the United States

It is a "choose life" ethic derived from Hebrew and Christian theology that functions in the operating room. It is often grounded either in the personal and vocational commitments of those who work there or in fear of the law (in the sense of custom). Irrespective of the motivation, the freedom of choice ethic is set aside when one is under anesthetic sleep. If someone arrests under surgery, resuscitation is built into the anesthetic apparatus and protocol. We safeguard against aspiration, sustain airways, maintain *nephesh* (the living soul, the breath of life). Though we warn persons in the informed-consent process of the risk of anesthesia death, we will do anything to prevent those deaths even if the patient has a nonresuscitation order and even if she sustains serious brain damage during the operation. How has this ethical policy evolved?

In recent years, roughly since 1960 when CPR became widespread, medical care for the critically ill and dying has moved into more and more intensive settings: burn units and the range of intensive care units; ICUs, CCUs, NICUs, SICUs, and step-down units. All of these special adjuncts to operating rooms are part of the heroic and protective sanctuary that has been placed at the center of the cathedral of modern medical care. These special places, using aseptic and antiseptic techniques and the armamentarium of life-monitoring and life-sustaining technology, protect the severely wounded and diseased against the insults of infection, lethal physiologic reaction, and death itself. By monitoring and modulating vital processes—blood gasses, electrolytes, nutrients, and pressures—we take hold of the vital balance of vitality/mortality, breath/stillness, sleep/resurrection.

The result has often been magnificent. One of our friends, a brilliant young professor at the University of Chicago, was recently struck down with bacterial meningitis. In a coma for days, he received the blessings of antimicrobial therapy and sophisticated homeostatic treatment, and recovered consciousness. Like Jimmy Tomelwicz, who fell through the ice on Lake Michigan and lay maintained in barbiturate coma for weeks until he could safely be eased up into consciousness from his hypothermic state, our friend's rescue was Lazarus-like— called back from the grave. Other victories are more pyrrhic. The battle may be won, but the war lost; and we are left with wounded and crippled semicorpses with sadly diminished lives. The ethical question thus comes into focus: can we allow death to occur under this marvelous system of control; or, if we admit the Dutch precedent, can we use this knowledge and skill to induce death in one who is ready to go? Equally crucial is the diagnostic question of discerning whether one can live well again or if grave morbidity has already ensued.

Is it possible that death under surgical anesthesia might be merciful, even heroic? I believe that countless human beings throughout the ages have had their wish granted that they die under anesthesia if they could not be made well. Perhaps this hope of either restored health or the peace of death was behind the admission to cool Orphic caves or Aesclepian sanctuaries in ancient times. These realms of sleep and dreams were thought to be places where healing gods or angels of death would visit. Whoever is appointed to come home should not be barred. Should DNR orders be suspended when one goes into surgery? I think not. Now that we need surgical procedures on dying patients to ease their passage—nerve blocks, relief of obstructions, feeding and breathing entries—need we negate one's readiness to die and refuse the currency of such directives should death's angel come at that time? Such allowance will be necessary, I might add, if we move as the sleep research protocol implies, to critical-care and terminal-care processes where we are constantly monitored. Some critics of my view argue that if death is desired by the patient, he should forgo the use of intensive settings, even hospitals. "Go home and let nature take its course." While I generally concur with this abstention, what Ivan Illich calls the fast from death-prolonging technology, why must we forfeit the blessing of palliative and sustaining support as we die? Can we not have the best of both worlds? For this reason I have argued against separate hospices for the dying, contending that we should integrate those beliefs and practices into mainline hospital care.

In the same critique of my view, some today are proposing that the operating room and intensive or acute settings only be used under certain circumstances. Reimbursement policies might be used to effect this triage. In a 1981 policy by the Department of Health Services of the State of California, it was recommended that only the survivable and those desiring to survive be admitted to acute hospitalization where intensive physician services, skilled nursing, sophisticated diagnostic services, even advanced rehabilitation and psychiatric service, were available.[11] The sad conclusion was "If you've given up, so will we." In addition to the inequality of such measures that affect only publicly funded patients and have no bearing on private patients—the controversial inference is that medicine has no business with the dying patient. While there is a certain Hippocratic wisdom in this view, I contend that the dying one is also the special charge of the physician and other healers. Otherwise, the doctor and nurse are reduced to magician/technicians or manipulators, to the loss of their pastoral role. In the coming days of rationing, cost cutting, and bureaucratically defined care, this ideology could wreak havoc.

Daniel Callahan sets before us the impending crisis and why it has come about:

> The power of medicine to extend life under poor circumstances is now widely and increasingly feared. The combined power of a quasi-religious tradition of respect for individual life and a secular tradition of relentless medical progress, creates a bias toward aggressive, often unremitting treatment that appears unstoppable.

> How is control to be regained? For many the answer seems obvious and unavoidable: active euthanasia and assisted suicide. If those (like myself) who strongly oppose this answer are to prevail in the years ahead, much will depend upon the success of physicians in addressing the kind of fear of dying in the company of modern medicine, ever growing, that lies behind the impulse to legalize euthanasia. That is where the most important struggle will be carried out. We will need a dampening of the push for medical progress, a return to older traditions of caring as an alternative to curing, and a willingness to accept decline and death as part of the human condition (not a notable feature of American medicine).[12]

Although I dispute Callahan's confidence that physicians can help us with our fear of death—and whether we should or should not "dampen medical progress," I concur with him that a renewal of a perennial philosophy of human freedom will be necessary to help us regain control of an awesome technology carried in relentless progressive momentum. In my view, assertive freedom, the yield of philosophical ethics, must be joined to appropriate communality and sacrifice, the ethical yield of sociology and theology, to carry us through.

Conclusion: Philosophy as Ethics

I contend that philosophy is an indispensable vector of ethics, contributing greatly to the humanistic dimension of our threefold comprehensive ethic (naturalistic, humanistic, theistic). It makes this contribution by setting forth rights, principles, axioms, and rules to govern our action. Philosophical ethics are by their very nature *surface* ethics, universalizable and therefore more formal and procedural. Freedom and justice, in philosophical meaning, do not define themselves. That substance is supplied by *depth* ethics, generally theological, which define freedom "for what" and the content of justice (e.g., justice as care for the disadvantaged). In public discourse in pluralistic cultures like ours, such procedural and formal ethics are necessary. Autonomy or self-determination, even at the formal level, is intersected and transformed by its antinomy, sacrifice; just as justice is brought to light in its dialectic with mercy.

Freedom is the value sine qua non of philosophical ethics. "If I can't exist on my own terms," observed Ernest Hemingway, "then existence is impossible." Have you ever thought what you can really do to another person who decides to resist your will and remain free? Parents feel this terror with rebellious children. Very few of us ever make the most radical commitment of freedom, but nothing could be done to coerce us if we did. You could silence a person, yet the mind remains free. Burning Nicholas Ridley and Hugh Latimer at the stake only extends their freedom and spirit. You can incarcerate one, and he can refuse to eat and drink. Suicide, as Camus hinted, is in one sense the ultimate expression of freedom. Sleep, mind control, and biological manipulation are powerful constraints of freedom, as Stanley Kubrick has shown in the film *Clockwork Orange*. The quadriplegic person has lost her freedom for suicide, unless "Whose Life Is It Anyway?'' has made its impact. Before Dax's[13] case, acute burn victims were not free to not be treated. Because of Dax, that has changed.

Philosophy can elucidate rights and duties, values and principles. Contemporary bioethics has given much attention to ''the right to die'' and ''the right to life.'' The obligation to preserve life and not to kill has been widely discussed. The principles of nonmaleficence, beneficence autonomy, and justice are formal and need the supply of substantive content. Together they constitute the perennial contribution of moral philosophy.

To summarize philosophy's contributions to mortality ethics we can search several meanings of one crucial right: the right to die. Should any power be allowed to keep us from our deaths? The fundamental meaning of the right to die is the freedom not to have one's life prolonged against one's will. A most heinous torture in the ancient and modern worlds was that reflected in the world of King Lear, to blind or burn or castrate the person without allowing him to die. Some cynics accuse modern medicine of maiming persons without allowing their release. The popular movement of ''living wills,'' ''advance directives,'' and ''powers of attorney'' is an attempt to preserve for us the right to die from what is feared to be some technical or legal necessity to continue doing what the person does not wish. When hospitals are thought to be places of terror rather than succor, something very serious has gone wrong. This first right, unfortunately called ''passive euthanasia,'' is now well-established. We cannot be forced to have our life sustained by life-saving surgery, chemotherapy, dialysis, or life-prolonging techniques if we deny consent. A second sense of the right to die is involved when we do not suffer a terminal condition. If death is inevitable because of underlying disease and if we refuse to intervene, that is a clear right. What if our disease is nonlethal? Take Lou Gehrig's disease (amyotrophic lateral sclerosis), cerebral palsy, cystic fibrosis, even chronic renal disease requiring dialysis. Here again, the right to die authorizes, I believe, ''letting go,'' refusing therapy, even having the terminal throes made easier as in the following case of Emily Bauer.[14]

Emily Bauer, a forty-two-year-old psychologist from the New York City area, struggled courageously to overcome, then live with, Lou Gehrig's disease. This chronic, relentlessly advancing disease leads to eventual paralysis and death. Well into the terminal course of the disease she was hospitalized and connected to a mechanical respirator, no longer able to swallow or breathe on her own. At this point she tapped out a carefully thought-out message indicating her desire to die. Hospital officials said they could not cease the treatments of feeding and ventilation. They did note that she visited home once a month and they could not control what happened there.

On the appointed day, the children, who had seen their mother days before, were visiting relatives. Mrs. Bauer was driven home with a portable respirator and placed on the couch with her favorite Bach music playing, "Passion According to St. Matthew."

"I had never seen her eyes so bright and happy in three years," said her husband. A few friends, invited for brunch, bid their farewells after noon when a doctor arrived. "See you soon," they said, knowing.

The doctor left the husband and wife alone for a while. Mr. Bauer read from her favorite poem, T.S. Eliot's "East Coker":

In my beginning is my end. Now the
    light falls
Across the open field, leaving the
    deep lane
Shuttered with branches, dark in the
    afternoon.

And Mr. Bauer found himself recalling, through tears, their life together. "I talked about the future," he said, "what kind of people we wanted our children to be, that I couldn't raise them her way but I'd try to do it our way and we'd climb those mountains together. We didn't talk about the disease or good times past. We agreed it was the end of a path we started together. She just wouldn't be there for the rest of the journey."

Then the doctor came in. He had explained the procedure, an injection of thorazine to make her sleep. She would not feel removal of the respirator.

Within two minutes, according to Mr. Bauer, his wife fell asleep, her hand in his. He recalls disconnecting the air tubes. "And then an incredible thing happened," he said. "She opened her eyes and moved her lips, a faint 'thank you.' Then her eyes stayed open, but they were empty. That was her gift. In that moment I got such an awe for life. I had thought of her as nearly dead before. But you realize, when it's gone, how full of spirit a living person is."

The first doctor left then. A lawyer, who had "just happened" to stop by unknowing friends nearby, was notified. So was the hospital. A second doctor, awaiting the call at home, was summoned to sign the document certifying, as far as he knew, death did not occur in any unusual manner and was due entirely to natural causes.

Beyond this kind of active-passive euthanasia, a third sense of the right to die is the act of suicide under conditions of health. Suicide when one is well is a personal and social tragedy. When despair creeps into one's inner or outer world, when the verve of hope and delight dries up and life becomes a dreary chore, we may find death the only way out, or sadly, in the psychopathological mode "the way to have the last laugh on those who have hurt us." Here the right to die, though worthy of our respect and if successful, forgiveness, should be vigorously challenged by the right to be protected, to be well—to be cared for and counted on. We often need to fight the all-too-easy "will to die" with an energetic "will to love" and affirmation of that person.

The final declension of the right to die is the most difficult. Does it entail the right to assisted suicide? This is the challenge of our opening cases, Adkins and Harper. Well into this century the state of Texas, and, it was thought, the state of Michigan, allowed this right. Today, in most jurisdictions, suicide is discountenanced as Blackstone's threefold offense—a sickness, sin, and crime, and assisted suicide is outlawed. To kill others or assist in the dastardly deed is forbidden unless, as we will consider as we go along in this book, it is justified by cause of war, capital punishment, urban politics (sociogenocide), or rationing. Killing except under carefully defined exceptional situations is not our right. Our duty is to insure life for one another and provide for its well-being. Paring, winnowing, purifying, and liquidating should be left to higher powers. As Darwin showed and Hitler set out to intensify programmatically, nature itself (natural selection) will provide the triage, disposal, and the survival quotient. We need not help.

"All men are afraid of dying," wrote J. J. Rousseau in *Julie*.[15] "This is the great law of sentient beings, without which the entire species would soon be destroyed." Death awareness and anticipation is the beginning of philosophy and all cultural pursuit. The normative significance of philosophy for mortality is that death awareness and acceptance is the beginning of wisdom. Because of our finitude and possibility we affirm a moral reality in life. Therefore rational principles such as freedom, beneficence, and justice and rational processes should guide human choices and actions. The primacy of the self and respect for other selves is the basis of all human rights and duties.

In the light of this orientation, suicide, one of the spectrum of issues in mortality ethics, has offered an appropriate field for the definition and elucidation of this vital parameter of values. Philosophy participates in the redemptive drama of reality where light overwhelms darkness (Enlightenment) and good is drawn from evil in its relentless demand for truth. But philosophy does not and cannot stand alone as a moral guide. It must be enriched by a range of other perspectives that activate other sources of insight in our consciences. We begin the process of extension to other pathways, thereby enriching and elaborating our ethical landscape by looking at that perspective on ethics that brings about our tension and dialectic on suicide cases. Those who decry the actions of Adkins, Kevorkian, and Harper appeal either to an authentic faith or what Daniel Callahan calls a quasi-religion. That theological ground then provides the ethos of our legal custom and professional morality.

2
Theological Ethics and Euthanasia

> The whole dilemma of humanity [is summed up in the choice
> between] to yield to and glory in the characteristics we share
> with other living creatures or alternatively to work at and
> glory in our capacity to transcend our creatureliness.[1]

Adkins, Kevorkian, and Harper spark sympathy, outrage, and
debate. Why? There must be an important fissure in the solid rock of our
moral tradition, and indeed there is. If the Unitarian faith were our
national religious consensus and if the philosophical ethics of suicide
prevailed in local law and medical practice, there would be no contro-
versy. But we are a society that is home to fundamentalist Protestants,
Catholics, and Muslims as well as Orthodox Jews. More importantly,
we are a society shaped not only by Enlightenment philosophy and
autonomy rights doctrine but also by theological ethics that have, from
Hippocrates to Surgeon General C. Everett Koop, given rise to what I
have called "holiness" ethics. By the holiness tradition (which I take
from the Hippocratic pledge as much as from the holiness code of Le-
viticus) I mean the cultural bias that affirms the authority of God in the
moral life, the sacredness of the human being, the purity obligations of
the healing professions, and a derivative secularized, quasi-religious
respect for life. Holiness doctrine may also compel technological
progress—but that is another story, harder to document, and must await
clarification in the chapter on the press of secular scientific ethics on our
endeavor.

In this chapter we will display the character of theological ethics as
they contribute to our moral life and as they are illumined by application
to the issue of euthanasia and other questions of mortality. Following

some further elaboration of the moral position that resists the assisted-suicide cases before us, we will wind our way back, then forward again to see the development of the theological ethics of homicide. After presenting the dominant themes of a theological ethic on euthanasia, we will propose some concrete ways of helping dying persons from the fields of pastoral care and practical theology. Here I will propound the view that our dying be made a more personal and parochial matter rather than continue to be a matter of public and professional control. Our purpose in this chapter will be to show that theology grounds an ethic that honors life yet receives death in due season, not when it is our whim but when we can discern the divine call in our soul and in the corroborative adieu of the loving community.

"In purity and holiness I will practice the art. I will dispense no pessary for abortion nor any deadly potient to those who ask for it." Familiar words from the *Oath of Hippocrates*. What is their source? Recent scholarship by Ludwig Edelstein and others finds the Hippocratic guild rooted in the ancient Pythagorean mathematical-mystical priesthood. They believed that numbers, music, mystical devotion, and healing touched the spheres of perfection, drawing eternal logos into temporal human speech. Against this background, the arts and crafts, including the art of medicine were mimetic activities in that they sought to pattern the perfections of the noumenal realm in the world of phenomena. Soul care, psychology, midwifery, herbal therapy, even the cruder arts of medicine and surgery were, in this vision, arts of holiness.

For this reason the christianized Roman Empire selected the Hippocratic mode of medical practice as its orthopraxy. As in the holiness moods of Hebrew scripture, reflecting the nonaccommodation phases of the life of the Jewish people, primitive Christianity forward into Constantinian and Justinian social order condemns other forms of healing practice as heretical. Perhaps it is the awareness of death and the privilege and fear of attending dying persons that evokes this sense of the holy. Rudolf Otto found in this primordial feeling of confronting the unknown of death the ground of the mingled sense of attraction and dread—the idea of the holy. Like the pastor or priest, the physician is aware that she stands on holy ground and that she handles that which is power-charged—the sacred.

The alluring and foreboding power of the divine in our experience corresponds to the imprint that death makes on our consciousness. For this reason we find in our mind an enormous reluctance, alongside proposed willingness to discuss euthanasia. We are repelled and attracted by death. We rightly recoil in horror if we think of euthanasia as the elimination of deformed or retarded children or as the eradication of those who are senile, mentally deranged, and incurable. Although legalized euthanasia linked to economic rationing in public policy might pose this dreadful prospect, when we speak of euthanasia we speak mainly of decisions by dying persons about the mode of their own dying. Euthanasia must never involve imposition of death on one innocent or unwilling. Though rough decisions to withdraw or withhold life-sustaining treatment must be made for incompetent persons, these involve passive euthanasia, often the withdrawal of respirators or feeding mechanisms, rather than any form of active euthanasia. In the case of Karen Quinlan, the question was to withdraw the mechanical ventilator, which was done. It was never a consideration to give her an injection of potassium chloride to stop her heart. In the cases of Nancy Cruzan and Sidney Greenspan, the issue was to discontinue nutrition and hydration supply and allow death to ensue. Many commentators have slighted or denied any significant moral difference, but there remains a consensus among moralists that voluntary euthanasia is a categorically different question from involuntary. Theology is grounded in sensations of shame and guilt, of reticence, dread, and respect. These impulses—activated as the realm of spirit confronts our mind—occur in the confrontation with death.

The roots of holiness doctrine as it shapes modern law and medical practice do not come from an inherent conscientious sense of the sanctity of life in the general community or even in the community of medical practitioners. Disregard for persons seems to arise more naturally than such special respect. We find ourselves today where we are vis-à-vis Adkins and Harper because Judaism participates in this ancient Near Eastern revolution of holiness, conveying it into the bosom of modern Western culture through its influence on Christianity. Our story of theological ethics about human mortality must therefore begin with Judaism.

Judaism

The essence of Jewish conviction about God, the human being, and killing can be summarized in two radical convictions:

1. homicide is blasphemy and deicide;
2. "the sanctity of human life is a belief that each moment of biological life is of infinite value"[2]

This starting point obviously differs from positions that emphasize human freedom or quality of life in decisions about ending or taking one's own life or that of another. The mathematical and philosophical construct of Rabbi Immanuel Jacobovits, that each moment of each person's existence is as an eternity and that to kill one person is to kill the whole human race or to save one for a moment is a messianic act of saving the race[3] is different from the Pythagorean system and somewhat at variance with biblical Judaism, which is less theoretical and more concrete and historical. All the same, these affirmations ring true with sanctity doctrine as it arises in the Greek Islands, the ancient Near East, and perhaps in Egypt in the period beginning in the third millennium, B.C.E.

Jewish commentary on the taking of life is focused on Genesis 9:5–6, an ancient judicial formula based in the conviction that the human person is *Imago Dei,* an icon or casting of God.

For your lifeblood I will surely require a reckoning, of every beast I will require it and of man, of every man's brother I will require the life of man. Whoever sheds the blood of man, by man shall his blood be shed, for God made man in his own image.

—Genesis 9:5–6

The passage, which continues with the command to "be fruitful and multiply abundantly in the earth" (v. 7), sets in poetic lyric the divine wish that holy presence fill the earth as the human family portrays the divine life. Defacing this presence or smashing it is tantamount to attacking God. This assault requires just retribution. This body of command and instruction clearly proscribes homicide and suicide. But, as Baruch Brody has shown in his very insightful study, its message on the question of euthanasia is quite complex. Numerous Talmudic texts put forth the imperative not to hasten your own or another's death. Texts also forbid contorting the dying process into one of prolonged suffering. Though the sad affliction of death is to be avoided by virtue of life love and stewardship and though we must not cause or assist death in another, in the end death is a blessing to receive in gratitude. Summarizing Jewish teaching in these matters, Brody writes:

1. Suicide and active euthanasia are prohibited because they are illicit acts of killing, but not because each moment of human life is definitely judged to be worthwhile. Many authorities concede that the death of some patients is a blessing.
2. As a result, it may well be prohibited to provide care which prolongs the suffering of a dying patient, and permissible to withdraw that care if it has been provided, although some authorities would limit that permission to a very few cases.
3. Because one may risk shortening remaining periods of life for the patient's benefit, one may provide active pain relief even if this risks the patient's dying sooner.
4. There is a suggestion among the most recent authors that a patient's wishes play a significant role in some of these decisions.[4]

The rich and nuanced teachings of Jewish medical ethics are found in the array of positions from orthodox, conservative, reconstructionist, and reformed schools. The orthodox commentators tend to emphasize the earlier standard texts while reformed commentators take into account new developments and data. The Christian moralist draws from this awesome heritage the simple truth that in life and death we belong to God. Indeed, as Ivan Illich has made clear in an unpublished work, it is wrong to speak of *life* as an abstract noun. There is no such thing. God is life. God imparts life to us. It is God's possession, not ours. The origination and destination of our living is Yahweh, and we are to respect the giving and receiving of our life that is offered. This is the meaning of sanctity doctrine, not some abstract ideology that insists on keeping persons perfused, nourished, and watered in a vegetative state for decades.

Augustine

Many cite Saint Augustine and his extensive reflections against self-killing in *The City of God* as the basis for a Christian proscription of suicide and euthanasia. I must say yes and no. On the one hand

Augustine, building on primitive Christian thought and the convictions of the early fathers, argues that life is precious, that it is providentially given and allotted for purposes mysterious to us. We therefore ought not to be tempted to take or offer our own life (as many early martyrs gleefully did, even arranged). Rather, we ought to endure tribulation and persecution with patience. It is God's way to make us holy. The greatest Christian philosopher since Augustine, the great Dane Søren Kierkegaard, struggling with the profound question of why God wills the wretched disease and agony of old age and dying, reflects in his journal:

> What pleases God even more than the praise of angels is a man, who in the last lap of his life, when God is transformed as though into sheer cruelty and . . . does everything to deprive him of all joy in life, continues to believe that God is love and that it is from love that God does this. Such a man becomes an angel. And in heaven he can surely praise God. But the apprentice time, the school time, is also the strictest time. Like a man who journeyed through the whole world to hear a singer who had a perfect voice, so God sits in heaven and listens. And every time he hears praise from someone whom he brings to the uttermost point of disgust with life, God says to himself, "That is the right note!" He says, "Here it is!" as though he were making a discovery.[5]

In this spirit, Augustine argues that the *summum bonum*, the ultimate human good and divine desire, is eternal life with God, not longevity here in wretched *civitas terrena*. The misery that Augustine pleads that we not flee is persecution for the name of Christ and hardships wrought by that confession. One wonders if the good pastor would not have a sense of pity were he or she to visit someone old and infirm who, robbed by illness of mental and physical strength, was ready to lay it down. Augustine chided us not to give up the good fight of faith and witness, not to struggle on seeking to retain failing physical vitalities. In invoking his powerful teaching against suicide as argument against contemporary euthanasia, we may be doing violence to the focus of his concern, which is viable witness in devotion to Christ. Permeating Augustine's thought is the imperative to love, as it is *caritas* which ultimately reflects *civitas dei* in our own city.

We need to move back behind Augustine and the early church fathers and teachers to reclaim the good news of primitive Christian proclamation that God in Christ has rescued us from the terrible plight of life and death separated from God, that death now holds no power against us as we confide and abide in Christ, and that our life is to be expended (given up) in the greater love of agapic service to others emulating the sacrifice of Christ. Despite Augustine, it is no false conviction that prompts the martyrs to receive death with such magnanimity and trust. They know that the fullness of this kingdom is found in suffering and trust and the bequest of eternal life is available only to death in faith. The watchword about this early band of believers, we need recall, was "see how they love one another," not "see how they take possession of their lives."

Summary of Christian Theological Thinking

At a recent meeting of the Eighth World Congress of the World Federation of the "Right to Die" Societies held in Maastricht, Holland, Derek Humphry, president of the federation, lamented the antieuthanasia feelings caused by the spread of world Christianity during the last 2000 years. "In [our] post-Christian times," he pleaded, "we must abandon the trappings of religion and allow new values to emerge."[6] It is not the spirit of Christianity that, in the words of another conference speaker, causes us to "deny another person a decent and gentle death." Rather, it is the secularized, inculturated residue of Christian faith, sadly expressed in popular prejudice, legal custom, and a legalistic version of medical practice. A close look at the sympathies within any congregation or religious communion would show this. The charge is similar to that which finds the church guilty of the depreciation of women and of the denial of civil rights to racial minorities. As Martin Luther King Jr.'s ministry exemplified, though the church in its formal life and its secularity is often an evil force, the church in its central conviction in the heart of its clergy and people is and always has been a most powerful force for liberation.

In our post-Christian world we need to hold on to those values that extol the sacredness of life and the worthiness of persons to receive our protection. In modern (Renaissance forward) Christian ethics, the programmatic condemnation of one who committed suicide

and, by inference, euthanasia (Augustine, Aquinas, Calvin) gradually
yields to a sense of understanding and mercy. The harsh condemnation
of the suicide to damnation was colored by the Reformation/Counter
Reformation diatribes where, in recollection of Augustine, both parties
accused each other of committing suicide (e.g., Luther's terminal walk
to Eisleben), thinking that they thereby repudiated their witness and
consigned themselves to hell. More representative of the spirit of the
gospel is Thomas More's hilarious utopia where he jests about fascina-
tions and fixations with bodily matters, or John Donne's sermon meditation on *Biathanatos* where on the basis of freedom in grace and
release from any need to cower in tribulation, he writes with the gay
insouciance with which he would preach his last sermon in his shroud.

> I have often such a sickly inclination; and whether it be
> because I had my first breeding and conversation with men
> of a suppressed and afflicted religion, accustomed to the
> despite of death and hungry of an imagined martyrdom, or
> that the common enemy find that door worst locked against
> him in me, or that there be a perplexity and flexibility in the
> doctrine itself, or because my conscience ever assures me
> that no rebellious grudging at God's gifts, nor other sinful
> concurrence, accompanies these thoughts in me, or that a
> brave scorn, or that a faint cowardliness beget it, whensoever
> any affliction assails them, methinks I have the keys of my
> prison in mine own hand, and no remedy presents itself so
> soon to my heart as mine own sword.[7]

I think the inclination of the Christian tradition at its theological and
personal best is to affirm that if Jeremy Taylor's holy living and holy
dying is followed, if we drive melancholy and depression from one
another in love, if we draw on the benefits of antipsychotic therapy and
counseling, and if we attend one another well in life's extremes there
will be no need for suicide or euthanasia. If we carefully worked
through the mortality ethics of Luther or Calvin, Barth, Niebuhr, Tillich, Thielicke, Ramsey, and Fletcher we will find a Christian ethics
focused on compassion for those on whom life in its disease and misery crashes down, a sympathy when they cry to die or be helped to die,
and a willingness to do whatever it takes to ease their plight.

As I wrote in the introduction, I have chosen to put final form to these thoughts that have been growing for years while on sabbatical at Oxford. In my mind England has been able to chart a careful course on euthanasia, avoiding the live-hard, die-hard, kill-hard ethos of Holland, South Africa, and Germany, and the technophilic and nomophobic (fear of law) ethos of the United States. With the hospice movement and a gentle ethic of care for the old and sick, which the National Health Service has not been able to destroy from the old provincial patterns of medical practice, England and Scotland have fashioned a more common-sense approach. It is my thesis throughout this book that good medicine, surrounded and animated by tender personal care, will obviate the need for medical suicide, PAS (physician-assisted suicide), and euthanasia. We will return throughout the book to the religious, cultural, and historical forces that create our problem and pose some meaningful resolution. With this cursory and preliminary description of an ethic at one level antithetical but at another concordant with that of philosophy, let us now turn to the contemporary issue of euthanasia and the spiritual and moral hope behind the search for a good death.

Euthanasia: the Vision, Problem, and Resolution

For we know that if our earthly house of this tabernacle were dissolved, we have a building of God, an house not made with hands, eternal in the heavens.

2 Corinthians 5:1

Beloved, now are we the sons of God, and it doth not yet appear what we shall be, but we know that, when he shall appear, we shall be like him; for we shall see him as he is.

1 John 3:2

In *Works and Day*, Hesiod recalled a day when people

lived in the time of Kronos when he was king of heaven. Like gods they live, having a soul unknowing sorrow, apart from toil and travail. Neither were they subject to miserable

old, but ever the same in hand and foot, they took their pleasure in festival apart from all evil. And they died as overcome
of sleep. All good things were theirs. The bounteous earth
bore fruit for them of her own will, in plenty and without
stint. And they in peace and quiet lived on their lands with
many good things rich in flocks and dear to the blessed gods.[8]

In words written about the same time, Isaiah of Jerusalem fore-
tells a day when, "No child shall ever again die as an infant, no old
man fail to live out his life: every boy shall live his hundred years
before he dies" (Isa. 65:20 RSV).

Two cases poignantly express the two-sided moral concern in the
search for euthanasia, good death. One illustrates our tragic tendency
to force people to outlive their lives, the other the temptation suicid-
ally to underlive our life.

William Bartling used to talk a lot with his wife, Ruth, about
football and basketball, fishing and camping. Today the
70-year-old Mr. Bartling cannot talk at all. Mr. Bartling is
suffering from five usually fatal diseases, and his case has
now become the focal point and test case for the national
"right to die" movement. A machine is breathing for him
through a hole in his neck, at a speed set by technicians.
Other devices are draining him and feeding him and monitoring him with electronic alarms and blips of light that move
across a green screen. Every two hours his throat is vacu-
umed. The doctors, the lawyers and his wife, who makes the
emotional daily pilgrimage to his bedside to hold his thin,
cold hand, agree that Mr. Bartling will never leave his win-
dowless hospital cubicle alive. Knowing his case is hopeless,
Mr. Bartling says he wants to die. He wants his breathing
machine turned off so he can slip into death naturally. But
the Glendale Adventist Medical Center refuses. Its attorneys
maintain and so far a state court has agreed, that turning off
Mr. Bartling's respirator would at best be aiding a suicide
and at worst a homicide. The hospital's chief attorney says
that the doctors' ethics outweigh a patient's right to privacy
or to control his treatment.[9]

Elizabeth Bouvia also wanted to die. Crippled by slowly progressing cerebral palsy, convinced that the flame was not worth the candle, she asked Riverside Hospital in California to admit her for care: pain relief and hydration, but to not feed her, merely to accompany her into a dignified death. In lengthy proceedings, the court—as in William Bartling's case—said it could not condone this suicide wish, that values such as life in the body, life-prolonging medical ethics, and becoming an unfortunate example to other affected persons superseded Bouvia's right to privacy and to refuse treatment. Bouvia's story took a surprise turn when on Easter dawn, after a night of soul searching at a Tijuana motel, she decided with the help of friends to carry on if they would pledge their help. Even with this newfound resolve ending a fifty-day fast, she still considered pressing her demand to be assisted toward a comfortable death.[10]

Two stories; a tragedy and a tragicomedy of sorts. Each case in its extremity points us to a golden mean between too much and too little—to the dialectic of clinging to life and resigning to death as we search for a personal style and public policy of good dying. The legal and moral impasses of the Bartling and Bouvia cases are symptomatic of an underlying uncertainty as to whether the achievement of a good death is a legitimate part of the biomedical project. In the seventeenth century, Francis Bacon advised physicians to "acquire the skill and to bestow the attention whereby the dying may pass more easily and quickly out of life."[11] Today we do not hear that admonition. We are not at all sure that euthanasia is a responsibility of health care providers, or that dying well (*ars moriendi*) is a proper personal discipline. Being immobilized by these cases and the thousands of other cases like Adkins and Harper, which they represent, also forces us to ask whether social policy can be so construed and clinical activities so organized as to facilitate our desires to die well.

Techniques for Prolonging Life

To move toward such a societal approach, let us first survey the techniques of life prolongation, cessation of treatment, and euthanasia. Analysis of the moral ambiguity of "preserve life"/"let die" decisions will then be offered. We will then scan the utopic history of euthanasia, seeking to understand our past actions and aversions to the practice and in that memory find moral guidance for today. Finally, we shall offer a synthesis and contemporary moral vision that appropriately responds to the modern crisis.

It is my hope that we will define euthanasia in the broad sense as the search for a better manner of death, rather than in the narrow sense of mercy killing. The latter definition is both provocative and pejorative and cannot lead to moral insight or direction unless it is seen as part of a broader fabric of concern. Sociologically, we have moved our concern from direct euthanasia policies to concern about "living wills" and "natural death acts"; from acts of direct taking of life to acts of withdrawing treatment or of not initiating life supports. In personal decisions, we are concerned with "dying well" rather than putting one another out of our misery. Our concern here will be to seek a salutary public policy and personal philosophy of dying and death so that active euthanasia will seldom be required. This will require a careful reconsideration of our deepest beliefs and values, as well as our practical strategies and decisions.

Mechanized Devices

A variety of technologies come into play as decisions are made concerning prolongation of life, cessation of treatment, and euthanasia. Bacon's vision of a battery of technological skills that would both prolong living and facilitate a more merciful dying has now been realized. Initially we must mention the mechanized devices developed in the euphenic project that are called into action in life and death crises. Dialyzers, cardiac pacers, and—perhaps most controversially—mechanical respirators are often utilized in the waning hours of persons' lives. The moral ambiguity of using life-support machinery is found when we confuse the purposes of "carry-through-crisis support," "chronic support," and "end-stage support." The mechanical respirator, indeed the entire cardiopulmonary resuscitative activity (CPR, direct cardiac massage, defibrillator, etc.) was created to carry people through a temporary breakdown, to allow normal function to resume, and then to withdraw the machine. Although the original iron lungs were chronic support devices for polio victims, the modern instruments were created for rescue and carry-through purposes. They were not meant to become permanent appendages. Often in medicine an act of utopic intent has a dystopic outcome. This happens, for example, when low birth weight babies are saved only to a life of blindness, deafness, seizures, and unfulfilled promise. It happens when persons at the terminal threshold are administered remedial measures that create debilitating bondage serving vital perpetuation and not meaningful life. Here the doctrines of iatrogenesis and medical fallibility call us to make decisions with greater care. The present moral and legal impasse represented by Bartling and Bouvia, Cruzan and Greenspan, allowing us to begin life supports but not to discontinue them, must be resolved.

Vital Substances and Interventions

A second range of life-prolonging powers is found in the array of vital substances and interventions that allow both monitoring and bolstering of critical functions. Pressors and other medications to hold to the fine line between hyper- and hypotension, antibiotics to aid in the fight against infections, substances to correct electrolyte imbalances, transfusion of blood ingredients, sedatives, and other pain-relief remedies, all of these interventions can prolong life; their usage can be withheld or withdrawn, allowing death to ensue; or they can be used as euthanasia devices, that is, intensifying morphine for pain relief with the secondary effect of depressing the brain's respiratory center and hastening death. These two groups of interventions, mechanical supports and vitality props, are controversial because they are fraught with dehumanizing as well as life-saving potential.

Ingredients of Life

More clearly benign and helpful, though not completely free of moral issue, are the ministries anchored in the four primal elements of the world: earth, water, fire, and air. Heraclitus and the other nature philosophers who built the foundation of modern natural science believed reality to be constituted by these four primal elements. Hippocratic and Galenic medicine translated these elements into the four humors that interplay in the human organism, in harmonious intermingling creating health, and in imbalance causing disease. The fact that these resources are natural and rudimentary implies the moral obligation to receive and provide these ministries. It is my thesis that sensible basic

ministry is appropriate. Mandatory and forced coercions of these ingredients of life sustenance, especially via technological entries, is more
questionable.

Earth

The good earth presents itself as a generous and provident mother,
offering up foods for sustenance and delight. In fruit, grain, and root,
and in egg, milk, and flesh, the sacrament of nature presents itself to
satisfy our needs. Through bread and milk, energy and protein for life,
we are sustained in helpless infancy, competent adulthood, and in
extremis. When persons are unable to feed themselves, a mixture of
earth's nutrients is prepared, flour and milk, sugar and pap, and gently poured into the person's throat from the invalid feeder. We have
examples of the invalid feeders, those small Aladdin's lamplike pitch-
ers, from the earliest periods of utensil making. Renaissance feeders
and painted Victorian porcelain versions exhibit the perennial custom
of feeding the sick and dying. This assistance could be received,
resisted, or rejected. Most cultures have the saying that we find in
early Ireland, "She turned her face to the wall." Today we wonder
whether we should force-feed persons like Elizabeth Bouvia in the way
we do fasting prisoners: strapping them down and force-feeding them
either with nasogastric (NG) tubes, intravenous lines, or G-lines (direct
parenteral gastric lines). With Irish Republican Army hunger-strikers,
authorities wait until the victim falls unconscious, at which point line
feeding is initiated. Should patients be treated like political prisoners?

A second moral quandary is created by the sophisticated means we
have for feeding the dying: NG tube feeding and IV lines with various
nutrient liquids. Now hyperalimentation and direct parenteral (G-line)
feeding replace the old invalid feeder offering its sustenance via the
enteral route. Since we can now sustain the living (or prolong the dying)
of babies and adults with severely compromised gastrointestinal status
(e.g., short-gut syndrome) and convey nutritional support to persons
with a wide range of threatening and terminal conditions, we will need
to use even this rudimentary ministry with nuance and discretion.

Water

It takes a long while to starve to death. But water is the elixir of
life, the nectar of the gods. We die quickly from dehydration. To sustain

fluid intake and kidney and bladder output is another of the basic life-support ministries of medical care. Today we can apply dextrose, saline, and other electrolytes to aqueous solutions and maintain the vital balance in cells and tissues. The baby at Johns Hopkins featured in the film "Who Shall Survive?" died of dehydration when parents refused permission to operate on the baby's duodenal obstruction. In the provocative euthanasia case of 1920, *The People v. Frank C. Roberts*, Roberts prepared a glass of water with the poison Paris Green at the request of his wife who committed suicide because of her incurable multiple sclerosis. Fluid overload or underload can quickly kill. Through the medium of fluids, narcotics can quickly pass the blood/brain barrier, and poisons can swiftly enter the bloodstream and do their deadly work. Perhaps the major form of suicide in the world is that of people "drinking themselves to death." The moral issues of hydration therapy are many and varied. Is death by "drying up" desirable or is starvation death easier? Dying of thirst is becoming a global crisis as we turn earth's surface into desert with irresponsible farming, grazing, and wood-hewing so that it can no longer support life. Jesus spoke of God as the "water" and "bread" of life (John 4:13, 6:48). In all the religious, literary, and moral imagery of our culture, bread is the staff of life, water the essence of life. We need to discover the delicate balance of provident and prudent use of liquids in living and dying.

We have noted three fundamental moral antinomies that animate and direct our ethical tradition: sustain life/accept death, honor personal freedom/serve community justice, seek health/abide suffering. We need to find a delicate balancing of these values in our baptismal ministries to one another. When do hydration therapies (cups of water) force upon people more excruciating deaths? Are we permitted to intervene when persons, in personal freedom, seek to drown themselves (e.g., obesity) or dry up (e.g., anorexia nervosa, self-dehydration)? Should blood become a saleable commodity, or should social justice and the "gift-relation" require the equitable, noncompensatory distribution (perhaps even compulsory appropriation) of this fluid? How to release our life (what some ancients called a drop of water) back into the eternal ocean, this is the fundamental question.

Fire

From the newborn incubator to the heat-moistened oxygen tent sheltering the cancer victim, we surround one another with warmth in living and dying. Keeping the baby warm is the antidote of love to the poison of exposure. In primitive tribes and in the Greco-Roman world, unwanted children were exposed to the elements. Today we move the bed into the corridor or a drafty corner, knowing all too well the teaching of Hippocrates on how air and climate, hot and cold, affect our health. We heat with blankets, vaporize with warm moisture, stimulate hyperthermia to provoke metabolism and immunological response. Conversely, we freeze tissue for procedures, use ice treatments for febrile states, induce hypothermia for open-heart surgery, force coma for drowning victims, and contemplate human hibernation and cryogenics to finally assault the destructive fevers of life. Serious, as well as transient, disease is often accompanied by fever and chills. We need to hold one another in warmth as we enter the cold and lonesome valley that lies this side of the Creator's warm sanctuary.

Air

"And the LORD God formed man of the dust of the ground, and breathed into his nostrils the breath of life" (Gen. 2:7). To revive and sustain breath in persons in extremis is one of the most impressive powers of modern medicine. Keeping the airways open, suctioning secretions, presenting oxygen through nasal canula, intubating the lungs, and beginning mechanical respiration are all rejuvenating and refreshing activities, albeit fraught with moral ambivalence. Oxygen lines facilitate the perfusion of tissues; but they also compromise the body's natural carbon dioxide buildup with its narcotizing, pain-killing effect. The mechanical respirator has turned many back on to renewed life. It has also linked many to the servitude of a machine that no one then has the courage to turn off. Cardiopulmonary resuscitation teams have revived many from the brink of death to further meaningful lives. They have also revived persons into perpetual comatose and vegetative states.

At many points in history euthanasia acts were accomplished by cutting off the air line, either by strangulation or suffocation. Anoxia to the brain brings swift death; and while asphyxia is not the most pleasant form of demise, it is better than other lingering deaths. The ministry of air and breath, of course, also has broad environmental and political implications. Much lung disease is caused by industrial pollution, cigarette smoke, and automobile emissions. The lungs, like great lakes, can rejuvenate themselves; but constant abuse destroys them.

Similarly, the ministries of breath have consequences for belief and fundamental values. Resuscitation is resurrection, revival from the dead, fraught with theological consequence. The biblical ethics of death has believed that God receives back the life given by withdrawing breath: the living soul. One can imagine a future day when artificial hearts perfuse, and artificial lung-oxygenated bodies sustain living brains or even wet nanocomputers as neurologic artifacts. Will this be an act of ultimate defiance or glorification of God? Science and technology are the fruits of human reason; in religious language, the instrumentation to think God's thoughts, to drive onward the divinely given progress that will one day fulfill human destiny and the purpose of creation. In humanist thought, fulfillment of the human prospect is the purpose of our life-support technology. Both moral visions agree in the necessity to resist fate, yet ultimately accept death. In Christian thought, we honor life in ourselves and in one another, yet yield to God who in Christ has taken the sting from death. In secular thought, we strive to ameliorate the pain of life, all the while accepting death as part of life so that evolution of this world might proceed. We live and die under God's mercy and God's wrath (see Ps. 90).

In summary, we presently find ourselves living in an age when we seek to use the benefits of modern technology to achieve healing and strength in living, survival through health crises, and comfort in dying. The miracles of pain medications, monitoring and diagnostic instrumentation, and curative and palliative treatments make possible greater controls over pain, sustained presence of mind even under powerful sedation, and rational judgments about end-of-life care. The rudimentary ministries of food and water, warmth and air must be extended to all. The advanced technological versions of those supports, as well as other advanced life supports (transfusions, antibiotics, mechanical respirators, and resuscitation) should be individually negotiated by doctor and patient in light of that patient's own beliefs and desires. Persons will have different notions about suffering, death, and what lies beyond death. Therefore, there will be variation in what is deemed appropriate—depending on personal beliefs, and beliefs and values specific to individual faith communities and voluntary associations. To maintain uniform clinical standards and equitable social justice in what is available to all people, along with an appropriate variability in styles of dying, will be a great challenge facing our generation as we develop our health-care systems and our belief communities.

Euthanasia: the Utopic Tradition

Across the ages various images of what is the "good death" have appeared. For the Hebrews, a blessed death was found in "happy old age" (Gen. 15:15) when a man "full of years" (1 Chron. 23:1) was "gathered to his people" (Gen. 35:29). Unfortunate death was death without leaving a legacy, too young, alienated from one's people, in a strange land. For the Greeks and Romans, a heroic or courageous death was desirable. In Suetonius's account of the death of Caesar Augustus, he records, "He expired suddenly . . . dying a very easy death, and such as he himself had always wished for."[12] One should die possessed of one's faculties, not subjected to the indignity of disfigurement or agonizing suffering. Even suicide was licit if it preserved life in dignity, poise, and mastery. Always tempering this ideal vision of a desirable death were proscriptions of suicide imbedded in the finer moral strains of the tradition. Although suicide is not specifically condemned in the Hebrew scriptures, the underlying affirmation is that God is the giver and taker of life (Job 1:21). In the Greco-Roman world, the lofty Pythagorean and Platonic ethics contended that the gods have placed persons at their posts and they are not to desert, even under trying circumstances.

In the early modern era, great utopian writers found in the benefits of science the opportunity to live long and well, not to be cut short in life, and to be guided to a gentle death. Thomas More's *Utopia* was a place where persons were gently eased from the burden of prolonged sickly and suffering existence by benevolent euthanasia. John Donne's great text *Biathanatos* allowed suicide as a voluntary form of euthanasia. A most interesting strain of the utopic euthanasia tradition is found the response of the church. Here again we see the same dialectic of love life/receive death that shapes the secular moral tradition.

Euthanasia and the Faith Community

To return to our opening excursus on Hebrew ethics, the Talmud tells the story of the old rabbi who lay dying in his second-story apartment. Prepared to die, he could not pass away because his pious congregation prayed outside on the street that his life be sustained. The old rabbi walked to the balcony, dropped a large flowerpot on the assembly, and disrupted the prayer long enough for death to steal in and deliver him to his maker. Other rabbinic traditions tell of the euthanasic customs of removing the pillow from under the head of the dying person. We may infer that this gesture would hasten the death of those with pillow orthopnea from pulmonary disease or congestive heart failure. In the Christian tradition, we also find the congregation petitioning, even practicing euthanasia. To pray for the welfare of a friend's soul, relief of suffering, and an easy death were commonplace throughout the Christian ages. Folktales from Europe, Scandinavia, and Great Britain indicate that direct euthanasia was often practiced in the chapel itself. The "Holy Hammer," made of stone, was kept in an old chapel in each district. "When it was needed or requested, it was secured and 'operated' by the oldest person in the village in order to crush the head of the dying person while all of the inhabitants prayed."[13]

It can be argued, I believe, that in today's litigious and morally afraid atmosphere, the faith community can and should have the moral courage not only to pray for good death, to faithfully attend those in terminal illness, but also to assist in the euthanasic act, at least in its passive form. I have observed across the years that it is those who love deeply who are able to let go, even to assist in the act of dying; while those of guilt-tinged alienation are immobilized and seek to "do everything possible."

To conclude this chapter we will look at new ways in which the parish might participate in the last days of its members lives. The underlying dialectic of honoring life and working for its prolongation, and of accepting the appropriate place of death in human experience is seen in the position of the churches on euthanasia policy. Beginning in 1945, the Euthanasia Society in America sponsored legislation to facilitate mercy killing of the incurably ill. Leading clergy, including Henry Sloane Coffin, president of Union Seminary, and Harry Emerson Fosdick, were moving forces in this movement. The bill proposed:

> (1) Any sane person over twenty-one years old, suffering from an incurably painful and fatal disease, may petition a court of record for euthanasia, in a signed and attested doc-

ument, with an affidavit from the attending physician that in
his opinion the disease was incurable;

(2) The court shall appoint a commission of three, of whom
at least two shall be physicians, to investigate all aspects of
the case and to report back to the courts whether the patient
understands the purpose of his petition and comes under the
provisions of the act;

(3) Upon favorable report by the commission, the court shall
grant the petition, and if it is still wanted by the patient,
euthanasia may be administered by a physician or any other
person chosen by the patient or by the commission.[14]

At the same time, the Archdiocese of New York termed the petition, "Anti-God, un-American, and a menace to Veterans . . . a
departure from the eternal moral law."[15] This dialectic represents the
polarity within which the sensible golden mean appears. In this *via
media*, we honor life in ourselves and in each other. We affirm the
continuity of all lives, irrespective of quality or status, oblivious to
one's wealth or value. A theological worldview is not contingent upon
anything that we are or have achieved. Our dignity is anchored in the
reality of God. In destiny we are also summoned to be in life until our
life is taken up by God. As the Pythagoreans and Platonists held, we
are not to abandon our posts. As Jews and Christians discover, God
has purpose for us in each moment of our living and dying, but our
utopic ethic allows us to relinquish our lives to God in due season. The
frantic attempt to resist death by any technological feat, no matter how
fantastic or dehumanizing, is an affront to the Lord who "gives and
takes life," who guards our "coming and going." In the modern
world, the vision of good death undergoes strange mutations. Ivan
Illich has characterized six stages of our cultural belief about what
constituted a "natural death":

(1) The fifteenth century 'dance of the dead'; (2) the Renaissance dance at the bidding of the skeleton man, the so-called
'Dance of Death'; (3) the bedroom scene of the aging lecher
under the Ancient Regime; (4) the nineteenth century doctor
in his struggle against the roaming phantoms of consumption

and pestilence; (5) the mid-twentieth century doctor who steps between the patient and his death; and (6) death under intensive hospital care.[16]

Illich is depicting both the optimal or desirable image of dying in a cultural period and the charade or cartoon by which a society caricatures that mode of death it fears. In the iconography of death we find a society's utopic and dystopic vision. Beyond these visions of good dying, we find the very modern expression of a good death coming in old age in full health. "Suppose we died young late in life?" poses Ernst Wynder, president of the American Health Foundation. This death will be like the "natural death" envisioned by the Marxist medical philosophers. No longer will we do ourselves in by deleterious lifestyles and inadequate health maintenance. We will all live to be old and well and then die suddenly from natural causes. This is a return to the gracious death of Caesar Augustus. It is not certain whether today's death in North America conforms more to Illich's dystopic horrors (sick in hospitals under intensive care) or Wynder's paradisiacal utopia of long lives, well-lived, culminated by sudden death in a hospital setting. Both tendencies seem still to be highly pronounced in our culture.

Scenes of a Good Death

What is the picture of good death that we should rightly seek and that is worth our earnest endeavors? This question, of course, hinges on our moral vision of the good and fulfilled life. It is that question, the rightful expenditure of our life story, that constitutes the search for the good life. For the time being, there seems to be a coincidence emerging between the good death that people desire and the ability of medical care to not impede, perhaps even to facilitate that desire. Sophisticated and targeted pain medication is now available. PCA (patient controlled analgesia) now allows the patient specific titration and timing of pain medication, moving us toward that yearned-for day when pain will not devastate and derange the poor sufferer. Living wills and natural death acts, hospices, and home-care programs are moving us toward that utopic day when we shall die well, accompanied by those we love, attended by those possessed with the gifts of diagnostic precision, prognostic truth, and therapeutic power. In that day we shall discover the wisdom of the words: "To every thing there is a season, and a time to every purpose under the heaven: a time to be born, and a time to die" (Eccles. 3:12).

A good friend and neighbor knew death was near when she relapsed a third time during the course of treatment for a breast cancer that had spread to the lungs, brain, and other organs. She asked that she stay at home, surrounded by her family, pastor, friends, and fellow parishioners. Her death was a parish and neighborhood event to the very last hour, as Brahms' *Requiem* was piped through the home.

This week in Oxford, I learned of the wife of a Reformed pastor in a small town who also is dying of cancer. She too has come home from the hospital and hospice. A small table with an open Bible and other mementos of faith stands near her bed. There is also a chair by her bed that is occupied twenty-four hours a day by a friend who is a member of the congregation. Sensitive to needs for the patient or family to be alone, this vigil, or better, companionship, sustains her through the end.

When my grandmother was dying in her small cottage in the hills of northwestern Pennsylvania, as a young pastor I asked her if she would like the family to gather now and then to read the Bible, sing a hymn, and pray. Though this was awkward for her grandson to orchestrate, she seemed pleased that her family marked her impending death with her, symbolized it in this manner, and lifted the experience to God in her presence. We needed it, she needed it. It supported all of us old German Calvinists who tend to avoid talking about these things, even before the One to whom we belonged in life and death, as we say in our *Heidelberg Catechism*.

Just a few decades ago we started transferring death from the home into the hospital. There is something of a reversal of this trend now, but the modern sociology of the family often makes it impossible. More and more people leave their homes and reside during their last few months or years in a nursing home or hospital-like facility. How might the church again become part of this experience? Let me pose several simple, perhaps controversial measures to take death back into the personal and parochial setting and get it out of the courts and doctors' workshops—the hospitals.

1. In our parish churches, synagogues, mosques, and other houses of worship, let us not only preach and teach on a regular basis about dying, death, and God's purposes through these culminating events, but let us have planning sessions: opportunities to lay out our wishes and enlist others to safeguard those wishes against any who would override them. The present fad of living wills, advance directives, and appointed powers of attorney, though crude and adversarial documents, are a starting place. Let us have parish dinners and put together these directives while we sit around tables together. In the Corinthian letters, Paul pleads with the congregation not to take our weighty moral matters to the law. Surely birth and death are such matters. We too need to work out these patterns of preparation and execution of wishes in the parish setting. We also need to offer the resources and the community care of the congregation to other persons who have no church home or who may not be believers.

2. When the process of sickness and dying begins in one of our congregants, let us put into motion this process of helping, consoling, grappling for meaning, providing meals, caring for children and guests who arrive from around the country, and just distracting to allow relief. If the home is a setting that is comfortable, let us bring the pastoral care of the congregation to that person, offering prayer, consolation, "good-time sharing," gratitude for life, and provision of any particular need. If, as is increasingly the case, appropriate home situations do not exist, let us set up parish houses, perhaps even with modest medical and nursing provision (church clinics are a good start in this direction), where persons may receive the grace of death in the presence of God and the members of the community of faith.

3. Finally, there may be a place today (in very limited instances) for the "holy hammer." At certain points in the history of the church, persons could come into the chapel and be put out of their misery with a blow to the head. We need not be so crude and use this Al Capone-like technique. That Dr. Kevorkian had to set up his thanatron in the back of his Volkswagen bus is a scandal. That Janet Adkins had to leave her home on the

West Coast is frightful. Could we not have situations where those rare circumstances in which one needs assistance to die—withdrawing the respirator from Emily Bauer, overdosing the morphine to Debbie, hooking up the thanatron to Janet Adkins—are done by and in the presence of one's community of faith? This is not the vicious mass suicide or homicide of Jim Jones in Guiana. It is a congregation attesting to the limits of our endurance of suffering, to the fact that by virtue of medical progress we have transformed disease into long, hard, chronic afflictions and away from the swift death of infection in years past. This corporate act would safeguard euthanasia from abuse and secure it ethically in the face of the law. It would be witness to the victory over death by the God in whom we trust. I hope in the years ahead when we struggle with this issue some congregation will be bold enough to try it and deliver the *coup de grâce* when such a desperate measure is required.

I firmly believe that making available such thoughtful measures as have been sketched in proposals one and two will almost completely eliminate the need for number three. But rare instances might occur. Better than changing our assisted-suicide statutes, let us try these familial and parochial initiatives. Dying care is now possible in relative freedom from pain, in alert consciousness, and in the presence of our friends. Why continue to expel it from the provincial hearth into the cold, sterile, intensive-care units of hospitals with lawyers or judges at the bedside deciding whether the plug can be pulled? This shameless parody of human and godly wisdom must cease.

3
Biology, Ethics, and Letting Nature Take Its Course

> The rules of conduct do not exist in splendid isolation, but are rooted in the very essence of living beings, just as the dictates of the Sermon on the Mount are rooted in the very essence of the living God.[1]

> "Nor dred or hope attend a dying animal.
> A man awaits his end dreading and hoping all."[2]
>
> William Butler Yeats

We have set in motion the dialectic on our question of prolonging and ending life. Natural reason calls on inherent and intrinsic rational purposes and asks, Why ought suffering be endured? It then affirms suicide when the self's pleasure and best interest is lost. Like the Stoics whom we noted affirmed suicide when nature dictated and who argued that moral life was "life according to nature" (*to kata physin zēn*), philosophy's god is often "nature" or the best we can find within ourselves.[3] Transcendent reason invokes *das Andere, das Heilige*. This wholly other reality rationalizes suffering as refinement and mandates sharply against the violent propensities of our nature. "Thou shalt not kill." As our conversation continues to unfold, let us now regress from philosophy to its more primitive, even more natural root in biology itself. Recent ethics, in a naturalistic vein, stress the animal impulses that prompt behavior by instinct. In striking ways, these imperatives often resonate with those prompted by higher moral reasoning. If ecology is the under-discipline of theology and eschatology is the over-discipline, biology may be seen to underlie philosophy as social polity (organizational anthropology) succeeds it. At this point a flow chart of our vectors of ethics might prove helpful.

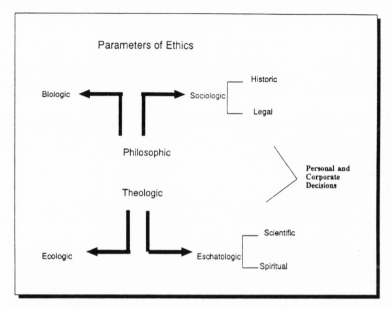

The most fundamental force that limits our life span is our biological being with its genetic structure, its evolutionary character composed of survival instinct, lethal propensities in body and mind, and specific strengths and vulnerabilities. Biology in individuals and the natural history of the collective species ensures the demise of each of our own lives and that of all creatures in right proportion and in due season. Whether by means of war, plague, or famine as external forces, or the inner forces of aging, sickness, or diseases, nature irresistibly has its way with us. The normative significance of biology for mortality policy, therefore, is that natural (bodily) and temporal (life span) limits must always temper those passions we have for avoidance, protection, and transformation of our nature. Born in the yearning of self-transcendence, cognizance of mortality is not only the root of science and progress, it is the root of religion and ethics. It is our glory and delight even as it robs us of the innocence of the animal.

As the great Russian geneticist Theodosius Dobzhansky, pioneer of the studies of drosophila, wrote:

Living creatures other than man are also mortal. Man is,

however, unique in knowing that he will die. Mankind, the human species has evolved from ancestors that were not human. A being who knows that he will die thus arose from ancestors who did not know this. The appearance of this new kind of being was an evolutionary event, certainly unprecedented on earth, possibly and even probably unprecedented in the cosmos. . . . Anxiety . . . in the face of death is . . . species wide in man. . . . People consequently strive for a union with, and for relatedness to other human beings.[4]

Love and interdependence are not the only virtues prompted by our premonition of death. Power and aggression are also rooted here. While by nature organisms (other than human beings) live and die by the benign rules of altruism, gene perpetuation, and the grim rules of selection and survival of the fittest, human beings resist these natural processes of refinement and elimination thinking, often audaciously, that they have risen above such brute and savage necessity. In a memorable passage in *The Descent of Man*, Charles Darwin gently chides us for making this assumption and exhibits the latent brutality of a biological ethic.

With savages, the weak in body and mind are soon eliminated; and those that survive commonly exhibit a vigorous state of health. We civilized men, on the other hand, do our utmost to check the process of elimination; we build asylums for the imbecile, the maimed, and the sick; we institute poor-laws; and our medical men exert their utmost skill to save the life of every one to the last moment. There is reason to believe that vaccination has preserved thousands, who from a weak constitution would formerly have succumbed to small-pox. Thus the weak members of civilized societies propagate their kind. No one who has attended to the breeding of domestic animals will doubt that this must be highly injurious to the race of man. It is surprising how soon a want of care, or care wrongly directed, leads to the degeneration of a domestic race; but excepting in the case of man himself, hardly any one is so ignorant as to allow his worst animals to breed.[5]

Darwin's awareness of dynamic evolution repudiated in his mind (and those of his precursors) the Aristotelian doctrine of static forms of creatures and convinced him scientifically of what farmers and herdsmen knew empirically, that a lineage could be cleansed from its flaws by selective breeding. The more basic imagination that this idea incited in Darwin was that inherited disease itself, that compound of all lethal flaws in an organism, might be eliminated through controlled breeding and husbandry. The fascination, hard to realize technically until our own era of artificial insemination, genetic analysis, and controlled gestation, drew on an assumption of Puritan scientists two centuries earlier—which must be examined before we outline the normative contribution of a biologic ethic for mortality.

The Puritans believed that there was an inherent causality between spiritual sin and physical derangement, degeneration, and death. This biological breakdown was in humanity and in all creatures as a result of humankind. Building on the Pauline/Augustinian concept of originally inherited and biologically transmitted sin, and the fall, and death-boundedness, the Puritans came to believe that corrupt lineage could and would be cleansed in the millennial renewal of life. This was occurring, they believed, in the restored world then breaking forth. In that ecstatic century when empirical faith and science erupted together even death might be conquered.

In the fall, human beings forfeited their natural immortality and also lost their intuitive intelligence about maintaining health and curing ills. Death ensued, if we use Walter Cannon's words, when we lost the "wisdom of the body." Animals retained this intuitive ability not to transmit flaws and to cure their ailments. Now in the seventeenth century a new human being, a new science, and a new medicine was expected as part of the great instauration of a new paradise. Prolongation of life was anticipated and, as Samuel Hartlib envisioned in his *Chymical Addresses*, "another garden will be found, whence shall be had herbs that shall preserve men not only from sickness, but from death, itself."[6]

Biological science since the Puritans continues to dwell on these normative ideas, namely, that death might be overcome and more certainly that death's precursors in disease and inborn errors of vitality might be flaws amenable to correction. Biological ethics, at least in its first phase among the Darwinist and evolutionary theorists, fashions the myth of biological Puritanism (purification), which reached such demonic proportions in the eugenics and euthanasia practices of Darwin's century and into our own. Though the vision of cleansing the gene line from death-propensity has waned in modern biological theory, the companion idea of the Puritans that lifestyle (nutrition, exercise, etc.) and therapeutics (paracelsian iatrochemistry and Harveian physiology) could save and prolong life has persisted. Modern biology and biomedicine now send us the equivocal message "resist death—but accept it." Perhaps this is where we should be in a contemporary bioethics. Roger Bacon in thirteenth-century Oxford said that we should strive for health and prolongation of life "finding the secrets of stores, herbs, sensibles," but we should also accede to the biblical life span allotment of 100 years. While he may have been slightly optimistic (+ fifteen years) according to recent calculations[7] the same ethical ideology is found in today's biological philosophy.

The genius of biological ethics on our subject of mortality is not found in its extravagant founding vision of death's conquest in the seventeenth century or in the harsh "survival of the fittest" ethic of the nineteenth century. It is found, rather, in the genial corroboration that evolutionary and biological ethics bring to our unfolding thesis of sanction for the exceptional taking of life in certain marginal situations. This forms a building block in the edifice of our philosophically and theologically mandated respect and compassion for human life.

Normative biological ethics is also found by a careful reading of the benign natural virtue of the biologic and psychologic instincts that pertain to extending and ending life. Let us now elaborate on these two aspects of biologic ethics and later see their relevance to the practical areas of dealing with human death—health policy built on our evolution of the human life span and clinical care of human beings as our biological strength fails and we near death.

Evolutionary Ethics

Evolutionary ethics are similar to environmental ethics and the ecological parameters of modeling that we will review in the next chapter. Evolutionary ethics are close to the sociobiology of human behavior—which considers the instincts, impulses, and feelings that so greatly influence our behaviors—and that will be considered later in this chapter. Many colleagues in ethics dispute my use of this ethical dimension. Ethics, they say, has to do with free choice, right and wrong, not the autonomous instinctive expression of genetically driven behaviors. Rote, conditioned impulses are not right or wrong; they just are. The simple fact that refutes this hesitancy is that we can distort and direct evolution. We modify evolution every time we refuse to let nature take its course, by removing the eye with retinoblastoma, by correcting the diabetes with insulin or islets. When we administer genetically recombined human-growth hormones to persons of short stature or elderly devitalized persons, we modify evolution—at least in its phenotypic manifestation. The achondroplastic dwarf or hormone deficient midget may get taller with recombinant growth hormone, but the offspring will not be altered by this change. That the person with youth-onset diabetes lives to be sexually active and produce offspring is a challenge to evolution's mortal force.

It is not the process of evolution or its meandering paths that are the subject of ethics. It is the mechanisms of the process. We could see our moral obligation somewhat in the terms of the earlier quotation from Darwin, not to impede evolution. In a somewhat cynical twist to this view, we could conversely argue that evolutionary ethics prompts us to exert fully (as its most highly-developed creature) our mastery over evolution. On this subject, I agree with Alastair McIntyre that the only ethical point to "designing our descendants" would be to design human beings that would no longer desire to "design their descendants."[8]

The evolutionary mechanism in the first place is a moral good because it allows new generations to succeed the old. To recall Dobzhansky, creatures that have premonition of death could only have come into being from those who developed that shadowy sense of mortality that we find in midrange primates and other animals like dolphins with an elaborate frontal cortex and language. Biological ethics thus impinges on eschatology by being the vehicle of fashioning the being that will be, but is not yet (*ontologie des noch-nicht-seins*, Bloch). In a similar vein, we may see that the evolving history of moral and spiritual consciousness is in some sense developmental. While conscience emerges more out of social-anthropological experience than biological evolution, we can see rituals of behavior including violence, retaliation, and altruism in those, our forebears in the phylogenetic chain, who forged the crude precursors of human ethics.

What are the mechanisms of biological evolution? Are they necessary conditions of natural law and therefore unpliable, or are they plastic and amenable to our influence and control? Some of the mechanisms of change in the organic world are simplicity evolving into complexity; homogeneity into heterogeneity; perpetuation of inherited and some acquired characteristics; struggle for survival; diminished reproduction at the higher levels on the phylogenetic chain; disease as the mechanism of mortality and therefore of invigoration and generational renewal. How would we evaluate these mechanisms in terms of the mortality ethics we seek to build?

Starting with the last and most problematic issue, the prophylactic and therapeutic challenge we make against disease: is this a salutary or dangerous action? Certainly vaccines and biologicals modify the unchecked interaction and penetration of microbial fauna and flora within human flesh and that of domesticated animals. According to any ethic, this intrusion against an evolutionary mechanism is justified, indeed is morally required. Take two examples: should smallpox have been eliminated by global introduction of the vaccine and should antibiotics be used for weak, elderly persons with bacterial pneumonia? In the first case, Darwin hinted, even though he knew of inoculations against smallpox by primitive peoples, that this was an imprudent course. It is true that the conquest of smallpox in our time has coincided with the significant increase of overpopulation and starvation, especially in Africa. But only the complete therapeutic nihilist would say that we should not have eradicated smallpox. Witnessing that blight, reflecting on its grim devastation across the ages and being able to prevent it made imperative, I believe, the risky inoculation that proved deadly to pioneer guinea pigs like Jonathan Edwards, president of Princeton University.

The modifications we have wrought in the microbial world—through sanitation, asepsis, inoculation, and antimicrobial therapy may return to haunt us some day. Indeed, that day may already be upon us with the frightful mutation frenzy occurring in the microbial creation and evidenced in the presence among us of sexually-transmitted diseases like the HIV AIDS virus and various oncoviruses. Still, we had to act. It was as if a great good was disclosed to the mind and heart of humanity by the God who imparts to us the secrets of the universe. In the discovery of the first vaccinations in Africa, through the costly and dangerous early attenuation and testing of the vaccine, through to the global dissemination just completed, we have witnessed a moral imperative that conscience could not deny.

We recently celebrated at the Radcliffe Infirmary in Oxford the first clinical use of penicillin forty years ago. The use of penicillin or erythromycin on pneumonic infections in old and sick persons may be a more complicated story. Denying Sir William Osler's "old man's friend" his due course was, and continues to be, an alloyed blessing. Evolution-wise it is of no effect unless such therapy might drain resources from pregnant mothers and thus disrupt procreative patterns. But this chain of casuistry is suspect. Antibiotic therapy in terminal cancer patients or emphysema patients may not be an unmitigated good. We may set these persons up for more protracted, agonizing, and intractable infections, say fungal infestations. We may check the infection but leave the patient physically and mentally damaged. Here again, though, we must acknowledge that swift and discerning use of megaantibiotics generally work well without a great residue of harm. To pull one child back from bacterial meningitis or save one mother with pneumonia is worth the world.

Attacking disease as the trigger of death in the evolutionary scheme is a matter of continual refinement in the ethics of biomedical policy. On balance, prophylaxis and therapy are goods we could not and should not resist. As for diabetes, PKU (phenylketonuria, a genetic disorder that can cause severe mental retardation in infants), and myriad other disease processes that we thwart and challenge with some deleterious effect to the gene pool and evolutionary process, the result may be ambiguous but it remains a moral duty to thus ameliorate present human suffering.

Next we discuss and evaluate the Darwinist mechanism of diminished fertility. Political hacks in dark taverns with a few drinks will always decry the fact that well-off people, well-educated people procreate less than those who are poor, especially black and Hispanic people. Their positions are so morally distasteful that they merit no comment. It makes even more ludicrous the following passage from Herbert Spencer, Darwin's predecessor who in many senses was the founder of early evolutionary ethics: "Humans have fewer offspring than herrings. The English have fewer offspring than the Irish."[9]

Certainly the Malthusians, who were Darwin's contemporaries, correctly noted with alarm how population explosion would threaten the evolutionary mechanism of a balanced birth and death ratio. Moral sensitivity to this problem will prompt us to prevent the catastrophic collapse into famine or resource depletion that will inevitably deal unjust death to countless human beings. Death that ensues from thoughtlessness is as grievous as that inflicted directly.

The biological reality of the struggle for survival presents a particular challenge to both the humanistic and theistic approaches to death ethics. Certainly humanist strains of political theory (Gentile, Grotius, Machiavelli, et al.) were more disposed to war in the spirit of Cicero than were the Augustinians and scholastics. Indeed the pacifism of Jesus and the apostolic church found great offense in the political realism of *res publica* doctrine, and to the Ciceronian ethic of harsh aggression and defense toward those who would threaten you. Even Augustine found self-defense no reason for killing. We might also suppose that Christians repressed the underlying aggressive and survival instinct in our biological being. In the spirit of the decalogue, which claimed "you are inclined by nature to kill, therefore you shall not kill," early Christians posited a violent nature within us (the flesh) perpetually at war with the indwelling spirit of God.

Today the "survival of the fittest" ethic is enjoying a mighty revival. From Jimmy Hoffa's trade unionist version "Eat or be eaten," to the banal advertisements that chime "you only go around once in life, so grab all the gusto you can," we are constantly bombarded with the brutal and bulimic versions of an evolutionary ethic.

That our moral frailties and possibilities are somehow consigned to us without our assent by heredity and environment is another significant challenge to ethics when viewed in an evolutionary perspective. Not only are we faced with a helplessness before a cosmic determinism in evolution itself, now we face a particularly and even more troubling determinism in the very foundations and lineaments of our own person. Some moral systems like Greek fatalism and Augustinian/ Calvinistic predestinarianism play on this perceived coercion about who we are and why we act as we do. I prefer David Hume's account. A man not untouched by Calvinism, he used destinarian doctrine to turn on his detractors and offer freedom in two different ways. On the one hand, if nature is transcendentally directed, then in living in accord with nature we are perfectly free. On the issue of suicide, he gave the argument a particularly biting twist by saying (against the Calvinist preachers who chided him on his suicide essay) that if God preordains and executes by his will all actions through us, then if we successfully commit suicide, that must be in accord with his will. In broader terms, as Augustine said, "God's providence is expressed through human freedom." To act in accord with our nature must be the highest freedom of the moral life, rather than some free-floating libertinism by which we may incline in whichever direction the wind blows. Actually the evolutionary concept of a hereditary and environmental (acquired) template informing our being encourages moral action and moral education because we can take confidence that we build on an inherent structure and direction.

The latter point of moral exhilaration ironically is the lasting impact of an awareness of evolution on the ethical life. If the mechanisms of evolution tend toward complexification and diversification, then range and possibility belong to the moral order as strongly as conformity and regularity. Modern chaos theory and indeterminacy physics allow that wide-ranging fields of action are found even in highly ordered systems. Evolutionary ethics therefore teaches us in our dealings with death that decay and degeneration may, in broader field theory, be an aspect of renewal and creativity. Nature may prescribe an allotment to our lives and an end to our days that may be as much cause to rejoice as to mourn. Biology claims that we are not only a part of nature itself, composed of the same chemicals and same primal genetic codes as all creatures, but we are unique, unprecedented and in some sense beings that will never be lost. Yet the apocalyptic devastation of megadeath as a phenomenon of evolutionary field process and the demise of those individuals who are sacrificed in the struggle for survival remains poignant and grievous.

Early this morning as I write, the U.S., British, French, and Saudi and Kuwaiti aircraft assault, which we fearfully anticipated, took off on their deadly mission against Iraq. Even an American residing in Britain cannot rejoice. Are we not witnessing the ancient and perennial ethic of the food chain where the stronger either devour or force the weak to cower? In this case, the small creature Iraq moved against tiny Kuwait and was in turn assaulted by the giant America. The shark has swallowed the bass who had swallowed the minnow. Just causes aside, it certainly has to do with asserting and repudiating power and with sustaining survival and livelihood against those seen as a threat to that well-being and dominance. An evolutionary ethic, another apocalyptic horseman, this time—war.

But what if war in the Gulf is not just war in Augustine's sense of an act of love in support of justice for the oppressed? The Kurds had been gassed, the Kuwaitis raped and ravaged, the Iranians brutalized, the Saudis threatened. When the staked out territoriality of a family of animals is transgressed, they strike out to recover and retain that preserve. When a weakened and vulnerable wolf bares his throat to one stronger, some gentle law of inhibition to his surrender prevents the more powerful from assault. Biological and evolutionary ethics displays both a forceful aggression in favor of survival and enhancement of one's sphere and a seemingly contradictory mercy for the vulnerable.

Friedrich Nietzsche emulated the aggressive impulses in the animal and natural world and the analogous assertive drives of the classical Greek and Roman warriors and states. He despised the contrary dispositions brought into the world by Judaism and Christianity: love, mercy, and pity. But biological ethics has shown us how altruism is in a subtle way edifying to the community. Violence is infectious and eventually turns on the perpetrator, "who take the sword, perish by the sword." The nonviolent resistance of Gandhi and Martin Luther King Jr. imitated a primitive naturalistic wisdom and intimated an eschatological theistic wisdom. The world this morning hopes that this natural and supernatural wisdom will prevail.

The Death Ethics of Animals and Primitives

All eyes are turned to thee, O Lord
To every one Thou givest food;
Thou openest thy hand and all are satisfied.
When Thou dost turn Thy face away,
All are stunned in terror;
Without their breath they die and turn again to dust.
Thou breathest on them once again,
And life springs up in them anew,
And the world is everywhere young and fair and beautiful.

From Haydn's *Creation*, after Psalm 145

The funereal, burial, and other rituals of death among animals are also constructive as we build a case for an appropriate human ethic of prolonging and ending life. Fire ants build a bridge of their carcasses across a fire so that those who follow can pass safely. There is an impulse of sacrifice and altruism built into that primitive instinctual structure as sure as there is an impulse to survive, fight, and propagate. Squirrels, rabbits, and other animals seem to go away to die when they sense they are moribund or are given this signal from the community.

As Haydn sensed in *The Creation,* the animals glory in their being and die with awesome innocence. In the same manner, primitive and aboriginal peoples prepare for and face death. The Amerindian goes out into the woods in the cold of winter, never to return! The Inuit elder is set afloat on the ice block by family and neighbors. Migrating peoples in the hunter-gatherer time of history apparently forded rushing rivers that would wash the weak and old away to their deaths, certainly a gesture to be understood in Darwinian evolutionary terms.

Animal ethologists like Konrad Lorenz and Edward O. Wilson have shown that while animals do compete even in lethal aggression for access to food, mates, or leadership, for the most part animals do not kill their own kind. Someone has tragically observed that rats and human beings are among the few animals that routinely destroy their own. Whereas infanticide and geriatricide come closer to a kind of natural biological ethic, suicide and homicide are rare. Human beings, not animals, have had to develop inhibitions against killing their own kind. Animals apparently need no such restraint. The ethologists have established that we do exhibit aggressive behavior toward our own species. Freud's theory of death instinct (*Todestrieb*) is drawn from the same biological side of his observation of nature. The male of the species is often vibrant and multicolored in order to assure both life and death by his flaming plumage. The male bird attracts both the female for mating and the predator to kill him. The aggressive energy needed by our prehuman ancestors to prevail in an environment now becomes a liability, says Konrad Lorenz, when militant enthusiasm (Mailer's lust for destruction; Fromm's necrophilia) enraptures a crowd, and losing all inhibition, they become a lynch mob.

Now the primal aggressive instincts are easier to exercise. Human beings do not have impressive teeth, claws, or strength. But like the pilots returning today from their "surgical strikes" on Iraq, human beings seem to have little sense of the destruction and death they have delivered. Pushing a button and releasing a missile or bomb load affects the aggressor far less than choking the enemy with your arms and hands. Before we move on to ethological and psychological theory to analyze homicide and homophilia, we need to offer a few remarks on interspecies killing.

Ethics with Animals

Reviewing interanimal lethal behavior raises the issue of how human beings treat and kill animals. Peter Singer, among modern ethicists, has offered some of the most thoughtful reflection on our treatment of animals. If we can reduce the fetus to subhuman status or characterize the black people as apes, we can desecrate and destroy them without pangs of conscience. When the sixteenth-century "just war" theorists in Catholic Spain justified killing the aboriginal natives of South America during the conquests, the objects of their subjugation were characterized at best as infidels to be coerced and at worst as savage, subhuman beasts to be hunted down. These human gestures of dehumanization and desecration imply that killing animals is morally licit. Singer questions the assumption of legitimacy in our killing and abuse of animals. This inhumane practice may lie behind our intrahuman insensitivity.[10] Drawing on Jeremy Bentham, English philosopher and founder of utilitarianism who takes the felicific calculus (avoidance of pain and maximation of suffering), Singer asks whether we are justified in causing animals to suffer and die. Should we be cruel to animals? Interestingly, such brutality is outlawed in the Noachite laws of Judaism in the same breath as the proscription of homicide. Should we experiment on animals to learn things that will benefit humanity? The last of the world's chimpanzees are now being sought for use in AIDS research. This may be necessary and good, but we will need careful protocols that will safeguard the animals from unnecessary pain. We will euthanize them when our work leaves a residue of pain or disability. Similarly, we shoot horses when they fall and sustain multiple fractures, and we put cats and dogs to sleep who endure terrible accidents or who become old and sick.

A poignant and telling incident has recently occurred in the war zone of Saudi Arabia. In the preparation maneuvers of U.S. artillery and tanks, a camel was seriously wounded. The Americans were forbidden to put the animal to death. According to Islamic custom, the owner of the camel had special duties to attend the animal in his death. This would be in accord with ancient Semitic moral law that shows humane concern for animals.

Singer questions if we take for granted the legitimacy of the food chain and the assumptions of the Darwinian ethics which, with corroboration from biblical ethics, has said that humankind has power to name and take dominion over the animals of the earth and the fish of the sea (see Gen. 1:26). While Inuits who may have no protein source may have a legitimate claim on the use of animal flesh, the rest of us would be wiser to limit our intake of red meats as all research on heart disease and cancer shows. The modern practice of specifically breeding chickens, cows, and other animals for human consumption has its own particular moral problem. The ethical power of our purview is that animal deaths must be delivered as painlessly as possible, their suffering taken into account, and a humble spirit of gratitude for their sacrifice for our table be constant.

The lesson we take from these comments on animal ethology and the ethics of using and abusing animals is that this arena, though having its own ethical integrity, is also a proving ground for establishing the ethics of how we treat other human beings. Although Hitler's last companion was his dog and the phrase "we shoot horses, don't we" has become a watchword for our benevolence for animals and coincidental contempt for people in the same straits, in general our sympathy for animals or contrary violence is indicative of how we regard other persons. When Hebrew law lists brutality to animals as unconscionable along with the spilling of human blood, the gravity of such violation is shown.

C. S. Lewis takes us back into a human ethic of care for the dying in his discussion of animal pain in *The Problem of Pain*.[11] In the case we are advancing step by step in this book, we argue that a sense of right reason will in exceptional cases allow us to end our own life and aid in the death of another. The spirit of mercy and love may allow this, and although a program of care will most often obviate the need for this, on rare occasions the need will continue—especially because of our aggressive need to prolong living in those under our care. Lewis helps us position our perspective again on a theological base as in this book we attempt to integrate religious and cultural ethics on these questions. We have argued that the basic purposive pattern that we discern in reality is that of suffering, death, and transfiguration. Death, war, even the execution of Jesus are the judgment of God (bringing righteousness from evil). This christological paradigm, symbolized by the crucifixion, contends that excruciating suffering and death take us close to the power center of what God is doing in the world.

Human pain and death is comprehensible and becomes explicable in the drama of sin, death, and renewal. Animal pain is inexplicable, "a plaint of guiltless hurt which doth pierce the sky" (quoted by C. S. Lewis, *The Problem of Pain*). It is not just the position of animals in the scale of sentience, nor their undeserving pain that creates the enigma of animal suffering. As we noted earlier, animals enjoy some naivete against suffering in the suffering of anticipated death. Animals also, as we have seen, may bear and share our human suffering vicariously. The deeper mysteries of animal sacrifice in the ancient world— Abraham's intended sacrifice of Isaac until the goat was provided, the lamb of God slain from earth's foundation (Rev. 13:8)—mean, in deepest sacrament, the compensation and judgment required in human violence as that is lifted up for ultimate correction and redemption.

We put animals to sleep to alleviate their misery. As we recall our discussion of sleep, anesthesia, and euthanasia, we remember that sleep undertaken in prayer and repentance detoxifies and restores. "If I should die before I wake," the prayer of parents with their children for generations, is tonight offered in Oxford and London, in Chicago and New York, in Riyadh and Baghdad. It is offered as expiation for the wrong within us that we sense deserves death. But morning comes and rather than the feared death, we are brought again to life and the unexpected reprieve, the awakening and resuscitation, the resurrection which God gives through sleep and arising (*wachen, auferstehen*), and this fills us with gratitude. The lion and the lamb shall sleep together, sings the eschatological prophet. Perhaps our reciprocity with the wild and the tame of this resplendent creation will show us some gentleness of ethic and some undergirding mythos about death and life by which we can rationalize our actions in this treacherous valley through which we must walk.

Brahms, in his *Ein deutsches Requiem*, chose to depart from religious versions of the death mass and fashion a national and natural song in the face of death. Brahms wanted to call it a "Human Requiem." Again the psalm (84) was placed centerpiece:

How lovely is thy dwelling place, O LORD of Hosts!
For my soul longeth, yea fainteth for the courts of the LORD;
My soul and body crieth out, yea for the living God.
—Psalm 84:1–2

The Biology and Psychology of Death: Instincts and Emotions

The next lesson we will draw from the animal kingdom for our kingdom of ends and means has to do with instincts and emotions that arise in our bodies and psyches, in turn animating our decisions and actions about death. When animals are threatened or cornered they exhibit what we call in human beings the anxiety response of fight or flight. Actually the behaviors in the face of threat, danger, and death present a very complicated pattern. We find withdrawal and escape as well as desperate flight. When uncovered or cornered, animals may not fight but bluff, deflect attack—even feign death. What we call protean maneuvers (after the Greek god, Proteus) are moves to bluff, camouflage, change our form in the confrontation with death. Moths change colors; opossums go limp, stop breathing, and appear dead; hermit crabs, with infamous haste, scurry away. One is reminded of the question put to the economist Kenneth Boulding after a university lecture on the theme of destructive aggression and exploitation by nation states. "What do you think it means when the Sermon on the Mount says: 'The meek will inherit the earth'?" the student asked. Boulding replied: "Those people who will be left standing when all the rest have killed themselves and each other are those who know how to back away at the right time." When survival moves like backing down fail, nature by selection has equipped animals with teeth, hooves, and claws. Indeed, one of the earliest extant forms of law, just beyond the law of the jungle, is *lex talionis*, the law of talons. Here we find the root for our word, retaliation.

In his masterful study *Sociobiology: The New Synthesis*, Edward O. Wilson summarizes the points we wish to make about animals, ethics, and gestures to end life:

> Fighting between animals of the same species is typically ritualized. By precise signalling, a beaten combatant can immediately disclose when it is ready to leave the field. . . . Ambivalence (to kill or back away) is a way of life in social creatures.[12]

The will to live and will to die, as I have shown in a previous book,[13] abide perennially and paradoxically in every living creature and are heightened in human beings. We resist death from disease, attack, or at the hands of some enemy. At the same time, there comes a point when we give in and "choose to leave the field." Discerning this important moment when it comes, is the primary task of pastoral care and clinical medical judgment. To this subject we turn next. Before that, let us extrapolate from these animal instincts and behaviors and look at the psychological impulses that arise within us in the face of death.

In a now classic study, psychiatrist Elizabeth Kübler-Ross verified from her clinical experience at the University of Chicago hospitals what had earlier been noted by psychologist Beatrix Cobb at the M. D. Anderson cancer hospital in Houston, Texas.[14] Persons confronted by the lethal insult of cancer and the awareness of immanent death experience a sequence of reactions beginning with denial, anger, and bargaining, and ending with depression and acceptance. On closer look, these universal and somewhat autonomic responses correspond to what we have noted in the animal world as responses to threat. These stages, or better phases (sequence may vary), also corroborate the "near death" studies which we have had in behavioral science for a century and from literature and anecdote for millennia. Persons who fall into the sea and almost drown, air passengers who crash yet miraculously survive or are rescued, report a liturgy of action starting with disbelief, resistance, fantasy and proceeding through to negotiation and surrender. Lifeguards working on the ocean shores often report that victims they have rescued from drowning, after resuscitation, will stand and hit them in the face, angry at being pulled away from what they later report was a strangely blissful state.

Building on these popular studies, we can position the awareness and confrontation of mortality within the richer depth and breadth of the emotional life by reviewing what we are coming to know about the neurobiological, psychological, and psychoanalytic dimensions of our mental life.

Psychologic Ethics and Death Response

In recent years we have learned from the neural sciences (neurophysiology, neurochemistry, etc.) that complex structural, electrical, and chemical processes develop at the mind/body synapse and discharge salutary and exhilarating impulses (endorphins exciting verve and creative energy) as well as negative and destructive impulses. Perhaps the focal science for our inquiry is neuropsychopharmacology. Two systems convey messages to the tissues and organs of the body. These messages signal repair and regeneration or breakdown and disintegration. The nervous system transmits electrochemical signals in two-way traffic circuits from brain to tissues. The endocrine system circulates chemical mediators to various tissues and organs from their sites of origin.[15] Hormones surge through the body and stimulate reproduction, growth, and development, maintaining homeostasis and energy storage and utilization. Modulations in and of these functions obviously incline the organism toward demise rather than invigoration. The profound questions of philosophical biology—whether organs have lifetimes, whether there is a genetically (evolutionarily) fixed number of cell divisions in the organism and in particular organs (the brain), and whether the triggers which at some point change the organism toward devitalization are correctable errors or naturally benign events—these are questions beyond the scope of this book. Suffice it to say that biologically we are born and programmed to live and grow and also to degenerate and die. Indeed, the two processes occur simultaneously with an exquisite complementarity.

Discovery in recent years of the salutary and deleterious neurochemicals—the endorphins, the neuropeptides—has begun an inquiry which will, in the years ahead, illuminate the benign and malign forces in our bodies and will show, most scientists think, a very subtle reciprocity between those biological energies that serve life and those that insure death. For the sake of our study, we note simply that these frontier sciences promise new insights into the dynamics of living and dying.

Structural characteristics of our psychological being and the range of emotions which we might label morbid and mortal feelings also afford insight into how we do and should respond to death in ourselves or those whom we attend. In general, we must first acknowledge in our conscious selves a hesitancy to confront, to bring forward in consciousness, to speak about the matter of death. We tend to evade the subject, move on to something else, send cards and flowers to distract and deny the morbid subject. Sociologist Geoffrey Gorer has gone so far as to label death the pornography (strictly forbidden taboo) of our time.[16] Life and hope and the correlative denial of death so surge through our being that the contemplation of death, either our own, or vicariously experiencing the dying of a friend or other person, insults our conscious and conscientious soul and we discharge the matter off in some other direction. In his *Confessions*, Augustine writes of the death of his best friend. It is a passage that speaks of the absorbing and consuming force of this experience in our soul that causes, perhaps not Augustine, but mortals like the rest of us, to repress the reality. We quote it at length because of his incisive description of the concourse of death sympathy in the soul.

> During those years, when I first began to teach—it was in the town in which I was born—I gained a friend, my equal in age, flowering like me with youth, and very dear to me because of a community of interests. As a boy, he had grown up with me, we had gone to school together, and had played games together. . . . This man was now wandering with me in spirit, and my soul could not endure to be without him. But behold, You were close at the back of those fleeing from You. You Who are at once the God of vengeance and the font of mercy, Who in a marvelous manner convert us to Yourself. Behold, You took the man from this life when he had scarce completed a year in my friendship, sweet to me above every sweetness of that life of mine. . . .

> Tormented by fever, he lay for a long time senseless in a deadly sweat, and when his life was despaired of, he was baptized while unconscious. . . . After a few days, while I was absent, he was attacked again by the fever and died.

> My heart was made dark by sorrow, and whatever I looked upon was death. My native place was a torment to me, and my father's house was a strange unhappiness. Whatsoever I had done together with him was, apart from him, turned into cruel torture. My eyes sought for him on every side and he was not given to them. I hated all things, because they no longer held him. Nor could they now say to me, "Here he comes," as they did in his absence from them when he lived.

To myself I became a great riddle, and I questioned my soul as to why it was sad and why it afflicted me so grievously, and it could answer me nothing. If I said to it, "Hope in God," it did right not to obey me, for the man, that most dear one whom [it] had lost, was more real and more good to [it] than the fantasy in which [it] was bade to hope. Only weeping was sweet to me, and it was my friend's successor in my soul's delights. . . .

I marveled that other men should live, because he, whom I had loved as if he would never die, was dead. I marveled more that I, his second self, could live when he was dead. Well has someone said of his friend that he is half his soul. For I thought that my soul and his soul were but one soul in two bodies. Therefore, my life was a horror to me, because I would not live as but a half. Perhaps because of this I feared to die, lest he whom I had loved so much should wholly die.[17]

Television interviews with the British and American pilots who have just returned from their predawn sorties over Iraq give vivid evidence of the mind's ability to short-circuit the reality of death. "I'm scared," said one still-trembling RAF pilot, "scared of dying, of failing my mission. . . . " The Americans were more distracted. "It's like a football game. When it begins you have the jitters, the weight in the stomach, but once you run a few plays everything's OK." "It [the brightly lit skies over Baghdad] was like a fourth of July I remember as a kid," said another.

This psychic phenomenology of resistance and repression when it comes to death accounts for the reticence of loved ones and friends, even doctors and nurses, to sustain open contact and communication with dying persons. This fact presents a twofold danger in the clinical setting. On the one hand, like pilots or anyone who must pass through great danger, we may wish to simply get it over with quickly. On the other hand, we may so abhor the confrontation that we absolutely refuse to deal with it and let it string on or force someone else to handle it. The threat of not-being and annihilation is the first intrapsychic reality that anyone of us who accompany and comfort the dying must come to terms with ourselves.

Love, it is said, is the antidote to annihilation and alienation. When we know that we are not alone, that someone cares, that we can come home, that God holds us near, then we can venture out, deal with threat, even face death in our own body or in someone we are privileged to serve. Love is such a powerful emotion that one thinks it must be something greater (see 1 Cor. 13). Love is also the antithesis of hate and rage, which are other natural emotions that often contribute to destructive impulses against others or ourselves. Anger and hate, like aggression, usually arise in us when we have felt insult or attack. The feelings therefore possess a basically salutary virtue of repelling danger and protecting the self. At the same time, the emotions often arise from misunderstanding, misinterpretations of others' actions toward us, and of course from psychopathological roots. Like the stress response and anxiety, anger therefore can have inward origins and may result only in self-harm. As Jesus said, anger kills (see Matt. 5:21–22). Indeed, the greatest danger of anger is that it becomes internalized and either destroys one's self through repression and compaction or it lashes out in uncontrollable rage against someone or something outside ourselves. Domestic violence, gang violence, and war are often the result of pent-up hostility that has not been afforded normal outlets of expression.

Perhaps the most psychologically insightful story in English literature of this human quality is Shakespeare's *King Lear*. In the first moving scene of the play, the die is cast for all that will follow. The simple and naive old king calls his three daughters before him to parcel out the realms of England as their inheritance. Allowing himself to be flattered by the duplicitous expressions of devotion of the two false daughters and finding insult in the honesty of Cordelia, he lashes out to disown his good daughter and lavishes endowment on the others who will eventually destroy themselves and him. The telling psychic insight of Shakespeare is the power of an *idée fixe*, a presumed insult and how we will recklessly and with bull-headed resolve persist in living out the unfounded anger and rage. Shakespeare, of course, gradually unfolds a tale of judgment where the evil is exposed and justice is done. He also weaves the story of gradual insight in old Lear using dramatic metaphors of blindness and storm. Anger and rage can be healthy and saving emotions if they are received as natural, allowed their proper expression, and if we remain open to their redemptive possibility. As Elizabeth Kübler-Ross showed, anger is the rightful response to the announcement of death. Its righteousness is verified as it runs its course and is transformed into serenity.

Shyness and shame are two of the emotions triggered by the vivid self-consciousness which occurs when, in Augustine's words, we see the "naked truth" and "naked deed" about ourselves. Living in England, a culture that C. S. Lewis contends seeks to cultivate reserve and goodness, one becomes aware of a deference, shyness, and civility in human encounters. The word heard most, hundreds of times a day, is "sorry." Shyness, as we learn from one of its pathological exaggerations—anorexia—is a desire not to intrude, not to be noticed, to slip in and out quietly without causing a stir. In Dickens' tales like *Bleak House*, heroes and villains fade into the dark crevices of buildings in London's streets cloaked so as to conceal who they are. Sherlock Holmes is often disguised in drab, baggy cloaks so that his omniscient self is not revealed. In life we clothe ourselves, cover ourselves in warmth so that, as in Genesis when Adam and Eve discovered their nakedness, we cover our shame. When we die we are stripped bare and stretched as a cold, naked slab on the mortician's block. One of the frightening anticipations of death is nakedness. This is why the open-backed skivvy we are forced to wear in the hospital is so humiliating. Embedded in the graceful emotions of shame and shyness is our death anticipation. We will all come to a time when we no longer wish to make an impression. We shall then be content with the impression we have left behind. What terrifies older persons or persons with Alzheimer's disease is that their closing impressions will be gross and distasteful. We want to be remembered with a smile on our face, a twinkle in our eye, a slight blush to our cheeks, a sweet scent on our breath and body, and our hair groomed. Dying cancer patients will often go to the barber or beautician even in their very last days—a reflection of our unquenchable human vanity and dignity.

The moral instruction this emotion provides us is the importance of noticing the time when one sick or dying wishes to be alone and to be left alone. Just as animals withdraw to hidden places to face their demise, so we come to the point of wanting to be left alone. When Dr. Henry Beecher, the great Harvard anesthesiologist, was dying of cancer, he wrote a final essay on "The right to be left alone." He was a man of enormous grandeur and grace, and I learned much about the *gentilhomme* through our association as roommates at the founding meetings of the Hastings Center. From a distinguished family of preachers, writers, and physicians, he knew well how to carry himself unobtrusively through and beyond this life.

Anxiety is another emotion that teaches us about death and how we ought to die and not die. Angst or *Sorge tragen* is also an emotion of being exposed, of meeting our end in the daily flow of experience. Brahms again takes the majestic psalm in his *Requiem:*

> *Herr, Lehredoch mich*
> *dass ein ende mit mir haben muss,*
> *und mein leben ein ziel hat,*
> *und ich davon muss.*

Lord, let me know the measure of my days before death that I may consider my frailty, that I must perish (Ps. 90).

In recent years we have rendered this and other deep historic emotions to be items of psychological management and manipulation. In a more profound sense, are they not signals within our being about who we are and where we are going? Certainly anxiety can become a clinical phenomenon when threats are imagined or exaggerated. But the healthy emotion is one that calls us to fully human awareness and vocation as it reminds us of limitation and mortality. In this day of Valium and antianxiety drugs, we run the risk of cutting ourselves off from the deeply salutary and constructive yield of this emotion.

To know our mortal frame is to find wisdom, to be able to care for others and to thirst for God. In Karl Barth's treatment of baptism (the universal ritual that symbolizes death and cleansing), he speaks of the rite of immersion when one gasps for God as the drowning person gasps for air. Anxiety is such a potentially edifying breathlessness. The child is anxious when mother does not come home. The student sweats and frets when she does not know if she will have funds to finish the term. The father writhes and tosses in bed when he fears losing his job. Anxiety is a premonition of loss and an emblem of death, the ultimate loss. Yet to count all as loss, Paul tells us, is gain (see Phil. 3:7, 8).

Anxiety, like shame, can trigger frenetic compensatory activity, sublimation by losing oneself in creative act (think of Vincent Van

Gogh at Arles), lashing out in violence or engaging in high-risk behavior. Death anxiety can cause the patient frantically to demand more and more treatment—surgery, pills, whatever. It can prompt a restlessness in nurses and doctors whereby they must "do something" and not just be there. Much of intensive-care medicine and end-of-life technology, I fear, is activated by the discomfort we feel in the face of anxiety and the compensations we make in our frenzies of therapeutic activity. Letting the panic yield its intended peace, numbering and measuring our days becomes the good antidote of serenity to anxiety, trust against fear.[18]

Two other emotions associated with mortality are guilt and grief. Guilt is in general the feeling that we have wronged someone and that wrong is not concealed. Putting the question of source aside, be it conscience, superego, taboo, or more likely the natural and wholesome structure of cause and effect and violation of the perceived inner and outer moral order, guilt as a phenomenon can weigh down on us, make us wish we were dead, inspire the martyr complex or inversely cause us to compensate and deny death. The patient in real trouble in the hospital is the one who has been the object of a medical mistake. Infused by guilt, the caregivers will go overboard to satiate their guilt, often doing more harm in the process.

Guilt generally can function in a healing way, opening to awareness the ways in which we wound ourselves and others (the old church liturgy of "falling short" or "leaving things undone" is much too benign, given the human condition). Guilt can therefore help us to live and die well.

Grief or mourning is a profound emotion associated with our self-perceived or vicariously experienced mortality. Grief is both sorrowful and sweet. The loss of a friend, a spouse, or a child is bitter and painful. It wells up the tears, it causes the whole body to shudder. I recall the heart-wrenching privilege I had a year ago attending our neighbors whose seven-year-old son had just been killed by a runaway car. The grief was acute and agonizing. The father, also badly injured in the accident, howled in grief in front of the congregation at the funeral I conducted. But then his bitter wailing would turn to laughter as he remembered the delights of playing with the young boy. Grief is good, says my colleague Granger Westberg.[19] It is a capacity rooted in our biological and psychological being that allows us to deal with loss. It heals and redeems. Our body and soul is ordered so as to receive loss and death in due season. Long evolution has prepared us to die, even by starvation (those who claim withdrawal of feeding is unnatural are mistaken), and the human organism is perfectly capable of confronting and conquering death.

Yet the majesty of grief is in its pain. No easy answer or comfort should impede us from walking its sorrowful path. Recently sitting in the south bank of stalls at Sung Eucharist at Magdalene College, our attention was drawn to the shaft of sunlight on the brass plaque above the opposite stall. It was the seat of literature don C. S. Lewis. Lewis is at his best, I believe, in his grief books. In *A Grief Observed*, he remembers:

> And poor C. quotes to me 'do not mourn like those that have no hope.' It astonishes me the way we are invited to apply to ourselves words so obviously addressed to our betters. What St. Paul says can comfort only those who love God better than the dead, and the dead better than themselves. If a mother is mourning not for what she has lost but for what her dead child has lost, it is a comfort to believe that the child has not lost the end for which it was created. And it is a comfort to believe that she herself, in losing her chief or only natural happiness, has not lost a greater thing, that she may still hope to 'glorify God and enjoy Him forever'. A comfort to the God-aimed, eternal spirit within her. But not to her motherhood. The specifically maternal happiness must be written off. Never, in any place or time, will she have her son on her knees, or bath him, or tell him a story, or plan for his future, or see her grandchild.[20]

Examination of our biological and psychological nature has provided us good and true moral insight. To conclude this chapter, let us consider two topics of health-care ethics at the end of life. First, we now look to the human body for our ethical wisdom. Discussion of the natural life span and the imperatives arising from that predictive data for clinical care and medical research will be the first application we will draw from biological ethics. Second, we will look at two recent initiatives from U.S. and British physicians to address end-of-life care ethics in a new way. In their clinical judgment, physicians seek to read what is happening in the body. Is it fighting on, wearing down, or giving up? Clinical wisdom about this vitality/mortality ratio is one of our best indicators about when to press on, when to stop, when to resist, and when to aid the dying process.

Life Span: Medical Imperatives

For many years a lively debate has occurred in the medical literature about the life span: Was it increasing or holding steady? Were we tending at the end of this century and millennium toward longer and healthier living or longer and sickness-filled aging? Recently the debate between James Fries[21] and Edward Schneider, et al.,[22] holders of the former and latter theses, has been joined by a Chicago group, Olshansky, et al.[23] Although Olshansky is focused on a statistical analysis that shows that we are now close to reaching the life span of eighty-five years, his clinician-ethicist collaborator, Christine Cassel, M.D., sounds a warning about the ramifications of the findings for clinical care. Her analysis resonates with Schneider:

> It is not clear whether a longer life implies better health. In fact, we may be trading off a longer life for a prolonged period of frailty and dependency—a condition that is a potential consequence of successfully reducing or eliminating fatal degenerative diseases. Current research efforts by the medical community are focused on prolonging life rather than preserving and improving the quality of life. An obvious conclusion, therefore, is that the time has come for a shift toward ameliorating the non-fatal diseases of aging.[24]

What are the ethical implications of our success in moving life expectancy out to the edge of the possible life span? It was decades ago when I remember hearing C. P. Snow, the British scientist-historian, reflect on the meaning of our landing a space camera on the moon. He said, "We now know that the only life we will ever find in this solar system is our own." Snow is less exuberant in his expectancy than Carl Sagan, but his point stands and it corresponds to what our intranauts into biomedical space are discovering. There are limits to the life span. Even if we made major conquests of the chronic diseases—cancer, heart disease, stroke, emphysema, etc.—the effect on average life expectancy would be negligible. We are left with only ourselves and we are invited to do well morally with what we have. Our manias for progress and transformation of human life will find some successes, but the great challenge will be to make good within the confines of what we have been given.

The crisis that has precipitated the ferment in medical ethics in our time and prompted books such as this one is nothing less than our frantic quest for conquest and control over human life unchastened by a wisdom to accept life as it is. We rush the dying into intensive-care units, intubate and wire them with myriad contraptions, and lose all sight and touch with the person on whose body we make that assault. Euthanasia should not be necessary if thoughtful, moderate medicine is being practiced. Coming to terms with life span, what scripture and tradition has termed our "allotment," is morally and spiritually beneficial for humanity as coming to terms with our personal deaths is for individuals. Our project should not be to "methusalize" our elders but to provide them adequate preventive and interventive health care out of justice and genuine respect. This will require a research enterprise that will address the real problems we will face as we age and an equitable delivery apparatus so that the present disgrace of so many of those we are called on to honor as they become old, sick, and poor all at once are dumped out of the purview of our care. The present health-care system, as we will see in a later chapter, provides too much for a few and too little for many. We extend the dying days of many of our loved ones perhaps two weeks too long, with very marginal accrued benefit. Easing off here and transferring our resource to safeguard the body at an earlier stage from crippling onslaught ought to be a health-policy priority. Two recent efforts in this direction deserve attention in this chapter.

In March of 1989 a dozen American physicians, including Dr. Cassel, formulated a report in the *New England Journal of Medicine* entitled, "The Physician's Responsibility toward Hopelessly Ill Patients."[25] A similar document was published by the *Journal of the British Medical Association* from a working party of the Institute of Medical Ethics.[26] Both papers set out to deal with the multifaceted problem that is the central concern of this book, the prolonging and ending of persons' lives. The Wanzer report set forth a multipronged care approach to the terminal patient and only in exceptional cases resorts to the question of physician-assisted death.

> Physicians have a specific responsibility toward patients who are hopelessly ill, dying, or in the end stages of an incurable disease. In a summary of current practices affecting the care of dying patients, we give particular emphasis to changes that have become commonplace since the early 1980s. Implementation of accepted policies has been deficient in certain areas, including the initiation of timely discussions with patients about dying, the solicitation and education in advance about their directives for terminal care, the education of medical students and residents, and the formulation of institutional guidelines. The appropriate and, if necessary, aggressive use of pain-relieving substances is recommended, even when such use may result in shortened life. We emphasize the value of a sensitive approach to care—one that is adjusted continually to suit the changing needs of the patient as death approaches. Possible settings for death are reviewed, including the home, the hospital, the intensive-care unit, and the nursing home. Finally, we consider the physician's response to the dying patient who is rational and desires suicide or euthanasia. [27]

Two of the participants dissented from the controversial section of the report. They were both colleagues of mine, astute experts in medical ethics and religiously devout men. Ned Cassem is a Jesuit priest and psychiatrist. He is an attending physician at the Massachusetts General Hospital where he directs ethics consultations. Ned personifies the genius of the Roman Catholic medical-moral commitment, which is to deeply cherish and safeguard the human person in whom life is found but also to receive death in its season as the gracious mystery of God. Jan Van Eys is a Dutch-American pediatrician, now chair of pediatrics at the University of Texas in Houston. Formerly he headed the pediatrics department at M. D. Anderson in Houston, one of the world's most advanced cancer hospitals. Like Cassem, Van Eys has reflected on the deep theological and pastoral aspects of medical care at the edges of life. He served on a commission I chaired for the Presbyterian Church, U.S.A. on these matters. Both of their dissents focus not only on the religious prohibition of killing but on their clinical sense that thorough and sensitive medical care, including palliative care, will make it unnecessary for any to suffer so badly that they will want to end their lives.

All of the physicians on record in this report possess rich clinical experience and seasoned judgment in dealing with terminally ill patients. From my own experience with half of the group, whose clinical skills I know well, it is certain that they are basing their moral convictions finally on the messages they receive from the voice of illness in the bodies and minds of their patients. The body can endure powerful insults from disease and from therapeutic countermeasures, for example, chemotherapy. The body has an exquisite sense of resistance, of hunkering down and regathering strength and continuing a will to prevail over disease by courage and strength aided by the assistance of surgery, drugs, psychotherapy, and the natural inclination of the body to heal and repair itself. The body also knows when the time has come to succumb to the force of disease and to accept the natural course. Even in the controversial passage, these physicians are responsible to this reading of bodily wisdom and integrity.

> All but two of us [J.V.E. and E.H.C.] believe that it is not immoral for a physician to assist in the rational suicide of a terminally ill person. However, we recognize that such an act represents a departure from the principle of continually adjusted care that we have recommended.[28]

Acceding to rational suicide as we discussed in chapter 1 is a strong moral position grounded in natural reason. Perhaps this is the best we can come up with in a pluralistic and autonomy-based society. My fear is that this development may lead to a medical practice where physicians and nurses see themselves simply as executors of patients' wishes to die when that seems appropriate in that person's own moral reasoning. I would point us to objective grounding in theological (the perceived receptive will of God to reclaim our life) and biological ("It's enough, I need help") realms as corroborations of the more subjective grounds of "rational suicide."

British medical practice, less heroic, more firmly grounded in centuries of provincial practice, where physicians know well the neighbors on their list, has also sought to ground its ethical views in such clinical judgment. That working party's report focuses on a presenting problem and a proffered response.

> The lives of an increasing number of patients, predominantly but by no means all elderly, are now being prolonged by modern medicine in states of coma, severe incapacity, or pain they consider unrelievable and from which they seek release. Doctors in charge of such patients have to decide not only whether they are morally bound to continue with life-prolonging treatment, but also, if no such treatment is being given, whether and in what circumstances it is ethical to hasten their deaths by administration of narcotic drugs.[29]

With an unexpected gusto reminiscent of David Hume, the report quotes John Donne's *Biathanatos:*

> Death therefore, is an act of God's justice,
> and when He is pleased to inflict it,
> He may chose His officer, and constitute
> myself as well as any other.[30]

The report concludes with recommendations similar to the Wanzer report.

> The majority of the IME working party may be formulated as follows. A doctor, acting in good conscience, is ethically justified in assisting death if the need to relieve intense and unceasing pain or distress caused by an incurable illness greatly outweighs the benefit to the patient of further prolonging his life.[31]

Again, while the spirit of this highly thoughtful and humane report is in accord with the thesis of this book, the moral reasoning is more questionable. The classical utilitarian view of ethics, known well to the British through John Stuart Mill and Jeremy Bentham, is like body wisdom when, in the calculus of pain and pleasure, suffering overwhelms the opportunity of any happiness and the body may say stop! Yet utilitarian or cost-benefit, pain-pleasure judgments are fraught with two dangers. In the first place, we can never gather enough factors into our calculation. The simple fact that pain blinds and distorts any capacity to measure calmly may mean that we will choose short-term relief over long-range well-being. Often in the medical care of serious disease very painful, obtrusive, and exhausting measures are needed to secure long-term gains. The second and more serious drawback of utilitarian ethics is that one person cannot judge what is best for another. As we have seen often in care for disabled or defective newborns, we say to ourselves that we would not wish to live like that or that the quality of existence is not worth it. But should our norms, expressed in serene health, be imposed on another? Whose life is it, anyway?

In sum, we can see biological and clinical wisdom moving in the direction of our thesis that on occasion we need to countermand our life-prolonging measures with particular measures to stop or even assist someone in dying. The raw biological material we have to work with should guide us into appropriate action. The question of what treatment or technology is there to be used should not be as decisive as to whether that procedure will aid a bodily recuperative potential or merely forestall or delay a bodily deterioration to which we should acquiesce.

Broad patterns and processes in the natural world help us to determine ethical action. In the biological realm these include evolutionary forces, biological instincts, psychological impulses, and clinical wisdom known by a close awareness of the body. An even wider perspective also teaches us our moral judgment when we view concerns ecologically. When the vast natural system is viewed as a whole, other imperatives come into view. To this we now turn.

4
The Ecological Background
of Mortality and Ethics

As is the generation of leaves, so is that of humanity. The
wind scatters the leaves on the ground, but the live timber
burgeons with leaves again in the Spring returning. So one
generation of men will grow while another dies.[1]

Homer captures here the broad cyclic and rhythmic pattern of life
and death that nature bestows. When we listen to Vivaldi's *Four Seasons*, sounding the throbbing of spring or the serene silence of winter,
our attention is drawn to the same truth. Schubert's *Die Winterreise* is
a song cycle about a journey through the cold and snow. But like Paul
Klee's painting of the same title, it is also about our inevitable journey
into death.

The ultimate natural context of our life and death is the cosmos,
the ecological envelope or environment that enfolds our being. We
consider the ecologic perspective in ethics as lying in the background
of theology because it is a kind of mythos or sacramental construct by
which we give not only position and bearing to all things but, by
means of this imagery, we also extrapolate their meaning and purpose.
In the sense of Saint Francis or Carl Sagan, the cosmos is something
of a sacred canopy within which we seek to line out all causality and
purpose.

In nature there is a necessary and benign death as well as that
which is violent and cataclysmic. These chaotic and disruptive episodes themselves are larger patterns of change. The meteor that may
have crashed into the earth and precipitated a dark cloud killing the
dinosaurs and much planetary life 65 billion years ago might be such
an event. The black cloud hanging over Kuwait from ignited oil wells

comes from human malevolence. In our day of biological, chemical, and nuclear weaponry, human malevolence might be able to release chain reactions within normal processes that will bring death, even megadeath, to humanity. Saddam Hussein decapitated the oil wells on land and on the Iraqi-Kuwaiti shelf, releasing into the Persian Gulf a spill four times greater than the Exxon *Valdez*. In his scorched-earth withdrawal from Kuwait, Hussein ignited a trench equal to 10 million barrels of oil a day. The cloud of smoke with its toxic carbons could blot out the sun over India and Japan and the spill might poison the seas. Ecological ethics would cry out against this lethal abuse of the life-giving biosphere. Biocide, destruction of the sphere of life, takes on benign (recuperable) and malign manifestations. We spray for mosquitoes to keep our summer evenings free from the pesky irritation. This intensifies adaptive mutation among the species so that a mounting arms race occurs with each new spray creating new mutant breeds. We do the same with antibiotics against certain pathogenic organisms, like pneumococcus and streptococcus. These organisms also adapt with subtle surface mutations and become resistant to our biocide. A relentless process of staying one step ahead is thereby set in motion.

Biogenocide, on the other hand, is deliberate contortion and usurpation of biological vectors to do harm and kill human beings. If anthrax or other biological weapons were released by vapor-spray bombs over Israel or Saudi Arabia, we would have known that our worst fears about biological murder had been realized. Chemical warfare from mustard gas to other forms of nerve gas uses natural vectors—aerosol, cutaneous absorption, and breathing to bring carefully calculated death. Similarly but less deliberately, we are poisoning ourselves slowly with our pollution of air and water. Both activities are targeted but are in another sense indiscriminate. Once toxins diffuse into the air or water, they are like the rain that falls on the just and unjust. Nuclear fallout killed hundreds of sheep in the Utah and New Mexico plateaus. A shifting wind can sweep our coal and steel-belt fumes and soot over Canada. An ill wind might blow Iraq's chemical cloud back over its own cities. We both control and are controlled by the regularity and caprice of nature.

In this chapter we will first consider the general themes of ecological ethics as they pertain to issues of mortality. We will then analyze two megaecocides and resulting genocides—nuclear winter and the greenhouse effect, or the perpetual summer of global warming. Finally, we will draw ethical guidelines from this perspective back to the clinical question of human deaths in the rationing of medical resources and of "setting limits." Our hope is to find yet another vector of corroboration to sharpen our moral sense about the appropriate and inappropriate prolonging and ending of life.

Ecological Ethics

Paul Taylor has written a provocative book entitled *Respect for Nature*.[2] Joining the train of moral persuasion going back through Schweitzer and Saint Francis, Taylor pleads that we stand back, attend with an awe and reverence, and respect nature. Schweitzer would have been offended by reducing God's verdant and picturesque creation to a technical abstraction called ecosystem, but he would approve of Taylor's dedication of the book to "the earth's wild living things." Nature exists in pristine form in the virgin forests, grasslands and marshlands that have never been exploited by human beings. Thoreau discovered this foreboding before a primeval world when he climbed Mount Katahdin in Maine. It was

> vast, titanic, and such as man never inhabits. Some part of the beholder, even some vital part, seems to escape through the loose grating of his ribs. . . .Nature has got him at a disadvantage, caught him alone, and pilfers him of some of his divine faculty. She does not smile on him as in the plains. She seems to say sternly, why come ye here before your time? The ground is not prepared for you.[3]

Nature also exists in various forms and stages of cultivation and civilization where human nature has made its overlay on this inhospitable substratum. Today most of the earth and even some interplanetary space bears the stigmata of people who have come. These visitors, like those European colonists to the new world beginning in the sixteenth century, have found its resources useful and have either left it rich and flourishing or depleted and trashed. Nature has been much altered by human nature. Breeding and hybrid farming has fashioned new specimens, yet this too is nature. Taylor's argument is philosophical, deducing arguments from foundational premises. We can view the natural world as the subject of our respect that entails protection and positive regard. Moving behind both act and rules philosophy, Taylor concentrates on an attitude or disposition of respect. A biocentric view of nature, which Taylor defends, is one where our regard for the world does not spring from what good we receive from it but from its own inherent worth.

Taylor does not go so far as to suggest that we deal with the environment as another person or certainly in any pantheistic sense, as a divine being. These views of a humanistic or mystic grounding of nature are not possible within the limitations of philosophy. They do, however, provide another reason for our positioning ecological ethics as a precursor of the theological.

When we resort to the biblical tradition of care for the earth, we confront something of a paradox. On the one hand, Hebrew thought demystifies and desacralizes nature. In contrast to the land faiths and fertility religions of Israel's neighbors in the ancient Near East, the Habiru worship God alone, not the sun, moon, stars, or fields. On the other hand, the biblical tradition understands land as a divine inheritance that we do not own and that we are to husband with tender care such as a husband cares for his wife. The connection between woman and earth, between Adam and *Adamah*, between the two fertilities, between sexuality and economics, though profoundly different in biblical thought than in Baal worship, is fundamental to any ecological ethics.

Walter Brueggemann,[4] from whom I borrow this insight, draws the stark parallel from the writing of Wendell Berry:

> I do not know how exact a case might be made, but it seems to me that there is an historical parallel, in white American history, between the treatment of the land and the treatment of women. The frontier, for instance, was notoriously exploitative of both, and I believe for largely the same reasons. Many of the early farmers seem to have worn out farms and wives with equal regardlessness, interested in both mainly for what they would produce, crops and dollars, labor and sons; they clambered upon their fields and upon their wives, struggling for an economic foothold, the having and

holding that cannot come until both fields and wives are properly cherished. And today there seems to me a distinct connection between our nomadism (our "social mobility") and the nearly universal disintegration of marriages and families.[5]

The ethical crisis comes when we no longer cherish but exploit mother earth, no longer reverencing but now utilizing her.

The rural community—that is, the land and the people—is being degraded in complementary fashion by the specialists' tendency to regard the land as a factory and the people as spare parts. Or, to put it another way, the rural community is being degraded by the fashionable premise that the exclusive function of the farmer is production and that his major discipline is economics.[6]

Ecological ethics within the biblical tradition holds economics and justice to be inseparable from the fertility and fecundity of the earth. We cannot reduce earth's growth, flourishing, and sustenance to technical "reproduction" and "management" any more than we can reduce our wives to objects of use (or abuse) that we eventually discard. Just as sexuality is holy, so the economics (house ethics) of our earth care entails sacred duty.

The first theme of ecologic ethics is therefore that of sacred trust for one beloved. Brueggemann summarizes:

When sexuality is connected to fertility, and when economics is connected to fertility, and when economics is connected to justice, we are close to the core of all biblical ethics, for the Bible insists that fertility is impossible without justice, that is economics cannot be separated from sexuality, nor sexuality from economics. We treat the land the way we treat women; "we" being dominant males who are historically owners of both.[7]

This complicated notion needs to be unpacked, since it is at the heart of the kind of organic ethics of creation and creature care and killing that we explore in this book. Ethics cannot be reduced to object manipulation or the application of static principles. We are involved through moral living in deep patterns of exchange (intercourse) and reciprocity with self and world (Heidegger, *"in der Welt sein,"* *"Umwelt"*). Sexuality and economics are not just incidental functions in the world. They exist in order to "bring forth" fertility and justice. The modern reduction of both fields to manipulable excitement (prostitution and promiscuity) or manipulable management (Wall Street) are profound distortions of the very nature of the betrothal. Sexuality is in order that love and life may come into being. Sexuality, including marriage and family, is a creative order, a procreative patterning or extending of the divine creation. Economics is the activity of ordering the world in life sustenance. Justice is the right ordering of the earth's fecundity so as to sustain the needs of all who dwell therein (inhabitants). Ethics in its inner meaning is fundamentally about habits or nurturing (nursing). Etymologically, ethics means habit(ations) or stables (ethos).

But this is not enough. The whole story involves cross fire as well (as Brueggemann rightly notes). Justice pertains to sexuality and fertility to economics. What can this mean? It is illustrated by the text from Ezekiel that ponders the ancient violation at Sodom.

> This was the guilt of your sister Sodom: she and her daughters had pride, surfeit of food, and prosperous ease, but did not aid the poor and needy. They were haughty, and did abominable things before me; therefore I removed them, when I saw it.
>
> (Ezek. 16:49–50 RSV)

Ezekiel is a holiness prophet and his prophesy belongs to the genre of holiness literature. As we noted in chapter 2 on the holiness tradition of medical practice, key ideas here are life as divine conception, assault as deicide, and the reproach of contamination and maintenance of purity. More important in this text is the connection of purity (chastity) with generosity. The sin of Sodom, as the sin of *pornē* in the Gospels, is not only prostitution. It is not giving oneself to life.

Dostoyevsky wrote of this truth when he developed the unforgettable character of Sonja in *Crime and Punishment*. Roskolnikov, wishing to believe himself a superman, violates all the goodness and order of the world by killing an old pawnbroker and her half sister. Sonja the prostitute, driven to this life by the poverty of her family, gives herself in saintly generosity to all and becomes the agent of Roskolnikov's redemption. Following him to his imprisonment in Siberia, through her kindness and nonrecrimination, she becomes a life-giver by opening his life to the divine realm.

To withhold oneself from love and life is to die. To hoard resources to oneself is to die. In the Gospels, the farmer harvested the fields, filled the barns and silos and then said "take it easy, our goal is satisfied." But the message came: "This night your soul is required of you. What now of your amassed wealth?" (Luke 12:20). The silos storing Scud missiles in Iraq and those storing Patriot missiles in the United States and Israel were built like the Gospel farmer's silos: on the backs of the poor. The delivery of missiles can only bring death. Yet amid our ambition toward death, God gives seed and field to the world for life to flourish and in that abundance to reach out and satisfy every living thing (see Ps. 145). Ecological ethics involves this kind of intimacy, fidelity, and care with the earth. Not an object to be manipulated, not a passive and pliable mass to be shaped to our will, but a living world for whom we must care as a friend. Ecocide at the rate we have inflicted it on earth in the last century is nothing less than matricide and ultimately suicide.

The ethic I advance is one where humanity is a partner to the earth, a position that attempts to avoid two dangers. The first is a resacralizing of the earth where, because of fear and false worship, we refuse to receive the gifts of life-sustenance that the earth means to provide. The other danger that a partnership ethic avoids is the domination ethic. In the Western tradition, as historian of science Lynn White has shown, we have subdued and taken dominion over the earth with relentless force. The spread of Christianity, claimed White, was responsible for the current ecological catastrophe.[8] A partnership ethic does not exploit and destroy the world to serve selfish human ends. It perpetuates life in nature as sustenance for human need. It ends life only as that ending aids renewal. We deforest an area selectively when that thinning will facilitate new growth. We allow natural fires to burn in great forests (for example the Grand Teton and Normandie's Sherwood forests this year) when that purging fire will renew growth.

The partnership ethic is one of interdependence. The world is part of a coherent universe. All parts cooperate with all others. The belief in creation allows that each particular creature lives and dies with particular and interactive purpose. For that reason sexuality can have intrinsic and cooperative meaning. Mimesis of divine creativity and multiplication of life is the originating purpose of fecundity. The interactive purpose with economics and justice arises as this realm of life interplays with the network of all others. Ecologic ethics, for example, requires that once the earth is filled, the mandates to be fruitful and multiply now be transmuted to the maintenance of birth and death equilibrium.

In its reverence for our God-created human home, ecology is a form of theology. We could survey the ecotheologies of the various world faiths: polytheistic, primitive nature worship, Judaism, Christianity, Taoism, Islam, Marxism, or secular enlightenment humanism. Since the ecologic crisis has begun within a Judeo-Christian context, which also created the technological and industrial revolution, let us look at the ecological premises of Judaism and Christianity with special reference to the ethical values of this worldview.

The earth is the Lord's and the fullness thereof,
the world and they that dwell within (Ps. 24:1).

The heavens are the Lord's heavens,
but the earth he has given to mankind (Ps. 115:16).

The first principle of biblical ecotheology is that proprietorship belongs to God and fecundity is provided by God. There is no Aristotelian notion of self-generating necessity in Hebrew faith.

Blessed art thou, Lord our God, King of the Universe who bringest forth bread from the earth . . . fruit that grows on trees (quoted in Brueggemann, "Land, Fertility, Justice," p. 45).

To be alive is to acknowledge the source of life. Commenting on Deuteronomy 17:6, "let the dead one be killed," Midrash Tanhuma explains, "an evil person is considered dead, for he sees the sun shining and does not bless the creator of light, he sees the sun setting and does not bless him who brings on the evening! He eats and drinks and offers no blessings."[9]

The orders of creation (*Sidrei bereshit*) bestow two ethical imperatives on human beings, the vice regents of the creation; forceful injunctions against despoiling nature and imperatives to develop and conserve nature. The first law condemns destruction of trees (*Bal talshhit* [Deut. 20:19]) and destruction of species (Lev. 22:20). The second requires settling and cultivation of the land. *Yishur ha-aretz* is an imperative to receive from earth the goods it provides for human life all the while sustaining the rhythms and balances of the orders of creation. Open spaces (*migrash*) and periodic fallow periods are requirements to insure the replenishment and perpetual invigoration of the land.[10]

Creation, writes Gerhard von Rad, is a saving act.[11] In its meaning inheres a process of providence for and enrichment of life. The earth also resists humankind's exploits. In the second creation narrative, the earth demands toil to yield bread (Gen. 2:15), and thorns and thistles confound our search for sustenance. The earth, in other words, extends both divine blessing and judgment to humanity.

If devotion, responsibility, economy, frugality, justice, and fertility are our response, life on earth will flourish. If we neglect, hoard, and destroy, the earth itself will turn against us. If we read the Hebrew words about subduing the earth (*rada and kabos*) as treading down or trampling under, the earth may recoil in vengeance or simply die away beneath us. If we interpret these commands as settling and cultivating, its bounty will continue.

In addition to intrinsic value, nature has instrumental value. Provoked or stimulated by human work, the earth has economic value. Crops, herds, fish, and minerals (Gen. 13:2, Job 42:12, Matt. 13:45) abide in the earth to be drawn out for human sustenance. Thanksgiving in part requires our constant commitment to replenish what we have received. The earth is our life-support system. Air and water, rain and sun, invigorate the biosphere and in turn sustain our life. The earth is also a thing of beauty and delight, providing an arena for aesthetic and recreational delight.

Human beings are creatures who can safeguard or destroy themselves, others and all around them. Our wonderful and terrifying freedom allows us to achieve a moral maturity by not succumbing to the *reductio ad absurdum* of our power of transcendence that is pride or being so absorbed in nature that is the sin of sensuality. The delicate equipoise of knowledge and power kept humble by identification and participation in all nature protects us from these two ethical errors.

The most dramatic examples of our inordinate and abusive pride against the environment are found in our capacity to effect nuclear winter or perpetual summer on earth. As we noted earlier when referring to air and water, earth and warmth, we can modulate these life-sustaining substances, thus prolonging or ending life. At the global level we may also have the power to elevate temperature or cool the earth and thereby devastate living beings.

Nuclear Winter

The morning news reports that an Iraqi Scud missile has hit in the residential heart of Tel Aviv killing at least three and injuring 100. One can imagine that the patience of Israel to not enter the conflict may now be spent and Israel will retaliate. The world only hopes that Israel will refrain from using a nuclear bomb as the other nuclear powers all refrained since the horror of Hiroshima and Nagasaki. These blasts, forty-five years ago, fulfilled Vedic prophecy of a world "brighter than a thousand suns" and set for the world a measure never again to be taken.

A nuclear exchange of great proportions (which the United States and Russia are capable of releasing) would initially create a hot explosive death that would melt and shatter the megalopolis on which the bombs would have been dropped. The light and heat would soon be replaced, however, by the death of darkness and cold. A blanket of darkness would cover the entire northern hemisphere and perhaps spread over the entire planet. The vast cloud of dust and smoke caused by the blast and consequent fires would blot out all sunlight, killing all plant growth and precipitating global famine. Temperatures would drop to below-freezing levels for a long period of time causing all fresh water sources to freeze and killing most domestic and wild animals on earth, as well as phytoplankton and zooplankton in the seas. The radiation fallout and toxic gasses would trigger instant or gradual death if any human beings survived the global winter. The scenario is no longer a Jeremiad from alarmists. It has been confirmed by the American National Academy of Sciences, the British Medical Association's Board of Science and Education, and other responsible world bodies.[12]

Lewis Thomas, the great physician-philosopher calls the nuclear winter projections "the most important research findings in the long history of science." The ecocidal effects that would follow the months-long winter would be biologically devastating. After the dust settled "a new malignant kind of sunlight with much of its ultraviolet band . . . capable of blinding many terrestrial animals"[13] would reenact the tragedy of Gloucester and King Lear where helpless animals and, any human survivors, like the leukemics of Hiroshima, could only wish they were dead.

Thomas goes on to describe the catastrophe that would be a holocaust, a dénouement of nature:

> Something else will have happened at the same time, in which human beings *ought* to feel the same stake as in the loss of their own lives. The elaborate, coherent, beautifully organized ecosystem of the Earth—what some people call the biosphere and others refer to as nature—will have been dealt a mortal or near-mortal blow. Some parts will persist, I feel reasonably certain, and the life of the planet will continue, but perhaps only at a level comparable to what was here a billion or so years ago when the prokaryotes (creatures like today's bacteria) joined up in symbiotic arrangements and invented the nucleated cells of which we are without doubt the lineal descendants.[14]

The lessons and analogies of this important ethical projection for our. more narrowly biomedical purpose are made clear by the former head of the Sloan-Kettering Cancer Center. Initially we note that physicians, especially the international fellowship of Physicians for Social Responsibility, have shown that the main disease threat to public health in the waning years of this millennium is the nuclear threat. The mania for conquest, the obsession with security, and the historic lust for war are now lethal behaviors. We may continue to have anachronistic military efforts such as we have witnessed in Iraq and Kuwait. Here, as in Panama and Grenada and on the Russian border of Afghanistan, all means of warfare, especially nuclear, chemical, and biological means, were not used. In a perverted twist, these war games or fantastic video games, are waged with a kind of seeming complacency, knowing that the nuclear capacity could be called on if it was ever needed. What the world will be like when fifty nations have nuclear capacity—and when nuclear warheads can be fashioned by engineering students in their labs and launched from shoulder devices, we dread to contemplate.

Second, we can take note of the way that our desire to live on and be secure can prompt us to frightfully destructive actions. The scorched earth option in war that Saddam Hussein exercised (withdraw from Kuwait but burn everything in Hussein's path) is not unknown in medicine. Just as General William Sherman made his lethal path to Atlanta to wipe up the U.S. Civil War, cancer patients often are left physically devastated after surgical strikes and the napalm of cytotoxic therapy. In war and in medicine, we need to learn both gentle and moderate measures of life-sustenance and life-prolongation. Our passion for survival and security loses meaning when we win the war but lose our life. The medical version of this military irony where the city was destroyed in order to save it is "the operation was a success but the patient died."

We must also learn in war as in medicine, in both fields of nuclear promise and threat, that the answer to health is not always fighting and conquest. A wiser approach is often found in that search for accommodation and equilibrium. Here, except for food-chain necessity, all creatures live and let live in mutually edifying reciprocity. If anything, latter-day warfare and medicine teach us that thoughtless benevolence to secure and save life may actually harm, destroy, and annihilate. The threat of nuclear annihilation, like our own extinction, is unthinkable. We therefore need to force this awareness into consciousness, deal with it openly so that we do not lash out subconsciously and irrationally to our greater loss.

The achievement of life sometimes involves the relinquishing of life. The rabbi, Jesus of Nazareth, knew this. "He who would save his live must lose it" (Matt. 10:39). The secret of saving life in our body and life on earth involves a self-effacement and mortification known to saints and mystics. This theologic wisdom emerges from ecologic wisdom. Saint Francis embodies the composite wisdom and his hymn to the earth and its creatures grows out of his own ascetic piety. In world affairs we are confronted today with the challenge of laying down our lives for one another in sharing earth's resources with one another rather than holding them to ourselves. The [former] Soviet Union and Eastern Europe now desperately need the assistance of the United States, Western Europe, Japan and Israel—the wealthy sector of the world. The developing nations of Asia, Africa, and South America need massive life-giving airlifts to achieve the bare minima that life requires. When the freedom to travel and emigrate becomes a universal human right as it inevitably must, the only way to avoid catastrophic depopulation of some countries will be international generosity. The moral secret of generosity and sharing is that we save and enrich our own lives by giving to others. The earth's enormous potential resource is symbolized by the nuclear secret now known to physics and genetics. The potential energy release of the atom is like the life release of the genetic code. Life's resource is abundant and sufficient, if we only discover the grace to give it away.

At the same time there is survival wisdom in the shield. Perhaps 200 million years ago a dense shield of ozone had formed over the earth sufficient to allow organisms to survive on land. Water creatures had long enjoyed the protection from ultraviolet radiation that the sea affords. Now the miracle of terrestrial life could begin. Here on this hot, harsh, and hard rock, floating on great plates amid the oceans, a new experiment of life was to begin. Now beings with large lungs, more complex dexterity and more complicated brains and neural systems could arise. It was these creatures so like God, yet so presumptuous in their arrogance, who found themselves one day in a position where the future of the earth was in their hands. And as this awareness of responsibility of prolonging or ending life shattered humankind's innocence, they were apprised that the hour was already late.[15] Picking up on this apocalyptic specter, Bill McKibben has written one of the most provocative books in recent years.[16] *The End of Nature* is an ominous prospect posed by the cognate threat of perpetual summer (greenhouse effect). As we noted in the earlier section on bedside ethics of life and death, we kill by cold or heat, by proximity or distance. We kill by not caring enough or by caring too much. Let us now ponder the significance of ecocide by global warming. McKibben's book is about our willful and unconscious damage of the ozone layer and our creation of the greenhouse effect. This frightful suggestion holds that we have already irreparably harmed mother earth and rendered her moribund.

Greenhouse Effect

One hundred years ago a Swedish scientist named Svante Arrhenius observed that in the early decades of the Industrial Revolution humankind was burning coal at an unprecedented rate so as to "evaporate our coal mines into the air." Arrhenius and scientists of his time knew that the by-products of combustion, including carbon dioxide, trapped infrared radiation that normally would be reflected back into space. He projected that if we doubled the amount of carbon dioxide in the air the temperatures on earth would rise nine-degrees Farenheit and calamities of a hothouse—rising waters, parched fields, and scorched animals—would occur. In the late 1950s other scientists confirmed that this, indeed, was occurring and if present pollution rates and rates of industrial expansion continued that we would double the carbon dioxide load in the atmosphere in fifty years time. When this insult is joined to the methane exhaust from earth (from domestic animals, termites, rice paddies, rotting garbage, etc.), nitrous oxide, fluorocarbons, and so forth, we see why we may have already turned earth into a steaming hothouse with the added danger of having punctured the ozone shield, exposing the fragile earth to dangerous ultraviolet radiation.

England in 1990 has experienced an extremely hot and dry year. Even though it has rained as we have come to expect, most days in our now two months sojourn in Oxford, farmers are alarmed and the reservoir levels are dangerously low. The official records, kept now for a century, show that the warmest years on record were 1980, 1981, 1983, 1986, 1987, 1988, and now presumably 1990. The critics of "greenhouse" theory say that this may just be a periodic phenomenon that will balance out when we can look at a 100-year span of time. Perhaps. But what if something is happening?

Statisticians are now saying that we have already witnessed an over one-degree Farenheit rise in temperature in the last century. This is three times the possible standard deviation and suggests that it is no accidental warming or blip on the screen. It is universally agreed now that if "endless summer" has not already set in, it will in the not-too-distant future. Perhaps the earth with its enormous compensatory and adaptive potential will react to the insult. Clouds may increase, screening solar radiation and diminishing the resultant warming. The deserts that we create by deforestation may better reflect radiation than did the rain forests they displaced. But the result of "greenhouse" will likely soon be upon us. Forest "dieback" is probably already beginning in Europe and North America (this in addition to trees killed by acid-rain) and more sudden "biomass crashes" may soon begin in the great southeast pine forests of the United States. Just as people do not die from starvation but from opportunistic infections or the diseases of vulnerability like cancer and heart disease, plants may already have begun to die from acid-rain toxicity or infestation. We therefore do not know if ecological calamity or routine evolutionary mechanisms like the end of an interglacial age is to blame.

In a synergistic crisis, we know for certain that chlorofluorocarbons have depleted the ozone layer of the earth between one and three percent in recent decades and have already created seasonal puncture holes in the stratosphere above the Arctic region and Antarctica. A small loss of this protective shield will scorch the skin, blind animals (as Lew Thomas predicted with a nuclear explosion that would destroy fifty percent of the ozone shield) and stimulate the malignancies caused by genetic breakage such as skin cancer and melanoma. That these malignancies are being seen with alarming frequency might be another piece of corroborative evidence that something is wrong.

Is it morally appropriate when we have fundamentally altered the environment creating intractable malignant melanoma, pollution-induced emphysema, perhaps heavy-metal triggered schizophrenia or Alzheimer's disease to deny persons the right to the compensation of suicide or even physician-assisted euthanasia? We have robbed the earth of natural law or unadulterated providence that lies behind those prohibitive ethics. We have inflicted on ourselves agonizing chronic and acute diseases that may morally justify some undoing of what has been done. The epidemiology of disease is shifting in our time from nature's infliction (e.g., infections) to human-made illnesses that may justify new moral responses at the end-stage of affliction.

> We have done all this by ourselves—by driving our cars, building our factories, cutting down our forests, turning on our air-conditioners. The exact physical effects of our alterations—even whether or not they will be for the worse— are for the moment beside the point. . . . In the years since

the American Civil War and especially in the years since the Second World War, we have changed the atmosphere—changed it so much that the climate will be dramatically altered. Most of the major events in human history have gradually lost their meaning: wars that seemed at the time all-important are now a series of dates which school-children can't remember, great feats of engineering now crumble in the desert. Man's efforts, even at their mightiest, used to be tiny compared to the size of the planet—the Roman Empire meant nothing to the Arctic or the Amazon. But now the way of life of one part of the world in one half-century is altering every inch and every hour of the globe.[17]

What shall we make of this twofold ecocide—nuclear winter and unending summer—one a latent, though not yet unleashed, sudden catastrophe, the other an already extant, gradual, but equally destructive force? What has it to do with our exploration of ethical responsibility in the prolonging and ending of life? These two cosmic phenomena bear out the aggressive and lethal propensities that we discovered in our psychic constitution. These developments also point to the terrible after effects of the so-called Age of Reason in the history of thought, when we threw off all moral constraints of nature and God and set out to remake the world in terms of our own will and pleasure. The events also portend apocalyptic and eschatologic themes to which we will subsequently turn. It is the theological context that is the foreground sphere of ecologic ethics that offers basis for some analysis and reflection.

Nature, like ecology, is a myth, an abstraction, a construct of the human mind. The splendid heartland of McKibben's book traces the development of this idea. The provocation of his thesis is that this frame of mind has now come to an end. But what of the fact that we have always found God in nature? Indeed, only in the religions of sheer revelation is nature not the instrument of divine speech and knowledge. The world in its order and splendor is where we apprehend God and are disposed to the ethical life. If nature has died, is God dead? Is ecocide ultimately a *götterdämmerung*—a deicide? Will the loss of nature cause us to lose our soul, our conscience, our immortality? Nietzsche found nature devoid of the face of God, and since the

Holocaust and Hiroshima, most of us miss the hand of God in the events of history. Can we ever live rightly in the knowledge of good and evil again? In McKibben's words, will the loss of memory (and hope) portend the loss of meaning?

McKibben concludes with the words of the great Puritan poet John Milton. Milton calls us to transcendent respect as the ground for earthly virtue. We recall it was the Puritans who first developed the enormous inquisitive intellect that would ground modern empirical science as well as the moral commitment behind this project to achieve the millennial obligation of consummating the good age of human benevolence inaugurated by Christ. Milton extols that cosmic wonder and earthly respect grounded in trust in God that is the mentality that can pull us back from the brink:

> The Maker's high magnificence, who built
> So spacious, and his line stretches out so farr:
> That Man may know he dwells not in his own;
> An Edifice too large for him to fill,
> Lodg'd in a small partition, and the rest
> Ordain'd for uses to his Lord best known.[18]
>
>   *Paradise Lost*

Jonathan Schell, in a more humanistic vein, summarizes the same wisdom in his section "the Second Death," in his remarkable book on the nuclear threat, *The Fate of the Earth*.

> Human beings have a worth—a worth that is sacred. But it is for human beings that they have that sacred worth, and for them that the other things in the creation have their worth (although it is a reminder of our indissoluble connection with the rest of life that many of our needs and desires are also felt by animals).[19]

An ecologic perspective on ethics realizes that human life is bound up inextricably with all other creatures. Our divine mandate is to care for humanity and all life on earth not only because of its own intrinsic good as God's creation but for its instrumental worth in sustaining the life of humanity and all creatures.

The nuclear and ecological age has made the human community acutely aware of death. But for the miracle of breath, death is the ground. The earth like human beings themselves, arose from nonlife and will devolve back to dust. Life is an epiphenomenon shimmering precariously on a foundation of death. "Nuclear death," writes Hans Morgenthau, "radically effects the meaning of death, of immortality, of life itself":

> It affects the meaning by destroying most of it. Nuclear destruction is mass destruction, both of persons and of things. It signifies the simultaneous destruction of tens of millions of people, of whole families, generations, and societies, of all the things that they have inherited and created. It signifies the total destruction of whole societies by killing their members, destroying their visible achievements, and therefore reducing the survivors to barbarism. Thus nuclear destruction destroys the meaning of death by depriving it of its individuality. It destroys the meaning of immortality by making both society and history impossible. It destroys the meaning of life by throwing life back upon itself.[20]

It is against this background of threatened megadeath, the transformation of the human soul towards death, and in light of ecologic ethics that we seek to describe the concrete ethics of medical care. In some sense the world of life and death best in our control is that close at hand. Our rightful shepherding of the resources of earth is reflected in microcosm now in decisions that must be made about how much we spend in prolonging life and in providing health care. The needs and desires of persons for long and healthy life are almost insatiable. Most societies on earth, including the national health-care system in the United States and particular jurisdictions (e.g., Oregon), are struggling with the issues of ethical allocation of scarce resources, setting of limits, and medical rationing. To these issues that provide an illustrative field for the relevance of ecological ethics we now turn.

Triage, Rationing, and Ecologic Ethics

Triage or rationing is indirectly a way of ending and not prolonging life. My colleague in medical ethics in Chicago, David Thomasma, director of the program at Loyola's College of Medicine, makes the claim that we already have in place a broad-spectrum policy of euthanasia by virtue of an allocation policy that dictates which medical services will be available (or withheld) from which communities of people. If a fundamental premise of ecologic ethics is that we must take from the world only what we know will be replenished, then some program of rationing—implicit or explicit—will be necessary. The theme of ecologic ethics —one we will meet again in our legal-social chapter—is that of distributive justice.

Deciding who shall live and who shall die often involves resource allocation and categorical decisions about groups. Developing house rules concerning availability of transplants or age-specific rationing (e.g., over age sixty-five dialysis is not available) are ways of rationalizing the resource capacities of the house (ecos, logos). That we are dealing with an ecologic or economic structure of values becomes clear when we realize we are dealing with trade-offs and the effects of one part of the network on another. When, for example, we discuss the issues of death and dying, the question will inevitably arise: "How can we spend so much money on the last days of persons' lives" (some estimates show that thirty percent of health-care resources are expended during the last days and weeks of persons' lives)? "These resources would be better used for mothers with children or to prevent disease in the developing world." When issues are framed this way, assessing impacts from one part of a system on another, we deal with ecologic ethics. "How," it is asked, "do we live responsibly within the web of life and the enveloping body of resources?" The question goes to the very heart of the moral meaning of words like economy and ecology—house management. Not only are all things tied together in a dynamic network, but ethical action, as we saw in the discussion of sexuality and economy, is tied in to claims and obligations created within this network.

Seen in this systematic way, the death of persons (*mors in homine*) and entropy in the cosmos are forces that maintain the stability and sustainability of the system. Ecologically speaking, we must all ultimately give our life to sustain life in the rest of the world. Ecotheology asks that we live in the world gently and respectfully, with a kind of Franciscan fraternity rather than dominating control and utilization.

The crisis comes in health-care economics because of the constant introduction of new factors into the system. As soon as we reach a semblance of equilibrium, some new element breaks into the system. Technological progress introduces daily new opportunities. The best way to treat a person who has just had an MCI (myocardial infarction) is to inject streptokinase or TPA (clot dissolvers) into the vessels. These limited substances are very costly (up to $1000) and simply are not available for everyone. It may eventually prove to be the case that every heart-attack patient might profit from temporary cardiorespiratory assistance with a ventricular device or an artificial heart. How can we continually incorporate new technological possibilities into the system while we seek to sustain its equilibrium and just application?

Public expectations and an aging population are other new factors that stress a system. In one way the suicide or assisted-suicide cases involving persons with Alzheimer's disease (e.g., Janet Adkins, Ross Gilbert) may be ways in which ecologic or equilibrium forces precipitate actions within such a stressed network. The incidence of dementia and Alzheimer's disease itself is the result of a more aged population whose vectors of disease and death have been altered by biomedical progress.

Three options exist for solving the crisis of rationing limited resources to meet overwhelming needs. Let me offer reasons for the unacceptability of the first two options and then sketch a moral apology for the third. Age discrimination would be the first option. An example of this approach is that persons beyond age sixty-five will not have access to dialysis for end-stage kidney disease. Daniel Callahan presents the most forceful argument for this position in his book *Setting Limits*.[21] Recognizing that aging is a natural and inevitable process, Callahan argues that once one has lived out a natural life span the goal of care should shift from resisting death to making life as comfortable and fulfilled as possible. If the laissez-faire option of personal free choice and buying whatever kind of health care we desire is rejected on the grounds of discrimination against those who are poor, this position is said to represent the most moral position because persons have lived out the life cycle and now are obliged to pass the torch to others. The flaws in this position are its arbitrary nature and its coercion. The appropriate life span probably varies with individuals, ethnic communities, and environmental conditions. To construct a norm of longevity from particular cohorts such as Japanese women in Alameda County, California, or Scandinavian women (both groups have hit the projected norm of eighty-five years) is to apply an arbitrary ethnocentric norm on all people. The element of coercion is also unfortunate and should be rejected in terms of a policy that allows choice.

The second option would involve across the board triage: either restricting certain procedures to all (the Oregon plan) or giving a certain health-care payment allocation to all persons, letting them use their chits for whatever services they wish. A plan that prohibits public funding for all bone-marrow transplants or all coronary bypass surgery has the advantage of everyone knowing the rules up front and assenting, however reluctantly, to those rules. But again it discriminates in unjust ways. Say a young person has a kind of aplastic anemia that will respond dramatically to a bone-marrow transplant and the efficacy and outcome of the procedure will be unequivocally good. An across the board policy would be unconscionable because of the moral violation entailed in particular cases. The standard amount policy also suffers from its injustice, since nature does not afflict us with disease in any equitable way. Some persons suffer disproportionate sickness and medical catastrophe and need more help than the rest of us.

The policy I would put forward allows for selective nontreatment of certain disease conditions where life's quality is severely diminished and where either the patients themselves or the patient's agent concurs with the decision about withholding, withdrawing care, or terminating life. Disease classifications we might put in this group are late-stage Alzheimer's, irreversible coma, severe dementia with physical immobility, severe neurological handicaps in newborns, and nonsurvivable malignancies. Let me illustrate this third and preferred ethical approach with an excursus on Alzheimer's disease.

Alzheimer's Disease and the Ecologic Ethics of Enduring or Ending Debilitated Existence

> Though wise men at their end know dark is right
> Because their words have no forked lightening they
> Do not go gentle into that good night
> Dylan Thomas, 1951, 1952

For we know that if our earthly house of this tabernacle were dissolved, we have a building of God, an house not made with hands, eternal in the heavens.

2 Corinthians 5:1

Dylan Thomas, struggling with the impending death of his father and father's indomitable human spirit resisting death even when it seems good, and Paul the tentmaker's serene confidence in a better home beyond the world of persecution provide a backdrop for considering what living well and dying well entails in the face of an intractable and debilitating disease like Alzheimer's. When one witnesses the crazed and frenzied disarray of what was once a noble and alert mind, now deteriorating above a still strong body, or when a person of sound mind watches helplessly as her own body deteriorates beneath, the powerful insights of this poetry and scripture afford comprehension.

Only when viewed against the sacramental ecologic mystery of the universe and the divine providence that same universe portrays can we fathom the significance of such experience. As Dylan Thomas watches the spunk of his own dying father and his restless will to live flying in the face of inevitable finitude and ultimate impotence, or the Apostle speaks of the eschatologic mystery of a more sturdy and amiable edifice prepared for us beyond in eternity when this building falls down, we realize that death is life's culmination and only the dissolution of the body will ultimately disclose who we really are.

These two texts affirm that the embodied person, though bent to the breaking point by frailty and finitude, retains *dignitatis*—upright and erect defiance—against a world that would bring her down. That dignity can be expressed in patient endurance or courageous ending. A health-care policy that focuses on human dignity should allow either option. Natural life proceeds defiantly against our efforts to end it and it dies away despite our efforts to preserve it. Ecologic wisdom encourages the same unpredictable and uncoerced nobility from those erect creatures whose bodies no longer hover along the ground but like the medieval cathedrals aspire toward heaven, whose eyes no longer are fixed on earth but beyond the horizon.

"So human an animal," wrote biologist Rene Dubos.[22] We wonder as we watch the massive oil-spill now washing into the beaches of Kuwait and Saudi Arabia with doomed black oil-covered herons still stumbling along in the slick black surf. Was it U.S. bombs or Iraq's sabotage that caused the spill? What matter—nature and its creatures suffer. The animals are sentinels of human ethics. They signal to us the humanity or inhumanity of our actions. The same is true of our treatment of severely impaired newborns or adults who have lost their minds. When the patient is muted by severe organic brain injury, autism, coma, or Alzheimer's disease, we are severely put to the moral test in discerning what is the best course of action to take on behalf of that patient. While it is true that in our litigious society we rest such decisions in the proxy agent of the patient, it remains true that we must discriminate between danger and benefit for the person who is mute before us. The reader will sense the dangerous ground onto which my argument is being driven. We feel an obligation to kill in mercy the domesticated animal who has been severely wounded by our intervention into its wilderness nature.

Take the race horse. To satisfy our sporting and gambling desires, we have selectively bred, fed, and trained that magnificent steed whose evolution James Michener traces so beautifully in the novel *Centennial*. We have bred creatures with massive upper-body strength and weight on tiny spindle ankles and feet. We have beaten and trained the wild horse into fleet-footed domestication across history until today like the dodo freak or an overpurebred dog, he cannot perform, stumbles when tripped in the driving pack, and fractures ankles and legs. Then in mercy we put him to sleep. Just this year it has happened frequently on the world's race tracks. Will we continue to inflict persons with greater burdens of pathological brain disorder and then put them to sleep when those burdens become personally or societally unbearable?

The greater technological intrusions of avaricious humanity into ecology's web of nature, intrusions such as nuclear destruction, carbon dioxide and fluorocarbon release, have evoked natural judgment on humankind such as potential nuclear winter and global warming. In the realm of health and disease, our unwillingness to accept natural and moral law has caused us to distort the epidemiology of disease so that the more benign lethalities such as pneumonia and heart failure are displaced by what *Science* magazine predicts will be the dominant Western diseases by the turn of this century: AIDS and Alzheimer's. It may be morally illuminating that persons afflicted with these two dominant diseases of the late twentieth century have spearheaded the demand for ethical justification and legalization of suicide and physician-assisted suicide. Could it be that we have insulted nature by our intrusions and that it has retaliated by giving us these diseases that rob us of insight and sight, those unique powers of beings with the large myelinated frontal cortex and unprecedented kinds of brains capable of memory, hope, conscience, prescience, and astonishing cunning. Richer, more complex, Alzheimer's and AIDS are neurotropic diseases. They attack the brain and its constituent parts like the eyes. Has nature robbed us of mind and sight yet left us half alive by not taking the life of our bodies? The tragedy of Alzheimer's disease is that the mind is destroyed on top of a yet-functioning body. In AIDS we are now developing treatments such as AZT that impede replication of the virus, allowing the body to survive, possibly even long enough to meet death from other causes, while nerve cells and the mind slowly die—bringing dementia and intellectual and aesthetic death while the body survives.

If there is any truth in this analysis, might it become morally licit, especially in terms of ecology, nature religion, and ecotheology to offer propitiary and expiatory sacrifice of the bodies of those thus afflicted through suicide and euthanasia? Hans Jonas has hinted in his intriguing writings on technology, science, and human experimentation that the grand enterprise of moral and spiritual faithfulness and arrogance may be a twentieth-century version of primitive animal and human sacrifice. To appease the gods we must offer sacrifice for our sins. Christians believe that Jesus has offered final and perpetual sacrifice for human evil and his crucifixion and resurrection have inaugurated forgiveness and renewal in human existence, world history, and in nature itself. At the same time, human nature participates in, indeed brings to life, this redemptive drama of suffering, death, and transfiguration. Could the persons who travail with these latter-day idiopathic (humanly induced) diseases: Alzheimer's, AIDS, perhaps persistent vegetative syndrome (PVS), somehow be the persona of this drama?

Let us continue our unfolding argument on Alzheimer's patients by rehearsing the following case that illustrates this suggested ethos of redemption:

In late August 1985, the elderly physician in a small New York town was arrested and charged with the second-degree murder of his patient and old friend Frederick C. Wagner. Mr. Wagner, who was eighty-one, had suffered from Alzheimer's disease for five years and had also developed gangrene in one foot as a result of ulcerous sores. He was a patient at Penfield Nursing Home. Staff members said that he was in pain and that he no longer recognized anyone.

On the morning of Mr. Wagner's death, Dr. Kraai, alone with the patient, injected three large doses of insulin into the right side of Wagner's chest cavity. He then indicated to a nurse that the injection was a vitamin B_{12} shot. However, several hours later, as Wagner's condition worsened, staff members became alarmed. By midafternoon, when it was apparent that Wagner was dying, a nurse called the state Health Department Patient Abuse hot line. At 5:30 p.m. Dr. Kraai returned to the nursing home and pronounced Wagner dead. By this time, the nursing home staff had notified the state attorney general's office, the medical examiner's office, and the state health department. Sheriff's deputies began their investigation and within forty-eight hours Dr. Kraai was arrested and charged with murder. Later the sheriff told reporters: "Dr. Kraai was overwhelmed with emotion at the deteriorating condition of his patient."

Less than a week later, Dr. Kraai was released on a fifteen-thousand dollar property bond. After minor prostate surgery, he waited at home to hear the prosecutor's decision, which would be evaluated after consultation with Wagner's widow. "There's no doubt the case will be prosecuted," the county district attorney said. "The question is how." However, two weeks later, apparently despondent over "mounting pressures" and failing eyesight, Dr. Kraai got up early one morning and injected himself in the leg with a lethal dose of Demerol. At 6:45 a.m. his wife found him lying face down in the driveway. When paramedics arrived, they pronounced him dead.

Shortly after Dr. Kraai's arrest, the sheriff had commented: "this is the saddest kind of thing. I know of Dr. Kraai. He was the type of doctor who still made house calls.'' Support for the doctor in Fairport—a town with fewer than seven thousand residents—had been overwhelming. Friends and neighbors had universally praised Kraai, who had practiced medicine for fifty years. Twice he had received Fairport's Citizen of the Year Award. "Dr. Kraai would take care of anybody in this village," the mayor said. "You were more than his patient, you were his friend."

Still, community support and the belief that he had acted humanely had not been enough, apparently, to keep Dr. Kraai from killing himself. Prosecution, a lengthy trial, and possible imprisonment may well have been more than a seventy-six-year-old man felt he could endure, especially a man in deteriorating health. As well, the knowledge that another seventy-six-year-old man, Roswell Gilbert, had earlier in the year been found guilty in Florida of first-degree murder for shooting his wife (suffering from Alzheimer's and a painful physical ailment) may have been discouraging. Perhaps Dr. Kraai feared the same treatment.

The president-elect of the medical society in Dr. Kraai's county commented, after the suicide: "As professionals, we have all been very sympathetic. . . . It was not Dr. Kraai's sole burden." A rabbi wrote of Dr. Kraai: "The very descriptions of [him] reveal vulnerability and decency. He made house calls and was not always particular about receiving payment. He carried food in his car to leave with the destitute hungry. . . . [He] rushed to relieve pain and [was] devastated by the suffering of others. He cared too much. He is a tragic figure like Prometheus. But like Prometheus he is also a giant.[23]

The moral action at issue in this case is neither that of patient endurance when faced with a debilitating disease such as Alzheimer's or the desperate act of suicide. This is a story of helping networks, of a Charlotte's web of care. Going off on one's own to commit suicide is a private kind of act with its own morality. Assisting suicide, drawing loved ones, or trusted caregivers in, makes it a reciprocal act, an ecological or ethological deed. This action of a doctor and his friend is one of collaboration, and cooperation. Nature and God demand that ultimately we live at the mercy of one another. A moral assessment of this kind of cooperative act (which is increasingly necessary when our mind or sight or nerve system is disabled—think of assisted suicides of paralysis victims [Elizabeth Bouvia], spinal-cord injured [Zigmaniac], or blinded persons [Dax]) as these cast light on the prior moral responses of endurance or self-inflicted ending.

A moral position that extols courage and endurance is often grounded in a theological philosophy of excruciation or martyrdom when one's death becomes holy to the Lord (Ps. 116:15). In this purview, the experience of suffering is seen to offer vicarious (sacrificial) participation in the redeeming perpetual crucifixion of God for a broken, sin-ridden world. In this view, taking up one's cross is the deepest vocation that life on earth offers. This purposive theology also encourages efforts to conquer diseases through research and therapy. In this view patience and pain [etymologic: *poena* (Latin), punishment; *pu* (Sanskrit), purity] produces long-suffering and victory. The nobility of this perspective should always be honored, extolled, and emulated. Yet we must also allow moral credibility for the option of stepping out or helping one out of this plight. This understanding, I argue, should be reflected both in personal ethics and in public policy.

This wide range of moral response, at least with reference to certain disease categories such as mental decapitation or the diseases of aging is made necessary by the changing face of disease in our time. Our scientific progress has fashioned a new pattern of health and disease in the late twentieth century. We have moved from an age of acute diseases—such as childhood infections, maternal-child deaths, pneumonia, to chronic diseases, human-made diseases, and the diseases of civilization. Now we succumb to vascular disease, cancer, arthritis, osteoporosis, dementia, and Alzheimer's disease. What is the ethical impact of this shift? Having repositioned the burden of morbidity and mortality that befalls us into this new range of human-made diseases, we must be prepared to take account of and make amends for what we have done. The aftermath of our technological contortion of the ecological web of life processes and of our deleterious lifestyles that violate natural moral law have yielded a fiercesome harvest. For example, we fuel the AIDS pandemic with dangerous habits such as sexual promiscuity and drug abuse. When joined to social apathy, neglect, homophobia, and absolute vengeance that has now reduced our inner cities into hovels of despair and degradation, we become aware that the crisis before us is not nature's caprice; it is of our own making. "We have met the enemy," said Pogo, "and he is us." How do we become responsible and ameliorative in the face of what we have wrought?

How does our responsibility for patients with Alzheimer's disease fit into this scheme? How does the epidemiology and ecology of this disease constitute a moral challenge? We all know personally courageous spouses who bear graciously with the bewildered loved one who wanders away, shouts obscenities, or violently turns against himself and others and must be tied down. We know the mute and brute suffering of these dear afflicted friends. We know of the infinite patience of those who watch over and care for them. We have all watched Roswell Gilbert, the elderly Florida husband who out of pity for his wife suffering from Alzheimer's killed her and was sentenced at seventy-five years of age to a twenty-five year sentence. We have reviewed the strange tale of Mr. Wagner and Dr. Kraai, a tale that evokes not so much moral revulsion but extreme pity. But what can we do to alleviate this burden? Do we take the law into our own hands and like Rudy Linares, who extubated his baby boy Sammy, ten months vegetative on a respirator, bear the consequences? Moral proposals abound imploring scientific ingenuity and solution, genetic alteration, finding biological predisposition in utero and aborting, economic constraint, new manners of burden-sharing, setting limits. Ethicists like Daniel Callahan, Leon Kass, Joseph Fletcher, and David Thomasma have put forth proposals that span this spectrum of moral positions. All these proposals see the ultimate resolution not as a technical, economic or legal matter, but a matter of ethics.

Alzheimer's disease is the yield of the bittersweet success of advancing society. Sanitation, hygiene, general prosperity, and prophylaxis have released us from the scourge of primitive and preindustrial infectivity and degradation. But anyone who would romanticize those grotesque "good old days" should read Daniel DeFoe's *Diary of the Year of the Plague,* which is as gruesome in its description of bubonic death as Robert Lifton's descriptions of nuclear death at

Hiroshima. Suppressing those plagues in some cruel and to our eyes improvident twist of fate has of necessity forced into human flesh the plagues of AIDS and Alzheimer's, since morbidity and mortality do and must, for ecological reasons, remain constant in any species.

Alzheimer's disease now affects three million middle-aged and older Americans. Related atherosclerotic and neurologic dementias affect fully one-third of this first-ever generation of aged pioneers. Like prostate cancer, which may become ubiquitous in old age, mental failure may come to affect almost every octogenarian. Rather than stature and honors that were bestowed on *Presbuteroi* (old wise men) in ancient oriental and Near-Eastern culture, now we bestow only broken down incapacity and often isolation and disgrace. This brave phalanx of warriors are the first in history to experience the new world we have created.

A range of ethical questions confronts us when we experience Alzheimer's disease in our families or among our friends. On the issue of setting limits or rationing that we have explored in this chapter we have an example of what I have called a disease-based triage or a policy based on futility. We have raised the possibility of patients or families opting out of treatment, even choosing deliberate death in the face of such nonrecoverable and personally devastating disease.

But while we may wish to allow and support this desperate action in the face of such frustration and futility, we need to find better and kinder ways to care for Alzheimer's patients, especially if the sickness is coming to affect so many people. In view of our underlying moral paradigm of suffering leading to transfiguration, can we find some way in which such disease and death become redemptive? Drawing from an ecologic and ecotheologic ethic let us comment on the care of the muted patient and the veneration of the aged.

Whenever the ethics of care for the demented, retarded, or Alzheimer's patients is discussed, the question of animal analogy is raised. Should we not put such persons to sleep as we would suffering dogs or horses? The poor creatures are dumb and mute and surely do not understand why they are being made to suffer. In one landmark ethics case a mentally-retarded victim of leukemia was refused chemotherapy as his family wished because, it was argued, he would not understand the inflicted pain of vomiting, needles, and hair loss that would arise from the treatment. We often mistake the inability to think and speak as the presence of death in the person. "She is gone," loved ones will say. "Mom is no longer here." "Sammy already went to heaven, just his body remains."

The fact that patients with Alzheimer's disease are *avoce*, voiceless, does not indicate that they are not alive. Perhaps like persons with the "locked-in syndrome" or under anesthesia, the inner experience may be intense. Just as sheep are led to the slaughter or sheep before their fleecers are dumb, we may exploit the *avoce* and leave them without advocates. There may be more sensitive and subtle ways to listen to and communicate with such persons. Nurses I know speak of gentle ways to respond to incommunicative persons by touch, song, and other stimuli. The astonishing experience related by some clinicians is that their patients are fully alive and rich in expression and gesture once you enter into their new language. The field of biomedical linguistics, communication with the near dead, even extrasensory perception and apparition recognition should be cautiously explored at this new frontier.

Finally we need to find the grace of acceptance, appreciation, and delight for those who falter and break down just as we need to throw out our pagan passion for perfection and sound minds in sound bodies while we accept our tragicomic stature at all stages of life. Shakespeare, in *As You Like It*, has Jacques depict the absurdity of each pretentious posture we put forward:

> At first the infant, mewling and puking in the nurse's arms,
> And then the whining school boy, with his satchel
> And shining morning faces, creeping like snail
> Unwilling to school. And then the lover,
> Sighing like furnace, with a woeful ballad
> Made to his mistress' eyebrow. Then a soldier
> Full of strange oath and bearded like the Pard
> Jealous in honor, sudden and quick in quarrel
> Seeking the bubble reputation
> Even in the cannon's mouth. And then the justice
> In fair round belly with good capon lined,
> With eyes severe and beard of formal cut,
> Full of wise saws and modern instances;

And so he plays his part. The sixth age shifts
Into the lean and slipper'd pantaloon,
With spectacles on nose and pouch on side,
His youthful hose well saved a world too wide
For his shrunk shank; and his big manly voice,
Turning again toward childish treble, pipes
And whistles in his sound. Last scene of all,
That ends this strange eventful history,
In second childishness and mere oblivion,
Sans teeth, sans eyes, sans taste, sans everything.

As You Like It II, vii, 143–66

We can conclude this chapter by rehearsing the images from Dylan Thomas and the apostle Paul with which we began. The text spoke of the paradox of being bent low in degradation in order to stand upright. A truth of ecology and theology is that the old must fall away, the seed must die, for the new to be born.

In ecologic perspectives our lives are rightly given over to the larger whole. The victim of Alzheimer's disease falls back on the larger dissonance and mystery of the universe. The victim of Alzheimer's or AIDS is also a hero, a priest. The primitive meaning of *priest* is one who is brought low in order to be lifted up—humbled to be exalted. The Hebrew word for priest, for example, *cohen*, comes from two Akkadian roots: *kanu*, to bend down, to do homage; and *kown*, to stand upright and represent. The Alzheimer's patient is a priest to the world by acts of intercession, derangement (chaos), and sacrifice. The *nabi* or prophet is one who endures madness in order to perceive truth. In their disorienting and disturbing plight Alzheimer's victims and their families contribute to the upholding arrangement and salvation of the world. In silence, the mute one bears the awful sound and fury of a disrupted creation. By gentle endurance he attests to the quality of grace and the finality of God.

5
Historic Ethics and Genocide

We are considering the ethics of dying, killing, and resisting dying. We have examined the ethics that come naturally to us and are rooted in the insistence of our being in biological nature and philosophical reason. We have also looked at two parameters of ethics where we accede to a realm beyond ourselves and yield to the power of theology and ecology. Though ecology is a naturalistic sphere of reality, the values it portrays and demands of us are often at odds with our inclinations. God asks Job: "Can you bind the chains of the Pleiades, or loose the cords of Orion?" (Job 38:31). The environment in some sense stands over against us in judgment and presents to us the often harsh and overwhelming requirements of a world we did not create for ourselves. For this reason we have positioned ecology as a value matrix related to theology. We now turn to another transcending sphere of human values—the realm of history. When we look beyond our immediacy to memory or hope, to historic or eschatologic reality, we tap other values cognate to theology. On the naturalistic path of ethics we will then proceed on to the sociopolitical sphere of value that is also an immanent and immediate sphere—a realm of the practical.

We suggested in justifying ecology as a theological cognate that it was a construct or myth to imbue a certain dimension of reality with meaning. History is similarly an evaluative artifact. History is a selected fund of those events and interpretation of events by which we seek to give meaning to what has gone on before. While late twentieth-century historiography has sought to be more objective, positivist, and free from the ideological biases of all previous historiographies (such as nineteenth-century assumptions of primitivism or progress [Comte, Hegel]), it still, of necessity, remains a discipline that seeks to make

108

some point, and thus is value laden. Indeed, for history to be morally instructive it has to draw lessons. Recall the oft-quoted wisdom of Santayana that those who ignore history are doomed to repeat it. One wonders today as conflict bogs down in the Middle East or Eastern Europe whether the exact opposite of the supposed "lesson" of the Cold War history of nuclear deterrence is in fact true. In that view the only prevention to war was the perpetual fear of the nuclear weapons we continued to stockpile. Could we not as easily argue on historical grounds that since Hiroshima and the surrender of the Japanese in 1945 that no war has ever been won or concluded without nuclear weapons. Unless you take seriously skirmishes like the Falklands, Grenada, and Panama, all other post-Hiroshima wars have been indecisive and finally unresolved—Korea, Viet Nam, Iran/Iraq, the African and Central American conflicts. Perhaps now the Allied-Iraq war over Kuwait will be the test as to whether any nation(s) can decisively conclude a war without resort to nuclear weapons. The moral lessons drawn from the history of killing are inevitably ambiguous, with, I would argue, one exception.

The history of genocide and holocaust has left an indelible imprint on the moral consciousness of the human race. The ethical sequelae of the Nazi Holocaust against European Jewry has given rise to our morality not only about war (Geneva and Nuremberg conventions, the latter strangely ignored, even now); to medical conventions (Nuremberg and Helsinki codes) and to the broader national-legal and global-legal convictions outlawing genocide. When in these agonizing days of early 1991, Germany and Japan decline by reason of pacifist law to become involved in the Gulf; then Turkey struggles to find its appropriate role in the conflict, and when Armenia seeks to resolve problems with its neighbors Azerbaija and Russia, the remembrance of holocaust and genocide become all-too clear. All of our sense of justice about earthly or heavenly judgment against such crime remains disappointed and we may be doomed again to repeat history's moral legacy. This time it is a war of European Christians and Jews against Arabic Muslims.

When we contemplate the Holocaust of the European Jews, we face one of the deepest mysteries of history. As Arno Mayer of Princeton University has shown, history's greatest enigma is fundamentally a question of theology. Judeocide across the millennia and the deicide of the crucifixion of Jesus hover in the dark background when we ponder the genocide of six million Jews in Europe in the 1930s and 1940s. Entitling his book from a text of Solomon bar Simpson in 1096, Mayer quotes:

> No one was found to stand in the breach.
> Why did the heavens not darken
> And the stars not withhold their radiance,
> Why did not the sun and moon turn dark.[1]

Metaphysical and metahistorical questions aside, deciphering the meaning of the Holocaust, its origins, motives, and methods and its aftermath in our evolving moral reflection about killing and euthanasia, is an urgent and compelling task. For example, do we today subject persons to interminable end-of-life suffering while in a coma or vegetative state because we do not wish to reenact the horrors of the gas chambers? Remember, as Robert J. Lifton has carefully documented, the concept of gas chambers began with euthanasic practices in medicine. Does our collective guilt in the Western world over the anti-Semitism and Judeocide, which stretches back to New Testament times up through the Crusades and into modern history, now prompt us to "stand in the breach" and destroy any power in the Middle East that threatens the security of modern Israel? We must reflect on the ethics of mortality that history teaches. Our case at point will be genocide, historiography, and the medical ethics legacy of the Holocaust.

The word genocide (*gens:* a race, tribe; *cide:* killing) was coined by jurist Raphael Lemkin as he sought to develop support for the United Nations "Genocide" convention passed in 1948. By definition genocide is "a coordinated plan of different actions aiming at the destruction of essential foundations of the life of national groups, with the aim of annihilating the groups themselves."[2] Beyond the prototype genocides of the Armenians in the second decade and of the European Jews in the fourth and the fifth decades of this century, Leo Kuper[3] groups a series of modern political and genocidal events as fulfilling this definition. These include: the Russian-contrived famine of the Ukraine (1932), the U.S. and British bombing of Hiroshima, Nagasaki, Dresden, and Hamburg; the massacres of the communists in Indonesia (1965) of the noncommunists in Kampuchea (1975), the slaughter of the Hutu by the Tutsis in Burundi (1972), the Tibetans by China (1950), and the Bangladeshi by the Bengali (1971).

Each of these brutal measures set out to deprive one categorical group of people of its right to live not only as individuals but as an entire group. The highly discriminate elimination of every last man, woman, child, and fetus of a given people was systematically attempted by Hitler's Germany on the Jews of the world. The opprobrium proceeding from this history will forever condemn any human attempt to exterminate any given class of peoples, be they poor black Americans (who die ten years earlier than their white counterparts), mentally-retarded babies, or classes of patients such as those with Alzheimer's disease, those in PVS (persistent vegetative state) or simply those who are older than sixty-five.

As we delve into the German genocide of the Jews and the related medical crimes of the Nazis, we receive an historic ethic related to the sacredness of life motif, of what we have called a holiness heritage. The historical lesson provides helpful guidance on the questions of contemporary medical killing. The lesson for modern medical practice made clear by Holocaust scholar Lucy Dawidowicz and others is not that we refuse persons the right to die or even aid them in that desire, but that we forcefully forbid forever the systematic elimination of any group of people and that we never take the life of a person against his or her will.

In a recent TV film, adapted from a Nazi propaganda piece, Raquel Welch stars as a young woman with a chronic degenerative disease who pleads and gains allowance from the state to have doctors end her misery by taking her life. I had to remind some of my students, who had viewed the program with great sympathy, of the historical context and the extreme ambiguity of the moral lessons to be derived. The response of my students was disbelief, having little recollection or historical knowledge of the Nazi time. I got the same dumbfounded response that I receive from my doctoral students who start out blithely on their research on topics in "the quality of life" until I remind them that this phrase also originated with the Nazis who sought to show that some persons did not possess adequate quality of life to be allowed to continue living. The concept of lives no longer worthy of being lived (*lebensunwerten lebens*) was the poisonous contribution of German hygienists and public-health advocates of our century.

In the late 1970s the sad plight of a pretty young woman named Elizabeth Bouvia was carried prominently in the news. Strikingly similar to the TV film starring Raquel Welch, Bouvia suffered from debilitating cerebral palsy and quadriplegia. An intelligent and articulate professional with a master's degree, she sought the right while under hospital care to be kept comfortable and free of pain but not be fed. About this same time Richard Lamm, then governor of Colorado, argued in the spirit of Daniel Callahan's view in the last chapter, that societal rationing of health care be initiated and that the elderly population sets us good examples by being ready to move on and die. As we ponder these issues of personal and public policy, the insights of historic ethics come mightily to our aid. History has an orienting moral power. It draws us to time-honored precedents of conduct and warns us against inhumanities that experience has taught us to avoid. As we characterize an historic ethic on contemporary questions of mortality, let us see how such memory has the power to reorient even a people who have become gravely disoriented.

Disorientation

The Holocaust in Europe in the early twentieth century brings to a demonic focus all of the mounting fury over life and death that twentieth-century humanity has assumed with its technology and bureaucracy. Behind the war and the gas chambers is a moral crisis that pervades all human endeavors including science, statecraft, even the realm of sacred duty. That something has gone wrong in modern civilization is expressed in symptoms bearing names like Auschwitz, Hiroshima, and Nuremberg. The word Nuremberg signals for medical ethics the turning point for its modern consciousness. The historical crisis that we are living through has pointed up our ethical bankruptcy and has made us painfully aware of this disorientation. As Elie Wiesel has said, Holocaust is the countersign of history. In this earth-shaping event, as Solomon bar Simpson anticipated a millennium ago, nature, history, even God alone, seemed to have abandoned their purpose. In this *countersign* even the *design* of creation and the *sign* of hope has been obliterated. We employ *sign* in this context in Paul Tillich's sense as that which participates in ultimate reality. It now seems as if a crisis has opened up in the contact of the soul and moral soul with its grounding reality. Even *logos,* the signature that opens truth to the mind and good to the conscience, is now shattered. The covenant of life with life is repudiated. The universe groans with the absence of God. Holocaust is tremendum. It opens the chasm of fear and dread; it evokes trembling, awe, and wonder. But crisis means something new is coming. In theological terms we face apocalypse in nature and eschaton in history; the disruption of judgment has broken into cosmos and order.

This profound sense of loss and disorientation undergirds the moral quest of our time. The search for moral direction, substance, and motivation is surely one of the marks of our era. This moral concern is universal and not provincial. We want to secure norms that will apply to all people and pertain to global consensus of economics, ecology, war, science, technology, and medicine. The Holocaust has taken on such universal significance because it happened in the heart of Judeo-Christian civilization, that very civilization which had brought universal history to the world, but out of the Greek and Roman *Oikumene*. Christian civilization—the now waning arrogant and secularized vestige of the Holy Roman Empire, *Corpus Christianum, Res Publica* unleashed the sin of the world, the new crucifixion of the Holy One of God. In a grotesque act of rational, technical, medical, political, ecclesial, cultural, and historical evil all humanity wandered astray and we lost our way in the world.

Our only hope now is to shun all pretense and in a great act of repentance and renewal of life before the God of Israel and of the Universe, examine afresh who we are, recover God's inaugurating, sustaining, and finishing purposes in history and in nature and reclaim our origination, constitution, and destination as a human family on planet earth. Then with a covenant of faith reestablished, as Israel was reestablished in the Deuteronomic reform, we can reestablish those derived covenants of life with life and offer protection and edification in the creation. If we fail, all that awaits us is to perish with the whole world in some final holocaust where the abomination will be the odor and smoke of nuclear, chemical, and biological destruction—and a bang, and a whimper.

To claim these reorienting ethics that history offers, we need first to note (in our dealings with death and our mortality responsibilities) how the disorientation became apparent. Death dealing by the Nazis was not only massive and gruesome but subtle and almost benign. Reviewing the vitalistic efforts that disguised the death wish and the more overt intentional killing can help us with ethical discernment in the difficult issues we now face. On the surface, National Socialist medicine was committed to life: hygiene, racial purity, prevention of disease, genetic health, prolongism in vital states, and opposition to abortion. But beneath the surface this cache of vitalistic efforts lay the unabashed assumption of Nordic supremacy and the will to subjugate or exterminate all others. The companion holocausts that are seldom mentioned alongside the extermination of the Jews were those of the gypsies, Slavs, and homosexuals. A new pure human being was extolled and this required the elimination of the old and the contaminated.

In his acclaimed study, *The Nazi Doctors*, Robert J. Lifton has shown that what happened to us in the early decades of the twentieth century was not an unprecedented, crazed aberration of a small, lunatic fringe. It was rather the outgrowth of a long evolving natural, pervasive, perhaps even necessary development of patterns of national power, biological vision, technical capacity to alter birth, life, and death, even religious belief that grew up in the Western world in the early modern age. The rationalization and organization of the new world and the struggles to consolidate world power all reflected a new concept of human nature and destiny. The Nazi time, Lifton contends, shows us clearly the people we have intended ourselves to become in the modern world. It is an ubiquitous and universal development not to be dismissed as an extraordinary break of civilized culture. It happened in the epitome of culture, science, the arts.

The extreme expressions capture our attention and evoke our abhorrence. In Nazi thanatology as in eugenics, clinical and social judgments were made. To follow our metaphor of signs, first, some lives were *designated* to be not fully alive or worthy to continue living. The *Lebensborn* movement sought to bring issue to superior offspring and sterilization efforts sought to eliminate inferior offspring. Abortion under the Nazis was a double-edged sword—forbidden among supposedly superior stock and coerced on those thought to be impure and inferior. Second, there was political and ecologic *resignation* that found in some lives a threat to the viability and vitality of the social organism.

In 1920 the jurist Karl Binding and the psychiatrist Alfred Hoche published their book, *Die Friegabe der Vernichtung Lebensunwerten Lebens*.[4] The permission to conclude lives that were no longer worth living was crafted out of a more basic biologic vision that defined vitality as mental and physical symmetry and power, vibrant consciousness and absence of disability and disease. Calling on his psychiatric background, Hoche developed a concept of "mental death" to apply to various states of psychiatric illness, brain damage, Alzheimer's, dementia, and retardation. "If already dead, kill them" became the cruel inversion of the Talmudic teaching earlier noted. Only now covenant faithfulness became the fateful and lethal sin.

This social resignation led to the final *consignation* of these nominally dead to the realm of the actually dead. Such lives were consigned to oblivion. Euthanasia was simply an act confirming what nature had already determined. Today when we use the theological language of worship, when we ask if further treatment is worthwhile, or whether one is worthy of being helped, we unconsciously use this dangerous vocabulary.

To *designate* our own life or that of any other person as worthless, unproductive, a burden, or less than fully alive is to fall into the trap against which history should provide ample warning. When persons decide to cease further efforts to live and to die, it must come out of a sense of gratitude and dignity of life. From the caregivers' side, letting go must provide a profound sense of respect and service. Inestimable worth, in other words—and not some desire to be rid of something unpleasant and burdensome—must ground all decisions to "let go."

How a society came to this moral position was a matter of historical development. Nazi death policies on eugenics and euthanasia claimed that the injustice of the Versailles treaty, policies they claimed were endorsed by world Jewry, had impoverished the German *Volk* and robbed the suffering nation of any possibility of recovering well-being. Third Reich philosophers and politicians talked of what we would later term genocide—*Volkstod*—the death of an entire people. *Gnadentod* therefore, mercy killing, was a healing of the wound that history and violated nature had inflicted on German society. The euthanasia deaths that rid the nation of the weak, helpless, dependent and excess mouths to feed, and the subsequent Holocaust and "final solution" were designed to shift the course of history back toward enrichment and development and away from degeneration and growing subservience.

Again, this kind of historic ideology is nothing new. It emerges right from the center of Renaissance and Enlightenment historiography that promised an unfolding process of human betterment, rational access to reality, scientific and technological (industrial) progress, and religion as the final blessing on this unfolding enterprise of power and progress. Beneath this facade of liberation was the suspicion that some people were assuming to themselves disproportionate wealth, power, and influence and in traditional anti-Semitism the poor and lower-middle classes sought to limit the influence of Jews in commerce, banking, the professions, education, and the arts. If the march to progress and prosperity was being hindered, it must be under sabotage by some group—the classic theory of scapegoat, as old as another Abraham. Arguing that it was the function of the state to retain control over life and death, Adolf Jost, a political economist, wrote in a 1905 work entitled *Das Recht Auf den Tod* that "the rights to death are the keys to the fitness of life. The state must own death—in order to keep the social organism alive and healthy."[5]

History as Ethics: Orientation

If history as it unfolds leads us in certain pernicious directions because of the way in which events cause value shifts among peoples and nations, history is also morally instructive as it shows us the harmful outcomes of these historically driven beliefs, values and behaviors. Machiavelli could claim with the authority of history that the prince who acts expediently will prevail. Other historians would argue that tyranny always backfires. When Princeton University undergraduate James Madison stayed on with the Scottish Presbyterian minister and president of the university, John Witherspoon, he read the constitutions of all states throughout history in the firm Calvinist belief that democratic forms would ultimately prosper while autocracies fail. Madison formulated the *Federalist Papers*, fathered the U.S. Constitution, and ultimately became president of the nation, serving those beliefs. History teaches ethics via memory. This fundamental truth is derived from religion: "Lord God of hosts be with us yet—lest we forget, lest we forget." Modern medical and thanatological ethics derive from the history that culminated in Nuremberg. Just as the Exodus from Egypt became the historical foundation of Hebrew ethics at Sinai and in the Covenant, and as the life and teaching of Jesus of Nazareth confirmed in his death and resurrection the decisive and constitutive moral event for Christendom, in like manner the Holocaust is

the turning point for modern secular ethics. Indeed, the historical contin-
uum of the expulsion of Israel, the execution of Jesus and the extermination of European Jewry form the threads of a singular moral fabric.

This is history seen in the light of an assumption and interpretation. All historiography seeks to distill or impose upon the mere stac-
cato of events some sense of flow and meaning. The scheme of
interpretation I am using is the dominant western Judeo-Christian
notion that history expresses divine action and human salvation. What
the Germans call holy history (*Heilsgeschichte*) is the interior meaning
of the exterior events. In this moral view of history, human suffering
is not absurd but is part of the larger fabric of evil that is coming under
divine judgment and being overcome by the power of redemptive love.
When the angel of death calls for Jean Val Jean at the end of the musical version of *Les Miserables*, he cries: "He who loves another has
seen the face of God." Jean had lived a life of justice, honesty, forgiveness and care, and had overcome the vicious and vindictive legal-
ism of the avenger, the constable, Javert. Love overcomes death in
holy history. It is an eternal force greater and larger than the temporal
force of death. Self-giving, sacrificial love interposes resurrection into
the crucifixion of the world and draws life into the death of the world.
History is a construct of meaning overarching particular events or
vicissitudes of life, bestowing ethical discrimination through creative
memory and hope. What was meant to be (and was violated in actual
events; justice and peace, for example), becomes the moral weight of
historical imperative. What could be (and what could be extrapolated
from benign or camelot moments of history such as the reign of Elizabeth I in England or Henry IV in France), becomes possibility to
work for.

How does history, particularly history viewed in light of Exodus,
crucifixion, and holocaust, influence morality? The impact is clear
regarding human death. The ameliorative reach of God into our suffering and death grounds imperatives to save and not to kill. The primal
NO against killing and YES for protecting life has resounded through
human conscience since Cain and Abel and is directed against all
forms of fratricide, homicide, genocide, infanticide, and suicide. Killing is to seek to expel God from the cosmos and therefore obliterate
the human soul within us. In a day of prayer for peace convened by
Pope John Paul II at Assisi, Italy, a Janist priest prayed fervently:

Whom thou intendest to kill is, in truth
None other than thyself . . .
Violence, in fact, is the knot of bondage
It, in fact, is delusion
It, in fact, is death
It, in fact, is hell.[6]

The same revulsion against causing death is also expressed by a respectful holding back when one is ready to die and nature or God's angel calls. Ivan Illich, in his masterful study *Medical Nemesis*, describes the historical mutations of our moral concept of how one ought to die. In the fifteenth and sixteenth centuries one stood in awe before the dying, who orchestrated their own passing. To stampede or impede one to death was then and remains now in this historic ethic, blasphemy.

Children could help a mother or father to die, but only if they did not hold them back by crying. A person was supposed to indicate when he wanted to be lowered from his bed onto the earth which would soon engulf him, and when the prayers were to start. But bystanders knew that they were to keep the doors open to make it easy for death to come, to avoid notice so as not to frighten death away, and finally to turn their eyes respectfully away from the dying man in order to leave him alone during this most personal event.

Neither priest nor doctor was expected to assist the poor man in typical fifteenth- and sixteenth-century death. In principle, medical writers recognized two opposite services the physician could perform. He could either assist healing or help the coming of an easy and speedy death. It was his duty to recognize the *facies hippocratica*, the special traits which indicated that the patient was already in the grip of death. In healing as in withdrawal, the doctor was anxious to work hand-in-glove with nature. The question whether medicine could "prolong" life was heatedly disputed in the medical schools of Palermo, Fez, and even Paris. Many Arab and Jewish doctors denied this power outright, and declared such an attempt to interfere with the order of nature to be blasphemous.[7]

Honoring life as it flourishes, recognizing and respecting *signa Hippocratica* (death signs) was the divine mandate. The death ethics of our civilization, enshrined in the Vedas, the scriptures and all modern testimony, is chastened by genocide and all of its precursors and analogies. These ethics affirm human sanctity, inviolability, and dignity. We translate this primeval moral apprehension of safeguarding and saving life yet ultimately conceding to death into acts of science, technology, reason, law, and religion. We offer AZT to persons afflicted with AIDS. We also honor their right at some point to say "no antibiotics for this pneumocystis infection," or to commit suicide.

I am offering a kind of ethic different from those we are accustomed to, derived from religious convention, analytic philosophy, social custom, or law. Though all of these sources contribute to a comprehensive ethic, I am positing a synthetic morality of mortality derived from historical crisis. Any ethic that pretends relevance for the human crisis of sickness and death must itself be forged in some crucible of crisis. We look at ethics in this way because we are dynamic and historic beings. Ethics must therefore be a living narrative. We have focused this ethic on the reality of human suffering embodied in signatory events such as the crucifixion and the Holocaust. We do this simply because this is the point, as in our own crisis of suffering, where the cosmic forces of good and evil meet and where the realities of right and wrong find definition.

In the human mystery of suffering, life, and death, when we come close to the "orient point," which demands that we not kill or deface any persons, we are confronted by a profound paradox. If we take life from God, we must die to God. The belief that we "die into life" is the ground for an ethics that forbids us also to interfere with persons meeting their own death. To honor life against death is also to honor death against life so that we do not prolong a person's dying. Historic ethics reorients us to a new manner of dying and death.

Reorientation

The orientation we have identified by focusing on an historic ethic offers new direction for the practices of clinical medicine and pastoral care. These callings, though now autonomous, are legacies of the classic priestly vocation, as healers are drawn to human care for persons in the extremities and ultimacies of their lives. With reference to clinical medical care, let us ask again, in the light of historic ethics, whether there is a role for the physician to be an executor and euthanizer? In pastoral care, let us look at the unprecedented challenge of ministry to the person dying of AIDS.

As we consider the role of physician and nurse in accompanying the patient toward a good death, we need to remind ourselves again of the archaic foundational premise of ethics in the Western tradition. God has chosen to afflict God's chosen people in order that the world shall not perish, but be saved and healed. Suffering and death are not absurdities but elements in the deeper spiritual and moral mysteries of reality. They are the way God accomplishes God's mysterious sacramental will. Rather than finding here another masochistic myth, we discover in Teilhard de Chardin's phrase that reality itself is cruciform. Therefore, in this spirit we have to learn when to live and when to die. As caregivers, we need to discern when to protect and prolong and when to expose and let go. In T. S. Eliot's tough language, we need to know when to care and when not to care. If this is the case, we may have to begin to think of the physician not only as the technological life preserver but in some sense as the sacrificing priest. Shall the physician execute death in case of capital crime? This question is being asked in cases of curare injection in U.S. capital punishment cases and in Islamic medicine for cases of adultery. In the summer of 1991 the American Medical Association again censured physician participation in capital punishment injections. The desire to condemn capital punishment and war complicity is morally noble. The companion desire to wash one's hands of moral complicity in a patient's death in the winter of life is not courageous but a cop-out. In a much broader, more troubling, but perhaps necessary way medicine in our day may be becoming the altar of human sacrifice. Shall medicine become the *Missa Solemnis?* In a world where war and famine, perhaps even pestilence and disease are losing their force as vectors of mortality, medicine itself may become that instrumentality through which persons are dispatched to their destiny and the divine economy is maintained. The technology of death dealing that was portrayed for all the world by Nazi thanatology may again be incumbent upon us for ecologic and economic reasons. Is it possible and desirable that a transfigured thanatology animated by compassion and free will rather than hatred and coercion will slowly become acceptable?

Self norms and public norms may require that we act responsibly in the face of death. Whether we like it or not medical care today often becomes a killer. Cancer treatment is a cause of cancer. Immunosuppression in organ replacement is a lethal force. Iatrogenesis in general is a major disease. Mutant viruses rampage and ravage in sexually-transmitted diseases. Human immunodeficiency syndromes (such as HIV), even the rather frightening new childhood mutant organisms like mumps and measles are the latest visions of the apocalyptic specter. Nosocomial infections in the hospital take their toll. In all of these interventions, the procession of nature has been transgressed and it howls out against us. All of these morbidities and mortalities are induced into the human condition by our apathies about health but also by our assaults on death. In the late twentieth century we have removed death into hospitals. Today it is DRGs (the withdrawal of feeding and hydration) even death induced by physicians, oncologists and anesthesiologists. The issue of whether end-points and cut-offs must now become part of medical care itself has become a central question in ethics. Today in Holland, the sixth leading cause of death is euthanasia. We cannot blithely condemn these developments. We may be entering an age where it will be necessary to die not only in the presence of but by virtue of medical care. If it is the case that we are to die under medical care rather than by accident, human violence, genocide, or the force of nature then we will have confronted the primordial meaning of suffering and sacrifice that we have considered as the essence of our moral comprehension. Human freedom has become the occasion for sin and the opportunity for redemption, thereby forming the matrix of responsibility.

There is a harsh terror that awaits one who helps another person to die. It is much easier to walk away or hope someone else will do it. It brings down upon one the bitter opprobrium of the society. Dr. Kevorkian, in the minds of many, is a killer like Saddam Hussein. Only his instruments differ. My great aunt, who was an anesthetic nurse, allegedly administered lethal morphine to her father and mother, who had been bedridden, suffering, and catheterized for more than four years. They were in their mid-90s. She called down the ire of family and friends. She did what was right and what the old folks wanted, yet she paid the price. If we begin a broader practice of euthanasia like this, the action will and should always be accompanied by guilt, uncertainty, and a plea for forgiveness. If it ever becomes easy and automatic, then our moral sensibilities will have been irreparably dulled.

This point of costly caring with one another into suffering and death leads to the final illustration of our thesis from the agonizing experience of pastoral care for those dying from AIDS. Death from AIDS is the contemptible, disgraceful death of our time. State officials in California have asked Mother Teresa to help set up hospices for children and adults in the terminal phase of this plague. The pastoral response to such acute need is the subject of recent essays, all of which call the churches' ministry to an abiding faithfulness rather than the more prevalent righteous indignation and retreat.[8] The tension in the churches' response is related to the mingled impulses of condemnation and understanding, nonjudgmental care. AIDS forces us to come to terms with human complicity in disease and how we therefore evaluate responsibility. The agony, desolation, and death from AIDS appears to us as merited or unmerited. The innocent baby infected by the mother, the unknowing recipient of a contaminated blood transfusion, or the morbidly compulsive and promiscuous homosexual, drug-abuser, or prostitute each evoke a differing response of imputed guilt, pity, and forgiveness. In addition to being just another natural force, AIDS manifests to us both the sin of the world and the brokenness of life in the cosmos. If homosexuality in some mysterious way mirrors the derangement found in nature itself, a degeneration that theology has called the cosmic fall, then our posture cannot be puritanical damnation but silent abiding presence before an inscrutable disgrace of life, the agonies and groans of which are soundings of a new world being born.

The reorientation to which we are called reflects on this corruption of the flesh as somehow captured in the cosmic drama of suffering, death, and redemption. It takes us back through the Holocaust to the Cross at the moral axis point of the ages. In Nuremberg we remember that the gassed and cremated bodies of European Jewry bore the sin of the world. They absorbed the arrogance, the pretense, the anti-Semitism, and the inhumanity of the human race. Like Jesus' death on the Roman tree, degradation of this flesh drew the stripes that would heal the creation (see Isa. 53). In Elie Wiesel's story, *Night*, the Jewish lad hung suspended on the gallows. "Where is God?" cried the old rabbi. "There he hangs on the tree."

Orienting and reorienting our life-saving and death-dealing in light of the Holocaust and its deeper meaning may be the sign of hope and despair for our time. Wiesel writes: "Thanks to this event, the world may be saved, just as because of it, the world is in danger of being destroyed."[9]

The old German hymn captures such morbid joy:

O sacred head now wounded, with grief and shame weighed
    down
Now scornfully surrounded, with thorns thy only crown
O sacred head what glory, what bliss till now was thine
Yet, though despised and gory, I joy to call thee mine.

What thou my Lord hast suffered, was all for sinners gain
Mine, mine was the transgression, but thine the deadly pain
Lo, here I fall my savior, tis I deserve thy place
Look on me with thy favor, vouch safe to me thy grace.

History as the Source and Content of Moral Consciousness

Hegel saw history as the "progress in the consciousness of freedom." History is a spontaneous and autonomous force and has enormous power to fashion the character and the content of the human moral soul. Whether history is viewed as divine judgment as in Augustine in the fourth century, as "the invisible hand" or "finger of God" as in the eighteenth century, or as a purposeless flow of events as in the twentieth, our moral beliefs and behaviors are shaped by history. Slavery, which was once self-evidently good and necessary, now becomes a scandal. The place of women in society shifts perceptibly as history unfolds. Euthanasia, once considered a natural custom, becomes an anathema to the conscience and then a tragic but necessary release valve from pressure of death-prolonging technology. History has a way of making ancient goods uncouth and rendering the forebodings of the past innocuous.

Today, history is understood not as a sequence of "atomic entities," self-sufficient and self-explanatory, as in the Middle Ages or as the divine plan unfolding as in the early modern period, but of experiences that we choose to remember in order to make sense out of what has happened to us. History in deconstructionist thought is broken out into the fundamental elements of a narrative. Events are meaningful only within their context. The English were poised to circumnavigate and colonize the world when Sir Walter Raleigh wrote his *History of the World*. The histories of Churchill or Toynbee are chronicles that trace the moral stories of a people or a civilization.

Can we ever say with Cicero, who upon hearing of the murder of Caesar, exclaimed "O noble deed!"? Can we condone the conspiracy of Dietrich Bonhoeffer, Hans von Dohnanyi, and others who in the July 20 movement sought to assassinate Adolph Hitler? Will the air force officers slain in the attempt on Saddam Hussein's life ever be heroes? The story is eventually told and full narrative reveals character. "History never repeats itself," said Voltaire,"man always does." Fallen human beings kill when they should not, and do not when they should. This might be the primary moral lesson of history. In holy genocide, Henry VIII ordered his commander to "sack Leith and burn and subvert it, putting man, woman and child to fire and sword without exception."[10] Hector Berlioz remembers bitterly in his memoirs that doctors refused to end the life of his dying sister:

> I have lost my eldest sister; she died of a cancer of the breast after six months of horrible suffering which drew heart rending screams from her day and night. My other sister, who went to Grenoble to nurse her, and who did not leave her till the end, all but died from the fatigue and the painful impressions caused by this slow agony. . . . And not a doctor dared to have the humanity to put an end to this martyrdom by making my sister inhale a bottle of chloroform. This is done to save a patient the pain of a surgical operation which lasts a minute, and is not had recourse to in order to deliver one from a torture lasting six months. [sic] When it is proved certain that no remedy, nothing, not even time, can cure a dreadful disease; when death is evidently the supreme good, deliverance, joy, happiness! . . . The most horrible thing in the world for us, living and sentient beings, is inexorable suffering, pain without any possible compensation when it has reached this degree of intensity; and one must be barba-

rous or stupid, or both at once, not to use the sure and easy means now at our disposal to bring it to an end. Savages are more intelligent and more humane.[11]

Ironies and inconsistencies abound as we scan the history of killing and the history of the ethics of killing. Perhaps this is understandable as we forever oscillate between a natural sympathy and a cultural inhibition, between a rational readiness to help me die and a religious reservation. We traffic between two realities—one holy and awesome in its demand, the other humble with its simple expedients. Perhaps to live truly and rightly involves double-minded schizophrenia. But now we must move on to areas where we find an even greater tension between our earthiness and our character as fashioned by eternity.

6
Legalistic Ethics and the Lingering Doubt about Withdrawing Life Supports

The law is not a source of ethics. Rather, it reflects, more or less adequately, the ethics of a society. It has become, however, the court of ethical judgment. Apart from some small vestiges of ecclesiastical courts, for example, rabbinic courts, canon law judicatories and the like, the secular courts are most often the arena where contested decisions of life and death must be resolved. Although I contend that such life, health, and death matters might be better handled in parochial courts, especially since matters of morality pertaining to birth, sexuality, suffering, and dying are more fitting in courts that combine judgment and counseling wisdom, for now they remain in the secular courts.

Because life and death decisions involve such deep questions of belief and value and since these decisions often hinge on matters beyond the courts' apprehension or appreciation—matters like divine command, religious law, suffering and immortality—legislative and court decisions in this arena have often been awkward and unsatisfying. In the cases of Karen Quinlan, Nancy Jobes, Brother Fox, Clare Conroy, Joseph Saikewicz, Rudy Linares, Sidney Greenspan, and Nancy Cruzan, among many others, we have witnessed the murky and unsettled nature of secular judgment in this value-fraught zone of our life.

To continue our discussion of Elizabeth Bouvia begun in the last chapter: she was young, terminal but not imminently so, demanding selective nontreatment (palliation but no feeding), in and out of public institutions (hospitals and nursing homes), debilitated with progressive cerebral palsy and quadriplegia, pressing her demands now in informal channels, then in the courts—a complex case to say the least. The courts tried to state the principles of judgment that would pertain in such a case. Obviously the issues of manslaughter, suicide, assisted suicide, as well as laws of medical battery and unauthorized touching were raised to see if they applied. As always in the law, matters of suffering and injury were taken into consideration.

When we turn to the deeper reflective reaches of law and jurisprudence, we see emerging the same kind of balanced wisdom between protecting and taking life that we have noted in the other spheres. The legal doctrine of battery, undergirding the requirement of informed consent, interacts creatively with the state's interest and obligation to protect life and prevent killing.

Turning to Elizabeth Bouvia, we find the measure of suffering to be crucial in the decision. The law considers such specific cases to be instructive or binding both in retrospect and prospect. Precedents are taken into account and deterring impact is considered in any medico-legal situation. In the 1984 case of *Elizabeth Bouvia v. the County of Riverside and Riverside General Hospital*, Judge Hews declared:

> A severely handicapped mentally competent person otherwise physically healthy and not terminally ill does not have the right to end her life with the assistance of society. . . . Preservation of life is the strongest state interest involved. . . . The plaintiff does have a fundamental or preferred right to terminate her own life and to terminate medical intervention but this right has been overcome by the strong interest of the state and society. . . . Our society values life. . . . Her life will be preserved by this decision. . . . [A] decision to accede to her request [not to be fed] would affect the medical staff, nurses, administrators and others at Riverside General Hospital. . . . Such an order would have a devastating effect on other patients [in the hospital] and other physically handicapped persons. . . . The integrity of the medical profession's ethics of life sustenance will be preserved.[1]

Later, attorneys for Bouvia alleged that a Lancaster Hospital violated her rights when they force-fed her in 1985. Seeking ten million dollars in malpractice damages, the brief contended that a person's freedom to choose death by forgoing life-sustaining treatment was an inviolable right regardless of the exemplary impact of the act. The fundamental question in *Bouvia* was this: in what sense shall a person's dying be treated as a sign to others? Does her decision signify failure and therefore discourage other victims and demoralize other caretakers? While jurisprudential discussion of *Bouvia* turned on harm to others or autonomy as the decisive issues, in the background was always her personal and our societal estimate and evaluation of pain and suffering. When in one's personal experience does pain and disability become unbearable? How do we accompany one another through and, in chronic and terminal condition, throughout pain? How shall those professionals who care and the society that watches respond in analgesic and ameliorative action? The significance of her decisions is not nearly as important as our regard for her suffering. If she cannot bear the agony, she should be allowed to forgo medical life supports—even intravenous and nasogastric feedings, respiration, and resuscitation. Given her quadriplegia, is it licit for a physician or nurse to aid her in passive euthanasia or suicide? The law might wish to remain silent on such an issue. We should not be deterred or immobilized by any values other than the patient's own good. Our technophilia, our paralysis in the face of litigation, or our misguided Puritan delight in another's suffering should not keep such persons from their deaths. Our moral inhibitions should not license, enlarge, and extend the suffering of others. A proper sense of the sacred—of the acceptability of death, of the unavoidability of mistakes and failure, and of the enduring power of grace and forgiveness, would lead us to act humbly, but boldly and decisively. This active responsibility should have displaced the legal protection and passive evasion that wished she would go away and do herself in in some dark corner. We belong to each other in covenants of life and death. As one completely helpless as Elizabeth Bouvia shows us, we all invariably are and indeed should be at one another's mercy.

What I wish to argue in this chapter on the law and antidysthanesia (allowing persons to die by withholding or withdrawing treatments that would prolong living) is that both thoughtful principles of mercy in the face of suffering as a feature of justice and the principle of conviviality can amplify the principle of patient autonomy and ground a humane practice of limited passive euthanasia and physician-assisted suicide.

Let us first review the basic principles of law with reference to the prolonging and ending of life under conditions of severe illness. Then we will rehearse a series of the very provocative cases that have helped shape a just and responsible legal context for end-of-life decisions. Finally, we will touch on several social and political matters that also influence this vector of ethics. We are concerned in this chapter to depict and offer moral direction to the surrounding society as it limits, facilitates, and influences the decisions individuals make at their life's end.

The Law as Ethics in Life and Death

The law walks a fine line between protecting and preserving life on the one side and honoring persons' wishes about when they care to die on the other. The latter emphasis is enshrined in laws about refusing medical treatment, the former in laws about killing or assisting suicide. Well back into the common law of England (*Slater v. Baker and Stapleton* [1767]), courts recognized that it was battery, assault, and trespass medically to treat a person over his objection. In the same era, Blackstone summarized the law of England as prohibiting suicide as a crime against self, king, and God. An Illinois decision in 1905 reflected the common law tradition on battery by saying "the right necessarily forbids a physician or surgeon to violate without permission the bodily integrity of his patient by operating upon him without his consent or knowledge.[2] Judge Cardoza delivered the definitive U.S. judgment on this issue in *Schloendorf v. Society of New York hospital* (211 NY 125 105 NE 92 [1914]) when he wrote "Every human being of adult years and sound mind has a right to determine what should be done with his own body."

The doctrine of informed consent has a more checkered history from the side of medical practice. Though "on the books" legally for the better part of this century and canonized in some idealistic texts back into the nineteenth century, medical practice in this century has largely ignored the standard, until very recently. Relying on clinical judgment as to what is best and being more compelled by paternalistic care than concern to safeguard patients' rights, doctors benevolently did what they deemed best for their patients and in some ignoble events even did blatant harm to unconsenting persons in the name of medical care. The reason the Nuremberg Medical Code (1947) enshrines "informed consent" in the detailed and demanding first principle was that this principle was benignly abused throughout medical practice in the 1930s and blatantly and abusively ignored in Nazi experiments and in more general medical work.

The legal right to informed consent and refusal of treatment has had a history not only of being consistently ignored but also of being constantly qualified. Jehovah's Witnesses may refuse even simple life-sustaining treatments such as blood transfusions, but minors and even the dissents of pregnant mothers are often overridden by court order. Social considerations for public health and safety such as vaccinations further check the right of individual choice to opt out. As we saw in *Bouvia*, even the integrity and morale of physicians, nurses, and other patients can give occasion to suspend the right to refuse. Finally, most of the difficult cases we will review involve a patient who cannot tell you her own wishes, and we are therefore left with the maddening vagaries of implied consent, agent consent, substituted consent, or therapeutic privilege.

Irrespective of these weaknesses in the legal tradition, the "right to die" has slowly taken on both irrevocable weight and currency. In *Griswold v. Connecticut*, 381 US 479 (1965), though ostensibly dealing with contraception, a broader "right of privacy" seems to have been established under the fourth amendment. *Roe v. Wade*, 410 US 113 (1973), the still fragile abortion decision, may also have contributed to a growing jurisprudential conviction about private rights over one's own body. *Quinlan*, 70 NJ 10 355, A2d 647 (1976) argued that the constitutionally based right of privacy forwarded in the contraception and abortion cases also extended to matters of refusing treatment as well as to withdrawing life-sustaining treatment. Before we move to the sequence of cases that have begun to clarify the legalities concerning prolonging and ending life, let us review the thought on the matter of a leading American legal scholar, Richard Epstein of the University of Chicago Law School.

Epstein's view, which we will elaborate and comment on in detail (because it shows, I believe, the way the law is moving) is built on a simple premise: the law exists for two purposes—to protect individuals and to protect society. Neither good is served, he contends, by the present criminalization of voluntary euthanasia.

Presently the law cautiously allows passive euthanasia in the name of the principle of informed consent just outlined. Doctors may, upon request of the patient, withdraw instruments like respirators, dialyzers, perhaps even instruments of nutritional technology, but not initiate such actions. The principle of personal freedom pertains unless overridden, says Epstein, by the principle of protecting society and protecting an incompetent individual. Euthanasia is a specie of suicide, not homicide. It is an act of aiding one in a personal choice for death over life.

> What external costs justify government intervention in the face of the patient's *consent* to euthanasia, either active or passive? Surely the patient does not seek to kill another person; he only wants someone to help him end his own life, which in his extreme condition he is unable to do by himself. Suicide, after all, is not murder, and should not be punished as such, or indeed at all. Accordingly, the physician who makes the lethal injection is not imposing his will upon another but is following the requests of a patient. Consent takes us a long way from murder, and brings us back to suicide.[3]

While such actions may wound and deeply grieve loved ones, they may also bring relief:

> At the end of life, some people want to die, not only to put themselves out of their own misery, but also to allow their friends and family to get on with their lives.[4]

Epstein dismisses too readily, in this case, the offense that euthanasia poses to the general moral community in its conviction of the sanctity of human life. He finds arguments based on that fear totalitarian. There is no weighty objection to be made against euthanasia from the good of others, he claims. The only remaining issue is incompetence. This, Epstein admits, is a serious issue. I concur with him here because almost all such end-of-life decisions are made by persons in severe straits—with dementia, Alzheimer's disease, disorienting pain from cancer, and the like.

Epstein then moves to very practical checks against irrational and incompetent suicides. "If we saw a healthy person seek death, we could make a pretty good judgment that there was something amiss, but undetected in his mental processes."[5] In the arena where such actions are made matters of formal contract: such as living wills, powers of attorney, he counsels with the wisdom of an experienced parent: "It is easy to stop a seven-year-old from making a contract that exchanges a thousand shares of IBM for a package of bubble gum."[6] But Epstein knows that euthanasia usually does not involve persons "in the pink of health." In all of the cases around the world that have challenged our conscience in recent years, the persons were desperately ill; they had degenerative disease that would destroy their body and mind if not now, then soon. Epstein concludes, therefore, that a strong case against euthanasia cannot be made on the basis of self-protection and other protection. Passive and active medical euthanasia and physician-assisted suicide, therefore, ought to be decriminalized.

Though these arguments are based on autonomy, many of Epstein's considerations involve the good to others. The law can best deal with personal rights. It has difficulty dealing with responsibilities and convivialities. Relieving the burden of the terminal care on other persons and the theological argument that we are not to stand by passively while the weak, hurting, and vulnerable suffer, add argumentive support to Epstein's view.

Perhaps the most agonizing case I have struggled with in recent years on the issue of passive euthanasia was a case that engaged both Epstein and the attorney at Rush-Presbyterian Medical Center in Chicago, Max Brown. In the case of Sammy Linares, both of these respected colleagues took forceful but diametrically-opposed stands. Baby Linares was crawling around the floor of his West Side Chicago home one afternoon while the older kids ran and played at his brother's birthday party. Spotting a broken balloon on the floor, the baby stuck it in his mouth. After a few moments, the parents saw the baby choking and turning blue. The father, Rudy Linares, ran with the child to the nearby fire station from where they were rushed to the closest hospital. Sammy Linares arrived in a state of asphyxia but with some limited brain activity. After transfer to the major medical center and many months on a respirator, the parents sought to withdraw the machine from the near-brain-dead child. Physicians and the hospital counsel opposed this action. In desperation, ten months after the child was placed on life support, Rudy came in one night with a gun, held the nurses at bay, pulled the breathing tube from his baby's throat, and held him until he died a few minutes later.

Max Brown, the ethically reflective counsel at Rush, interpreted Illinois statute as not allowing such withdrawal of life support when complete brain-death was not present. Epstein and eventually the county coroner, Dr. Robert Stein, felt that such action was licit. The case pointed to the equivocal nature of law in this field. Seeking to preserve both patient and parental proxy right to refuse treatment or withdraw treatment already in place and the contrary value of protecting life and serving society's interest in preserving life, the law in the case had bogged down in internal contradiction and moral paralysis followed. The background of ethical reflection on which law is ultimately based continues to evolve. In Chicago, the state's attorney's task force, created after the Linares case, recommended policy and a statute that would allow institutions to withdraw such life supports without legal jeopardy.

For many years before, cases like Sammy Linares' would have been decided quietly by physicians and families without any legal or public-media attention. In recent years, though, we have come to an impasse as a society while we have sought to step back and ask about the ethical and legal propriety of such decisions. Over the last twenty years, a sequence of clinical cases have been taken into the courts to try to define the moral direction of the legal tradition and the ethical consequences of new circumstances under which people die, conditions such as sophisticated life supports, respirators and technological modes of maintaining nutrition and hydration. Let us now review this train of cases with the attempt to show a slowly evolving legal consensus that corroborates the thesis of this study that passive euthanasia in general and active voluntary euthanasia in exceptional circumstances are ethically acceptable.

Cases Which Have Refined the Legal Ground for Euthanasia

In *Quinlan*, to which we have already referred, the Supreme Court ultimately decided that surrogates for a patient (stepfather and mother in this case) could decide to terminate life-sustaining medical treatment since the constitutional right to refuse treatment belongs to both competent and incompetent persons. In a very crucial legal precedent, the court decided that the only way to justify such a proxy decision, however, was to offer evidence that the patient herself would want it this way if her views were accessible. This element in the legal judgment set the stage for the importance of advance directives in future situations. Focusing the decision on rights of privacy, the only moral criteria available to the law, the court decided that as in *Griswold* and *Roe*, a person's right to privacy did encompass the decision to decline or withdraw medical treatment. The *Quinlan* court placed moral authority for such decisions within the context of the patient-doctor-family relationship. *Quinlan* also established the desirability of having hospital ethics committees available to aid such decisions, again emphasizing the personal and immediate locus of authority in such matters. The court suggested that if the physicians indicated no hope for the patient's recovery, if the family was unanimous in their judgment and if the ethics committee concurred, treatment could be withdrawn and the parties remain free from legal liability. *Quinlan* made formal and explicit what had long been the informal practice of families and their caregivers.

In 1977, one year after *Quinlan*, legal thinking evolved one step further in *Saikewicz (Superintendent of Belchertown State School v. Saikewicz*, 373 Mass 728, 370 NE 2d417 [1977]). Joseph Saikewicz, a sixty-seven-year-old mentally retarded man suffered from leukemia. His guardian sought to spare him from the painful and perhaps lethal course of chemotherapy. Again the court decided that refusal of treatment, even in the case of an incompetent person, was acceptable. The court in this case added two ingredients to the ethical legacy of death and dying law. It sought to determine as closely as possible the "wants and needs of the person involved." In this case, the court felt that Saikewicz would not understand the suffering caused by the chemotherapy, and since the treatment had a good chance of not working and at best would not alter the terminal prognosis but only delay it, concurred with the contention of the court appointed guardian to withhold treatment. This case caused wide dissent, not only because of the substantive decision to withhold treatment, but because of the procedural decision that held that all such judgments should be made by an adversarial, judicial proceeding.

In a salient commentary on the case, Paul Ramsey asked whether "the ethical rule in practice for normal adult patients would be that such treatment should be *offered* . . . *given* to normal patients who because of age cannot themselves refuse treatment or *protected* in such patients by courts against any private decision to withhold them.[7] Ramsey was troubled by the apparent fact that nontreatment was coerced in Saikewicz. His critique points to the ambiguity that now starts to build up in this body of cases about whether treatment or nontreatment should be the initial bias. Battery and consent law subtly assumes that no treatment is to be preferred and that burden of proof lies with those who would proffer treatment. The question of this starting point is well taken. The difficulty with Ramsey's position is that only two options stood before Joe Saikewicz—coerced treatment or coerced nontreatment. In my view the questionable immediate prognosis and the certain long-range terminal prognosis justified the court's decision.

Beginning in 1980, a more conservative mood set in in U.S. medical jurisprudence regarding decisions to prolong or end life. Many reasons can be given for this noticeable shift in public policy. Obviously we were beginning a Reagan decade in national politics with its decided shift of persuasion against abortion. Whether "linkage" of this issue with euthanasia is evident might be disputed because the political philosophy of conservatism also has a strong strain of libertarianism with its correlate "right to die without governmental interference." A second development that may have influenced a new mood was the dramatic proliferation of medical ethics activity. In my estimate, in 1970 there were at most 100 persons in the United States who called their professional work "medical ethics." By 1980 medical ethics was a growth industry, with that many "experts" in Chicago alone (over 200 now belong to our fellowship, Chicago Clinical Ethics Program). Based on journal subscriptions and estimates at the national think tanks that have come into being (Hastings and Georgetown, among others), ten to fifteen thousand persons now worked in the field. Again, this broad interest is ambiguous in its impact. While sympathy for patient concerns was widespread among these professional ethicists, in my experience the increased attention to such issues, writing about cases and ethics committee activities itself chilled the willingness to let people die even after quiet and careful deliberations between physician and family. A final outcome of attention to these issues at the level of clinical ethics meant that they now often ended with a call to the hospital attorney, which usually meant counsel to do nothing that might pose legal jeopardy to the institution.

In *Satyr v. Perlmutter*, (379 So 2d 359 [Fla 1980]), the court confronted what would seem to be a baseline case of a mentally competent, terminally ill man seeking authorization to discontinue life-prolonging medical treatment. Perlmutter, seventy-three-years-old, suffered from Lou Gehrig's disease, which slowly takes away one's ability to breathe and swallow. On a mechanical ventilator in the hospital, he sought with the concurrence of his family, to withdraw the ventilator from his tracheostomy, an act that would promptly end his life. The attending physicians and hospital refused his request, citing fear of liability. Perlmutter's legal case against the doctors prevailed at all levels of the Florida judiciary. The new and unfortunate implication of the case was that the law now made it a legal precedent that such matters, heretofore resolved locally, should become legal matters. In this case, the court should have offered guidance and refused to hear the case, saying that it was not a matter for legal jurisdiction. Moving in the same moral direction, the Florida legislature at the same time as resolution of the case, passed the ''Life Prolonging Procedure Act,'' which established guidelines for declaring refusal of treatment in advance when persons suffered from such chronic, debilitating and terminal diseases.

Again, the end result of this act was unfortunate. It further insisted that such personal decisions of prolonging and ending life be made items of official legal record and adversarial process. As in the early experience of natural death acts (e. g., California in 1976), construing human dying as a legal matter created the paradox that those who had requested living will acts would not be resuscitated when they should have been, and those who had not requested (the vast majority) were resuscitated when they should not have been. The age-old experience of the law becoming an incitement to break the law came into frightening effect. If the courts had refused to hear *Perlmutter* and rather counseled withdrawal of treatment as extant procedure, Linares and so many subsequent grueling abuses of patient's death freedom might not have occurred.

But the die was cast. By virtue of advancing life-prolongation technology, the proliferation of not only bioethicists but clinician-lawyers and the disabling fear of litigation on the part of individual families and institutions (in 1990 our university's medical department practice plan expended one third of its total income on malpractice insurance), a new pattern of response had been set.

Despite the bewilderment and confusion (fueled by opportunism) of the period, an ethical position continued to evolve. In *Conroy*, (98 NJ 321, 386A 2d. 1209 [1985]), a nephew sought to have a nasogastric feeding tube removed from his eighty-four-year-old aunt with organic brain syndrome and limited life expectancy. With deteriorating circulation and poor bodily health, she had developed leg ulcers that required amputation. The court-appointed guardian refused. Although Mrs. Conroy died during the prolonged litigation and the case became moot, the courts refused the nephew's petition, moving the burden of proof in an unprecedented way from the historic right to refuse treatment to the presumed obligation to continue treatment unless the court superimposed a countervening right to stop. This subtle shift in U.S. jurisprudence continued to vex us down to the present *Cruzan* and subsequent cases. In the after-the-fact decision confirmed up through the New Jersey Supreme Court, it was decided that the right to refuse life-sustaining treatment was restricted to incurable and terminally ill patients who are either brain dead, permanently comatose, or vegetative. The more traditional right of persons, even through proxies, to refuse treatment with its obvious corollary to withdraw treatments already in place had been eroded.

This case ultimately led us around again to *Bouvia* where, we recall, for a constellation of reasons, the state's interest in preserving life assumed priority over the patient's right to refuse treatment. Late in 1987 another New Jersey case seemed to position legal precedent back within the broad stream of "allowing to die" tradition. Nancy Ellen Jobes, a thirty-two-year-old woman who was irreparably brain injured during an operation to remove a dead fetus following an auto accident seven years earlier was extubated from her feeding apparatus at the request of her husband. The court decided that family members were best suited to make substituted judgments because of their familiarity with the patients' philosophy of life and death and their intimate bonds with her. Though the Lincoln Park nursing home contested the withdrawal, the family pastor said that the family had bid her farewell years ago. The tradition of moral precedent of allowing passive euthanasia seemed back on course until *Cruzan*.[8]

The first significant legal decision in this sequence that has proceeded the full judicial route up to the U.S. Supreme Court is *Cruzan*. With very fuzzy strength of precedent, regional, the Supreme Court, then finally again regional courts vacillated between allowing loved ones to withdraw Nancy Cruzan's feeding apparatus and refusal of same. The U.S. Supreme Court finally conceded authority to the provincial jurisdiction that then allowed the petition for withdrawal. On December 14, 1990, the trial court in Carthage, Missouri, ruled that Nancy's parents might authorize withdrawal of her gastrostomy tube that provided her with nutrition and hydration. Twelve days later, on Christmas evening, she died. The case seems to give added momentum to the tradition that had come under some question that competent and incompetent persons have the right to have life-sustaining treatment withheld or withdrawn if that is their wish or the proxy expression of those closest to the individual.

A bird's-eye overview of this intriguing judicial and legislative timescape shows a deeply conflicted moral resolve on the matter of prolonging and ending life. We do wish to preserve what we have identified as a philosophically grounded and natural law sanctioned right to depart this life when it seemed fitting to that person or when in the best construction of proxy loved ones, it seemed to be "what one would have wanted." On the other hand, there has emerged a guarded caution against that same tradition based on classical sanctity doctrine compounded with a medical tradition against suicide based on property rights of lords over subjects, and more recently, on a fear of rampant unconsented medical murder and a related fear of establishing precedents that would lead to taking persons' lives for unworthy reasons. Since deep and positive values are found in both of these persuasions, it is likely that such oscillation will continue in the legal review of the subject of prolonging and ending life. It is furthermore probable that the expectation will grow that such matters must be taken to law. I will continue to argue, throughout this study, that this is wrong and dangerous. These decisions should remain matters of personal and family decision in concert with their physicians. If any contextual corroboration of such privacy and sanctuary is required, it should come from ethics committees, one's faith community and not from the criminal-court system.

Social and Political Matters

The reasons for positioning decisions with the family become even more important as we see the way in which other political concerns are now coming to impinge on decisions about human mortality.

Let us now review a series of concerns where forces proceeding from the body politic impinge upon human death. We lead into this topic by quoting former Dutch Catholic Sister Ms. Takken, now director of the Pacific Institute of Bioethics in Santa Barbara, California. After a lengthy interview in the journal *Hippocrates* on the subject of euthanasia in her homeland, she turned the discussion to the related political issue of care for the elderly. According to the article:

> Takken worries most about the effect of legalization on the ever-increasing numbers of elderly. With health care costs beyond the reach of many Americans, the elderly may feel pressured to ask for mercy killing simply to spare their families the crushing financial burden of hanging on—making euthanasia less a personal choice than a social responsibility. And those families, knowing the realities, may not be terribly eager to argue the decision.

> So who would fight for the patient? Nobody, Takken believes. Hospitals and nursing homes are struggling to contain costs. Medicare is on the skids. The elderly only use up what little resources exist, she says, and what better way to trim costs than offering the gentle death. In the 1930s, the rationale for mercy killing was racial purity; in the next century, perhaps, it will be budget considerations. A useless eater is still a useless eater.

> "I know a nursing home administrator here who just loves the old-timers and is really dedicated to them," Takken says, walking out onto the cabin deck where there are bright flowers all around and golden pastures under an endless California sky. "But he's beginning to say, 'What's the use. Kill 'em.' Every day he fights a system that won't pay for their care. The place stinks, there's no money. The patients feel useless in a use-oriented society. But what's he going to do, put them out on the street? It only takes a little morphine, and he has a real hard time thinking, 'No, don't do it.' "

> "Euthanasia is the perfect Band-aid. But what we should be doing is taking a long hard look at the inequities in the system."[9]

Care of the old, the poor and most often the old-poor in our society adds a critical complication to our question of prolonging and ending life. On the one hand, as we have noted earlier in this book, the funding crisis in U.S. health care arises in part because persons choose, or the system forces them, to extend their dying a few weeks or a month too long. The inordinate percentage of the health-care dollars spent in the last days and weeks of persons' lives (some estimates up to thirty percent) is increasingly questioned in a society that cannot insure even basic preventive and sustaining medical care for all of its citizens. Do we again face the paradox of a policy and clinical practice that keeps some people living (or dying) too long and in the same stroke deprives others of their rightful chance to live as long as they could? Crudely put, are we now killing those who deserve and wish to live and refusing death to those who are ready? Is the guilt about the former feeding the expiation of the latter?

The Thatcher era in Great Britain has had the same effect as the tenure of her ideological counterpart in the United States, Ronald Reagan. In the recently released report, *Health and Welfare: A Review of Health Inequalities in the UK*,[10] the link between poverty and premature death is again established. To begin with, infant mortality among the poor is twice the rate of that among the middle and upper classes. West Indian women in London experience precisely the same quotient of infant mortality when compared to whites as black mothers in Chicago. Among adults, the rate of cancer, heart, and lung disease is similarly disproportional to those who are poor. The causes of this increased morbidity and mortality are varied. Poor diet caused by inadequate incomes, lifestyles, and patterns of drinking, smoking, and drug abuse also take their toll. Habits deleterious to health seem to thrive where desperation, lack of opportunity, inadequate education, and chronic discouragement prevail. Systemic factors also contribute to this sociogenic mortality. Hospitals in the East End of London are decrepit, Dickensian structures, reminding the visitor of Chicago's 100-year-old Cook County hospital. Both have leaking roofs, outmoded equipment, and more importantly, a public edifice that says, to paraphrase the Hallmark cards ad, "We don't care enough to give you the best." Limited access, waiting lines, delayed procedures, and operations, and again the discouragement that comes from having to work so hard to find care, all conspire to bring early death to the poor. They simply give up.

The social-ethical culpability for this neglectful induction of death in old people is greater than that limited matter of our refusing death to those whose lives are inappropriately prolonged. The care stipulate of social ethics in Judeo-Christian culture is concern for the poor, weak, and vulnerable. This bias toward the oppressed, which is the basis of all welfare measures in those societies shaped by the mercy ethics of that tradition, imposes a demanding ethic. This is especially true since goods can be insured and evils avoided with simple provision of the necessities of life: an adequate living, food, shelter, and health care. Where this is provided, as in Sweden, Israel, or Japan, excess and premature mortality disappears.

Society in the modern world has assumed some responsibility for sustaining the health of its people. The most basic provision for this protection involves police, courts, and armies to thwart and punish those who would kill citizens. Secondary provision for life and against death is imbedded in efforts such as proscription of suicide and euthanasia and the supply of health care. Questions must be asked about the priorities among life-giving, life-sustaining, and life-protecting measures of a society. Homicide is now well into the top ten causes of mortality in the United States. Preventing deaths by reason of violence by banning hand guns would prevent many more deaths than efforts to prosecute cases of euthanasia. Nutritional support for mothers with babies would have far greater effect than the money spent by hospitals for legal services to protect themselves from the few negligent accidents and deaths brought about by medical care. We might ask, in other words, what are society's legitimate purposes in the prolonging and ending of life?

At the level of state and national governments, we also need to ask about the respective amounts of public resources that are devoted to shortening as opposed to preserving lives. Symptomatic of the scandalous immorality that any statistics would reveal in this matter is the news this week that European and U.S. support of Oxfam and other African famine-relief efforts will be pared back in order to financially underwrite the costs of the Persian Gulf war. In terms of social justice, we have progressed little since Dickens' day when ten-year-old children were condemned to premature deaths by their thirteen-hour work days in the cotton mills of Northumberland in order to improve the livelihood of the mill owners, provide subsistence living for workers, and enhance England's commercial preeminence in the world. While the measure of life given against life taken may on margin be positive, the margin is slight. Governments, in sum, may be less committed to life-saving and death prevention than we pride ourselves in proclaiming.

The societal inconsistency may be seen in the fact that most states have passed "living will" enactments to protect the "right to die," while for the most part they inadequately reimburse poor inner city hospitals for medicare and medicaid charges. A coherent "one cloth" policy of life affirmation or a socially recognized policy of tradeoffs would be more understandable, rational, and ethical than the present approach of saving the few and damning the many. Perhaps as with our strictures against abortion, we may be working out propitiation for residual social guilt for our general disregard and abuse of children. To a social ethicist, it is not incidental that the Hyde amendments limiting abortions for the poor (those whose health care is publicly funded) coincide with the awareness of the children whose lives were quenched by our military policies in Viet Nam or our domestic policies in cities like Chicago. Unfortunately governments and societies rarely think systematically, weighing effects against other effects.

With this proviso duly recorded, what has been the ethical adequacy of the main aspect of social death policy in the 1980s—the living will acts? As we noted in our rehearsal of the specific case histories that punctuated the 1960s through the 1980s, judges often recommended that states formulate guidelines and policies to obviate the need for every end-of-life decision to end up in court. Eighty percent (thirty-nine states) enacted living will laws during the 1980s. Generally called "Natural Death Acts," "Living Will Acts," "Life Sustaining Procedures Acts," or "Death with Dignity Acts," the statutes commonly contain some or all of the following provisions:

- Advance declaration may be made with personal instructions (which procedures one wishes to forgo, donation of organs, etc.)
- Provision made for another person to sign if first party is unable
- Physicians enter living will into medical record

- Health-care providers and institutions are immunized from prosecution
- Testified by competent witnesses
- Terminal condition of patient is medically verified
- Penalties provided for physician's failure to comply
- Special permission to withhold or withdraw artificial nutrition and hydration
- Physician given right to conscientiously object and refer patient to other physician
- Will does not impair or restrict other rights

Like the anatomical gift act, one sees the impact of uniform statutes that contain the elements adopted by the several states. In recent years, these statutes have been augmented by states adopting durable power of attorney acts, which also follow a uniform paradigm. What is the import of these measures on the end-of-life decisions that people face and on the terminal care-giving institutions? At this stage, I see only problems. In the first place, lawyers now displace pastors, nurses, and social workers as the dying and death counselors in hospitals and nursing homes. People are scared to death that they do not have the properly executed documents, that these have been filed in the proper places and with the proper individuals, and that the hard-enough choice of their own dying will be complicated by these added gesticulations.

Second, there is a bias in the statutes toward those educated and persons of means. The suburban hospital serving a community of middle-class college graduates is much more in the business of having living wills enacted and on file than is the poor inner-city community. This inequity is exacerbated by the fact that poor people more often face death at the hands of anonymous doctors (residents) and nurses in university teaching hospitals, rather than under the care of long-known family physicians in the towns and villages.

Another severe moral problem occurs when dying and death are increasingly being seen as matters of legal and adversarial definition and decision rather than personal, familial, and pastoral experiences. Do the acts help us achieve a better balance between the values of sustaining health and life while it is viable and worthwhile? Do they assist us to resist incessant death-denying and death-defying compulsions, to receive death in due season when one is ready and the prospect of recuperation is gone? The data is not yet in. Large scale studies, sponsored by the Robert Wood Johnson Foundation and other agencies, are now underway. How do people die? Under what conditions do persons spend their last days and hours? What constrainings, coercions, and facilitations do patients and their families experience? Is the intervention of law into this profound and sacred zone salutary or intrusive? Are persons' rights and wishes being honored, violated, or ignored? Are doctors practicing therapeutically sound and ethically wise medicine or are they being coerced to follow other nonhumanistic values?

These questions remain as our society experiences the overload of rapid advance of life-support skill and other diagnostic and therapeutic technology. They also sharpen in the presence of an increasingly enlightened laity demanding participation; a slowly evolving coalescence in ethical tradition; rapidly diminishing economic resources to do all that could be done; a law that seeks to offer protection without intrusion, and above all a populace that wishes to go toward death with magnaminity, courage, and dignity. How well we will do will depend on two future tendencies that are making us the kind of people we will be. To these we now turn as we explore the scientific-clinical future that is our natural propensity and the religious eschatology that might be a spiritual future as these offer a moral vision to guide us.

7

The Ethics of Secular Eschatology: Death and the Scientific Future

"I've been dead once already and it's very liberating."

> Jack Nicholson as Jack Napier who, after falling into
> a chemical vat, has reconstructive surgery and comes
> back as JOKER in the film *Batman*

At the conclusion of this study, the two paths of tradition converge and sustain a dialectic of tension. The natural and empirical tradition, which we have traced in the biological, philosophical, and political strain, gradually develops a secular position over against the religious tradition, especially when religion exploits and banks on human fear and premonition of death to perpetuate its ministry. As long as people die, they fear death and cling to the other-worldly salvation promised by the church. In vivid contrast to the early Middle Ages when faith, in fact, encouraged science, investigation, vivisection, and experimentation later became suspect. The church's rejection of Galileo or Darwin is based not only on those incipient sciences' presumed assault on cardinal doctrine, but on their implied prospect of displacing hope from beyond this world and the church's vested dispensations now to hope in life, health, and this world.

The Puritans and the empirical science they sponsored despised the Roman church's subjugation of persons' faith, hope, and devotion. The Puritans also rejected the Galenic and Thomistic captivity of science in favor of the investigative approaches of Vesalius, Harvey, Paracelsus, and a whole company of enthusiastic immortalists. A new world of empirical, deeply personal and felt faith was available, unconstricted by church channels. The same renewal offered a new world of salutary, redeeming, and life-prolonging science and medicine. An enormous hope was born in the hearts of people that the ancient scourges, degradations, and killers would be overwhelmed by the combination of scientific acumen, technical virtuosity, and human concern. The plagues were beginning to wane, a more general prosperity was felt, and learning advanced. While the extraordinary hope of the church fathers that life span, which had originally been set at 1000, had abated, 200 years was not out of the range of possibility. Seventeenth-century utopic texts outlined the medical prospects in this new millennium. Bacon's *New Atlantis* (1626), Platte's *Macaria* (1641), Chamberlen's *Poor Man's Advocate* (1648), among other texts, set forth a prospect where faith, science, and benevolence would converge to bestow health and perhaps immortality on all people.[1]

Because of a secularizing trend, humankind today has "come of age." To extend Dietrich Bonhoeffer's image, the humanistic challenge is now to become religious in the "worldly" way. We must hope rightly in order to act well. This eschatological hope in its secularized version remains vital to this day, having animated three centuries of scientific progress. Modern medical hope still follows the basic lines of seventeenth-century anticipation with thrusts in mechanical discernment and replication of bodily processes, iatrochemistry with its desire to understand what we would now call the cellular and subcellular processes, both vital and mortal, and the conquest of disease, particularly infections, malignancies, and idiopathic diseases of bodily deterioration. As we project the scientific and biomedical future that awaits us, we need to examine these broad areas of prosthetic therapy, cellular biomedicine, and the ability to impede, even check the course of disease. The moral thread running through the discussion is that we are gaining control over those morbid and mortal forces that injure and harm us. In this process we are assuming control over death, by facilitating some causes and forestalling others. We are gaining the long-sought and at the same time, long-avoided, power to define and delineate dying. The age of elective death will be one where human beings will deliberately choose the time, place, mode, and manner of death. We will help one another along in the adventure of death.

Let us outline these three pursuits: (1) support and replacement of failing bodily parts and processes, (2) modification of our metabolic and other vital substance and process, and (3) the fathoming and overpowering of disease. Let us then see how these historic ambitions may change the environment of human dying in the near future, say the next fifty years.

Impending Iatromechanics

Iatromechanical thought abounded in the sixteenth and seventeenth centuries. From Leonardo Da Vinci's fascination with the movement of limbs and joints, to the more fundamental and theoretical formulations of the body-machine by Descartes, the age was intrigued with the ways in which the body worked. Today's achievement in artificial organs and transplanted body parts is the heir to that tradition. Vital process focuses in these sectors of the body—the head, chest, and belly. What is the state of the art in supporting and refashioning function in these three zones?

Head

In an episode of the television series, *Star Trek*, Spock and the space crew return to earth at some future date. One of the crew incurs a terrible head injury in an accident. He is placed on an operating table and with precise diagnostic instruments, the nature of the injury is discerned. Without any trephination or messy neurosurgery, the injury is remedied, the trauma reduced, and the alert mind and brain restored. One of my first severe tests as a young pastor occurred when a young man, father of two children, was rushed in an ambulance to the small county hospital across from the manse where we lived. His car had been hit by a speeding train and dragged 100 yards. The only sign of trauma to the young man was a badly injured head. Skull films and clinical examination showed severe injury, crushed skull, massive bleeding, and edema. The doctor attending in the emergency room told me to prepare the family for his immanent death.

Today, although we might not alter the outcome, we are closer to *Star Trek*. We can see clearly what is going on with computerized tomography—sectional slices of the brain can be visualized and the exact nature and extent of the injury can be mapped. We can introduce or sustain coma or slowly bring one up from unconsciousness as in the case of drowning victims. Neurologic microsurgery can repair or recircuit vascular damage and resect lesions or tumors. Sophisticated procedures can activate or mute sections of the brain. The cavern can be reconstructed without while the vital organ within is repaired and protected from further harm. Though a prosthesis for the brain remains a long way off, in many ways the computer and other cybernetic devices already replicate the brain's function. Eye movements (a function of the brain) can trigger feedback signals that can perform functions like calling for nursing aid for a person with quadriplegia. The intriguing technology of night vision and jet pilot activity in the Persian Gulf war showed us the awesome prospects of technological counterparts to the human brain. Regrettably, it also shows why we could not resist the temptation to check it out in action, and the technological imperative, "It's there, use it!" was one of the unworthy precipitating causes of the war over Kuwait.

The brain and mind play a crucial role in end-of-life decisions. We have focused great attention for decades on the definitions of brain death as criteria to judge both cessation and beginning of life. Are the brain waves, those few of the many, which we can read flat? Is ventricle blood flow diminished? Do the corroborative neurological signs and reflexes—pupillary, laryngeal, ocular, aural, muscular—signal vital reserve or death? If the brain is dead or near-dead, is it permissible to withdraw life-support machines or to "harvest" organs?

We have also come to associate distinctly human qualities with the brain and mind. Is a person whose body pumps along perfusing a brain in vegetative state really a person? If the brain and mind are destroyed, even in cases such as profound dementia, Alzheimer's disease, retardation, and severe spasticity and palsy, can we stop the sustenance of hydration, nutrition, and perfusion to the supportive body? Loss of the mind, we have come to believe, justifies withdrawal of those supports that otherwise viable "human" beings deserve. Technological replication of the brain's broken signals to the supportive body beneath is at the root of our bioethical crises. When the brain no longer supplies regular and operative vagal stimulation to the heart, we can apply a pacemaker. When the respiratory center drive is diminished or becomes erratic, we can apply the respirator. Rather than giving in and giving up when any of the myriad brain-body interfaces fail, we provide some substitute. In the future I think we will weigh more carefully whether to intervene acutely and certainly chronically with the organismic vitalities and mortalities animated at the synapse of brain and body.

Other areas of brain and mind care must include atrophy of neural tissue and structure, tumors, disturbed neural electrochemistry, and psychiatric and psychological disorders. A great challenge to humane and ethical end-of-life care in the future will be to protect and enhance this vital link we call brain-mind as the seat of not only physical vitality but sensation, feeling, thought, memory, communication, and a sense of worth. Right now our skill at body maintenance and repair has moved along with great strides (because of its comparative simplicity) while mind care has lagged behind (because, in part, of its complexity).

We will need in the future to better read the mind and brain of the person. The mind that shifts from will to live to will to die should be read as offering a powerful moral message. When I think of the frantic efforts I have made to deny, to cheer, to avoid the subject when I have been called to the side of a dying patient either as a minister or as an ethics consultant on the medical service, I realize how hard it must be for a dying person to get across the message: "I'm ready." We will need that combination of historical, psychological, and spiritual discernment to know when life-weariness is appropriate, when one wishes to withdraw, when one's journey with God nears home. Then we will need the self-insight, the self-mastery and grace not to forbid, not to hasten, but to remain faithful, receptive, and near.

Chest

Iatromechanics pertain even more dramatically to the chest. Care of the heart and lungs constitutes the focus of most critical and intensive care. The full complement of this vital interactive system has been transplanted, the heart alone with modest success. Pioneering versions of the artificial heart, ventricular assist devices, and gas exchange systems are now at various stages of development and implementation.

Life and breath have always been known to reside in the breast and chest. When the English physiologist, William Harvey, sought to understand the inner secondary circulation of blood from heart to lungs, he waited for hangings in the Oxford Corn Market. When beat and breath had ceased in the corpse, he would attempt to revive that center of life. Today these mechanics of revival focus in emergency rooms and intensive- and critical-care units. Today blood gasses can be continually monitored to show health of the inspiration/expiration quotient as well as the vitality of the internal exchange mechanisms. Pressor drugs can bolster failing blood pressure and maintain vital equilibrium in this system. The cleansing mechanisms of the lungs can be aided by fluid manipulation and suctioning. Indeed, all of the forces that maintain the dynamic turgor of this vital axis—neurologic, hematologic, cardiac, pulmonary—can be monitored and bolstered.

The obvious ethical quandaries that arise as the chest fails are cardiopulmonary resuscitation and the permanent introduction of prosthetic heart or lung substitutes. Take the case of Nancy Cruzan, a somewhat typical emergency-room decision. The accident has occurred, the heart has stopped, perhaps from trauma or bleeding, and the brain has been deprived of oxygen for some short time. But it is a cold winter's night and hypothermia has cryo-preserved organs and tissues. The emergency-medical technicians reach the scene of the accident, immediately introduce CPR, and the heart and lungs again surge blood through the body and head. The body comes back to life but the brain has been damaged. When, we are forced to ask, is CPR appropriate?

During recent years I have served on official bodies creating ethical guidelines for resuscitation for the Hastings Center[2] and for the American Association of Chest Physicians and critical-care physicians.[3] In each of these documents we tried to answer this question. Values such as patient well-being and assessing whether CPR would benefit or burden the patient; patient self-determination; the ethical integrity of health-care professionals and justice or equity were marshaled to assess the appropriateness of action. Often in emergency situations where there is no awareness of advance directives or time to do exhaustive prognostic analysis or even diagnostic assessment like APACHE (intensive-care checklist of morbidity like APGAR in newborns), health professionals are trained automatically to attempt to revive and stabilize. This sometimes leads to blessed life rescue and often to prolonged projection of a debilitated course of dying. The percentage of resuscitated patients who eventually leave the hospital well is extremely low. New follow-up mechanisms are now incumbent upon us. I often advise my physician colleagues in ER and ICU medicine candidly to inform the family that while resuscitation and life support (ventilator) will be placed with every hope of recovery, they are also placed with the firm commitment that they will be withdrawn after a trial period if the sustenance is futile and there is no significant recovery.

In the near future we will have available elaborate cardiopulmonary life-support systems in hospitals and perhaps in remote and mobile sites. All of the necessary diagnostic monitoring and modulating apparatus will be there as well. The unit may have artificial heart and lung machines that can maintain corporeal circulation and perfusion for short or long periods. These devices will seek, as the prototype iron lungs did, to tide the patient over—carry one through a traumatic crisis, (e.g., polio) then be disengaged as one's own vital powers were restored. But the vista of Barney Clark, permanently appended to an artificial heart, and Karen Quinlan to a respirator remind us of proper and improper use of these devices.

In the future, good care of the person in institutions of acute or chronic cardiopulmonary care will require that the whole body and mind be embraced in sensitive diagnostic and prognostic efforts and that the classic but somewhat forgotten abilities to palpate and oscillate the chest be restored. The ability to listen and hear the voice of the body—both in its message of vital capacity and in its quotient of death and life urge must be honed again. The body emits signals through heart and lung; but also through eye, hand, and skin it emits the voice of struggle, of healing, of illness, or of impending death. Observing and heeding such *signa Hippocratica* will be essential to both the triage work that will give persons entrée to ICU and care once in that sanctuary.

Belly

A consultation came from a community physician. His patient had received surgery for an abdominal malignancy one year before. The primary site was unknown. Perhaps the pancreas, bile duct, or some other hard-to-diagnose area. Some metastatic spread had been resected and a bypass of the affected area had been placed. Now the malignancy had reached a new untreatable and intractable state. Treatment had allowed the patient to move toward a more advanced and proliferated state of disease. Now what? The case reflects on the ethical issues involved in current and impending iatromechanics of the belly. Kidney replacement via transplantation and functional subsumption via dialysis is an advanced and successful medical skill. Still at some point fifteen percent of dialysis patients decide to stop treatment and accept inevitable death. We have witnessed an era of pioneering liver transplantation and segmental donation. Multiple transplants in children with biliary atresia has raised some questions, but the procedure has moved from the realm of experimentation to the brink of standard treatment. In the case mentioned, the temporary blessings of circumventing intestinal or urinary obstruction led to later, more grievous, problems. Ought we then not to perform the procedures? The moral position emerging in this book is that we ought to use medical and surgical technique to palliate and relieve obstruction and any remediable cause of severe distress. This willingness should also be followed by a willingness to aid the dying process at the more complicated disease state that inevitably follows these interventions.

Enteral and parenteral nutrition will offer direct portals of entry when peripheral and nasogastric entrée fail. One day carriage transplants may succeed in lifting out the entire thorax, chest, and belly and replacing everything from esophagus, heart, and lungs down to the intestines. If the problems of trauma, neural viability, and rejection are mastered, why not? Mechanical intervention into the head, chest, and belly are now in a rapidly advancing period of progress, but a horizon of limitations already appears. Bench surgery may remove, repair or replace injured or diseased parts, but mortalities in this region of the body eventually overwhelm vitalities, even if the mind remains alert. The extensions—legs, arms, hands, feet—are less crucial to survival and may perhaps be more amenable to prosthetic or orthotic replacement.

Trauma surgeons in great medical centers located in such cities as Chicago, Los Angeles, and New York are masters at putting shattered bodies back together. If heads are protected by helmets, seat belts, or air bags, bodies can be pretty well broken apart, blown apart, shot through, and yet still be salvaged. The challenge of the future of iatromechanical medicine is tied up with neurologic regeneration and the transplant and regeneration of tissue, which we will presently consider. Above all, the availability of these techniques to all in equitable fashion will present formidable challenge. A post-Civil War photo in Alabama shows a large field filled with all of the still-living Confederate soldiers who had lost legs from wounds and infection in that state. The cost for their care alone consumed one-third of the state's meager budget. Such ecologic and economic constraint may ultimately confront what we can scientifically and technologically offer.

Iatrophysical and Iatrochemical Medicine

The second field of scientific progress toward prolonging life has been the promise of iatrophysical and iatrochemical medicine. Understanding the bodily processes of degeneration and decomposition, the problems of cell and tissue loss and injury, the toll that defensive (e.g., immunological) responses take on the body while performing their salutary tasks, all challenge bioscientific knowledge and technology. Take one of the major diseases of aging: rheumatoid arthritis. While we may one day discover that this spectrum of disorders falls into the category we will next deal with—the pathogen incited disease-like infections—for the time being it seems to be a disease with genetic propensities and onset related to general immunologic hypersensitivity and over-reaction, as well as the wearing down of the body, perhaps triggered by microorganisms or other insult. Something starts going on in the body that alters and accelerates the production of "rheumatoid factors" which deposit in the joints of the body, and induce inflammation and the resultant pain and debility.

The scientific future will confront this disease and other bodily deteriorations with a range of iatrochemical maneuvers. We may simply hold things in check with antiinflammatory drugs, which are certainly one of the blessings of scientific biomedicine. We might discover and eliminate dietary, environmental or lifestyle factors in the induction and proliferation of such disease. We might reach back into the genetic roots and propensities of the disorders and either alter the genetic structure or mute the phenotypic display, thereby alleviating symptoms but not the underlying disorder. We may develop sophisticated target medicines that can selectively move to the site of trauma and offset the deleterious process. Interleukin II for cancer and Erythropoietin for kidney failure are examples of such potent and expensive medicines. We may develop nanotechnology, which will allow us to sluff off degenerate tissue and regenerate healthy cells. By understanding the breakage and repair process of DNA, we might develop restorative procedures that will cure such diseases.

For the time being this utopic future will elude us. With every significant scientific advance against disease, we will most likely introduce new environmental causation that will call new morbid forces into play. Trading off infections will yield the new infections of retroviruses and sexually transmitted diseases or displacement from elsewhere on the spectrum of morbidity like Alzheimer's disease. These diseases of collapsing biochemical vitality will therefore remain the signals of mortality in our bodies. Diseases of the central nervous system, joints, and connective tissues, the hematopoietic, hepatobiliary, endocrine systems will continue to be the death we carry in our bodies in the foreseeable future. Dealing with these chronic illnesses with courage and creative compensation, beating them at their own game, masking their morbid and mortal effects, and eventually choosing good deaths in the face of them will be the challenge of the near-range future.

Fathoming and Overpowering Disease

Can the same be said about the range of diseases that depend on external insult-triggering internal-vulnerability conditions like infections and cancer? Religious and literary wisdom has always drawn us back to scriptural truth that we are fashioned from dust and to dust we return. This great recycling process of dirt (Adam) in the world is insured by the ubiquitous fauna and flora of the microbial world, which is forever with us, within and without. This "army of God" (Cotton Mather) ultimately releases pathogenic heat, bringing our death and that "cold sullen stream" of our dissolution. When Job cries, "though worms destroy this body—yet in my flesh shall I see God" (Job 19:26), his eyes have well focused both into and beyond the soil of this world.

Before the modern era, infections were thought to be inescapable human destiny. Before inoculation and antibiotic therapy, and even to great extent thereafter, "the old man's friend," Sir William Osler's euphemism for pneumonia, and related infections held sway over life and death. Eschatologically speaking, they were either God's messengers signaling and delivering death, or foreign invaders to be defended against, attacked, and defeated. The "weapons" with which tuberculosis was "attacked," Susan Sontag reminds us, were sun, air, rest, and hygiene, none other than Hippocrates' "airs and places." In this militant view, the physician conducted *bellum contra morbum*, the war against disease upon and within the battlefield of the patient's body. This warfare, as Sontag comments, often left a scarred and scorched battlefield. As we engage the metaphoric evils of illnesses like TB, cancer, and AIDS,[4] we were working out our dualistic and apocalyptic eschatology, becoming warriors against those invading or occupying armies. The metaphors have been "good and evil," "light and darkness." The Simingtons of Texas have constructed a whole field theory of psychological warfare against cancer—envisioning our good white soldiers or cowboys chasing the black-masked bandits. This mental model is meant to marshall immune response (white killer cells) and the body's strength against illness. The trouble with this approach is that retaliatory and vindictive campaign as with the Iraqi conflict may win the war but lose the peace.

Each time we introduce antibiotics into the human body we make the body different, be it penicillin for a suspected strep throat or some new antiviral medication to impede the cytomegalovirus that may in turn stimulate atherosclerotic entrenchment. Indiscriminate prescription of antibiotics to appease parents whose kids had colds in the 1960s and 1970s may come back to haunt those same children as adults as we find their resistance compromised. We become refracted against antibiotics and slowly the organisms develop resistance. A better approach is to seek a gentle symbiotic compromise with the world of germs and only attack them when they pose serious threat. Seeing diseases, even dread infections, as enemies causes us to disgrace the host body and invite disgust on the affected person. This has been the case down through the ages from the ancient lepers to medieval victims of the plague to persons with TB, cancer, and now AIDS. As Sontag acknowledges, her mission is to calm the imagination not to incite it.[5] The genius of the scientific approach to medical eschatology is to demythologize it and strip it of its transcendent meaning and terror.

One of the most difficult areas of care of dying patients today is the management of infections. They are so simple to diagnose and to treat. Routine blood cultures can be drawn and if certain bacteria or fungi grow, the proper antibiotic can be targeted. Should the team ever order routine blood work-ups for patients who are waiting to die? Is it proper to monitor for infections without the concurrent commitment to treat them when found? When one's system is vulnerable and resistance compromised, is it a moral and humane act to wage war against particular infections knowing that the subsequent enemies will be more irascible and cause greater suffering? Can one request the nontreatment of infections in living wills or advance directives? Like some of the antipathy toward withdrawing food and water, antibiotics are often seen as basic, obligatory, humane care where the right to refuse treatment should not pertain.

Infections in the future will also be amenable to stalling or staging tactics. In the sixteenth century, syphilis was a raging infection that killed quickly. Now its virulence has waned and it spreads out over primary, secondary, and tertiary stages. AZT and other antiviral agents may not "wipe out" the invading occupant, but it might keep it in abeyance for a long time, perhaps long enough for the patient to outlive it. Cancer also can seed at one time (the asbestoses and silicoses, for example) and not manifest as a palpable tumor until twenty years later. This fact of latency and control of the mode and manner of manifestation might be another scientific fact that will add dimension to our unfolding thesis. If we can place malignant infection and neoplasia into holding patterns, will we not be able to turn those mortal forces on when we wish and bring about intended death? Will we one day use voluntary germ warfare? A few authors have tentatively suggested that medical care today ought to start thinking about guiding the terminally ill person along toward death, not inducing it, but collaborating with morbidities and mortalities already *in situ*. If we can treat a head and neck tumor so that we forestall a death by brain metastasis in order to facilitate it by liver metastases or erosion of a carotid artery and exsanguination, are we not choosing a better course among sad options? Natural law ethics, experienced in Roman Catholic medicomorality, evaluates differently the act of allowing and accompanying a dying process from the act of killing. Such ethics also allows the tragic necessity of selecting a lesser evil.

Before we leave this chapter dealing with the constitution of scientific method and a scientific future to ethics, we need to note the liabilities that this same method imposes on clinical care. Arnold Toynbee locates the implicit danger posed by a method emphasizing materiality and specialty on a profession that must deal with human beings in their birth, living and delight, their suffering, sorrow, and dying.

The modern Western attempt to work out a psychic science on the lines of a preexisting physical science may put western psychic science in danger of being misled by a false analogy.[6]

In the west within the last three centuries, medical science has gone the same way as science in general. It has taken an analytic, selective and specializing turn. The medical specialist limits himself to dealing with some single organ or with some simple human malady. The specialist does not deal with all of the person whose organ or malady he is treating.[7]

Physicalism, materialism, biologism, and vitalism as univocal medical philosophies have the danger of ignoring the complementary dimensions that constitute reality in its fullness. Dimensions of mind, spirit, and eternal transcendence save science from claiming ultimate understanding and control within its method. They also insure a magnanimity and acceptance in the face of finite knowledge and inevitable mortality.

Specialism poses an equally ominous threat to ethical medical care. Knowledge of the particular part requires the bracketing of everything else in the whole. Yet we almost retreat to superficial understanding of the whole in order to retain a comprehensive perspective. Only two solutions are possible. Teamwork may allow us to perceive and care for the whole being as numerous specialists interact with one another. The other option is to seek such deep insight into the microcosm that it discloses the macrocosm. Eighteenth-century idealism believed that if one really fathomed one thing in particular it would convey the knowledge of the whole ("Flower in the crannied wall if I knew thee, I'd know all in all").

Science seems to be moving in this holistic direction, thus making its contribution to ethics indispensable. Take Bobby Alford at Baylor College of Medicine, chair of the department of otorhinolaryngology. Bobby is knowledgeable and honest enough to say that he can really only be a "nose" doctor. To move to the frontiers of knowledge and therapeutic skill, it is impossible to deal with ears, throats, noses, and the interstitial tissues. But just think. The study of the nose involves the olfactory sensation, forcing the doctor to comprehend the function of the entire nervous system. The opthomologist must be an expert on the visual cortex of the brain as well as a scholar of vascularity, renal function, metabolism, and most other synergistic biological processes. Study and help of the particular, in other words, cannot fail but lead us back to the whole.

Do we need neonatologist-neurologists or family practitioners to deal with maternal-child care in poor neighborhoods in the cities. Our enormous bias now says forget the specialist, give us the generalist. Our entire program of educational funding, licensing, curriculum development and fellowships is rapidly moving in this primary care direction. But is this the way to go? Is it not the case that we will need the specialist in neurological viability of a neonate who also understands the emotional needs of the mother, the impact of the home and environment, and the interplay with all features of personal and family health? Good medicine, in short, must be so specialized that it rises again to levels of comprehensiveness. The ethical impact of future scientific medicine will be to see the greater in the lesser and the lesser in the greater.

The Structure and Momentum of Science and the Future of Death

The rationality and progress of science seeks to realize both the possible and the desirable. In a fundamental sense science has no control over what comes next within its experimental reach. Knowledge unfolds somewhat along predictable and hoped-for lines but in a larger sense, new knowledge is serendipitous and surprising. In an even more telling way science is value neutral. The proverbial, "if the mountain is there climb it, wherever it leads" characterizes scientific endeavor. Recent breakthroughs in the history of science such as the nature of the atom with the phenomena of fusion and fission and the unraveling of the DNA molecule weren't planned, they just happened. The knowledge happened to be there for the taking and the human mind had been made ready to see it by long preparation. If one cannot accept such realistic and objective epistemology, perhaps we can say that the human mind in its awesome facility to model what it takes in experience reaches sufficient elaboration and refinement to say that things seem to be and work in this way.

The practical point often made on the basis of this assertion is that scientists discover, technologists (engineers) apply, and politicians use or abuse. This obviously is too simplistic. Implicit in the act of knowing is both the benefit and the danger of the discovery. Even pure knowledge is value fraught. The discovery of the nuclear and molecular basis of matter and life is of such profound implication. "We physicists," said Robert Oppenheimer (not the engineers or the Enola Gay bombardiers), "we physicists have known sin." Oppenheimer also said that what was "technologically sweet becomes irresistible." Knowledge is compeling, intriguing, and inviting. In Isaac Newton's words (after the Puritan scientists), science was "thinking God's thoughts after him." The lure of science and knowledge is built into the nature of the human mind and the receptive logos resonance of reality. In a strange way the existential dilemma posed by the apostle Paul and Martin Luther, "the good I would I cannot and the evil I abhor I do," and "*non posse non pecatta*" (it is impossible not to sin), applies to science. It is impossible to say no to knowledge. Bitter experience has also shown us that the sequel of practical application always follows every idea. Throughout history until today, it is the case that everything we could do, however abhorrent, we have done. Even the horrors of nuclear detonation, and chemical and biological warfare have been realized even in the face of enormous taboo and fear. Probably the ultimate test of this scientific-technical necessity will come early in the next millennium when we will be able to set in motion an unending nuclear chain-reaction or the nucleation and cloning of a human being.

The ethical case we have sought to make in this book is that giving and prolonging life is good unless it is moribund life, and that ending life is wrong unless it is a liberating, redeeming death. I have argued that nature, intelligence, our common life, and God elicit from us such moral response. Science and technology is the focus of the rational dimension of ethics. The awesome fact of science is that it can be life-generating or life-degrading. The science of the physical universe yields knowledge that can be applied in creative or destruction directions. The life and human sciences also offer explanation and control that can be put to healing or damaging purpose. Into the formal structures and purposeless momentum of science must be poured some substantive ethical direction. It will be either benign or malign, or more likely some admixture of good and evil. The surest guide for humane and godly science and terminal-care medicine is what we will call eschatological ethics. To this we now turn in the final chapter.

8
Death and the Sacred Future: Eschatological Ethics

Requiem aeternam dona eis, Domine,
et lux perpetua lucent eis.
Kyrie eleison, Christe eleison,
Pie Jesu, Domine, dona eis requiem;
Agnus Dei, qui tollis pecata mundi, dona eis requiem.
Liberame, Domine, de morte aeterna, in die illa tremenda;
In paradisum deducent angeli.

Gabriel Faure, *Requiem*

The sabbatical visitor to Oxford is surrounded by an embarrassment of riches, intellectual and cultural. Among these is the unique privilege of hearing the mass sung daily in splendid Evensong or Sung Eucharist. One may receive it at my College, Christ Church, with its classical cathedral school choir. On another occasion one delights in the robust and haunting choirs at Magdalene or New College. I sat one evening in the darkened center vestibule of New College Chapel while the choir sang Poulanc's *Mass* (sometimes one needs more dissonance than Bach or Mozart). My chair was so close to Epstein's statue of Lazarus that my coat rubbed against it. This monument of stone rises with the enigmatic release of a Michelangelo marble as the swirling-shroud-wrapped body arches with bent neck toward heaven. I was told that former Soviet Premier Nikita Krushchev visited this fourteenth-century chapel, and was so moved by this statue that he dismissed his entourage and sat there in meditation through the night. Death and life—the drama of the mass perpetually reenacts that story. Now it is Poulanc, or Britten, Mozart, Schubert, Byrd, or Palestrina. In a few weeks the orchestra and choir at Christ Church will offer Mozart's

161

Requiem Mass in honor of those dead, and now dying in war. A short trip up to Coventry Cathedral cannot fail to bring to mind the first performance there of Britten's *War Requiem.*

Hans Jonas has reflected that the primal riddle confronting human beings is not life but death. I always thought that wonder at life was the original question. Certainly well into the modern era persons were so surrounded by death that the grace of life excited a gratitude unknown to moderns in the age of penicillin. But Jonas must be right; thankfulness for life proceeds from an awareness of death. Death calls for an explanation, as all stories of human beginnings attest. All metaphysics and religion find their grounding in the primal enigma of death. Why does it happen? What does it mean? Where does it lead? How ought one to go about it? In this concluding chapter let us trace through a spiritual eschatology of death that is the mass, and the more basic human pathos that Teilhard calls the "mass on earth," which the religious mass symbolizes. Then with the aid of the thought of Ernst Bloch and Hans Jonas let us see where the soul of modern humanity is tending and what is the substance of its hope in the midst of death. Has the implicit deicide of modern philosophy and science robbed us not only of hope but of the moral direction supplied by hope? Finally, we will characterize the impact of eschatologic ethics on the death decisions that await us.

Death and the Legacy of Hope

The somber and dreary fatalism of the preclassical Greek writers like Homer left death as the tragic necessity at the abruptly short end of an heroic life. But it was the Hebrew vision of Yahweh, not the Hellenic concept of constant nature or capricious deity, that introduced the human race to a horizon of hope. This hope has fostered both a courageous life and faith and a sense of resignation in face of life's problems. Richard Rubenstein, the Jewish theologian somewhat associated with the "death of God" school, has written in Nietzschean mood:

> 'Eschatology is a sickness'. . . .It was our Jewish sickness originally. We gave it to you [Christians]. You took us seriously. Would that you hadn't!. . .If you are a Christian, you

cannot avoid it. If you become post-Christian, choose pagan hopelessness rather than the false illusion of apocalyptic hope.[1]

The passage recalls the epitaph on the tombstone of Greek writer Nikos Kazantzakis:

> I have no hope, I love the earth, I am free.

Hope is a two-edged sword that can either sharpen or sever ethical action. As we have seen, apocalyptic hope (nature is being transformed) inspired Puritan science to refashion the world as a millennial scientific utopia. Through the medium of Hegelian idealism and Marxian materialism, a lively secular hope with a vibrant vision of liberation of the oppressed was let loose in the world sustaining a latter-day sequel of humane revolution throughout the world. Yet even this liberation is sullied. Consider the independence revolution that occurred in the Baltic republics of the Soviet Union in the early 1990s. Here the ambiguities of freedom were poignantly expressed as release from central government tyranny, together with a desire for less collective concern and more self-aggrandizement.

In eschatological hope, the Benedictines of the Middle Ages fashioned the cultural and agricultural technologies and the servanthood means of distribution that would bring prosperity and longevity to the modern world. Hope also brings a *contemptus mundi*. The oppressed have always been soothed against rebellion with the opiates of religion. The African slaves sang, "this world is not my home. I'm only passing by." Cancer patients may distort a hope for miracle and yearnings for the world to come into a therapeutic nihilism and neglect their symptoms. Eschatologic ethics, as hope philosophers and theologians have shown, implants in the human spirit a dissatisfaction with what *is* in favor of what *could be*. A passion for the possible engenders an attitude of waiting and working. Both serene acceptance of death and frantic work to overcome it are born in apocalyptic (nature miracle expectation) and eschatologic hope. What are the origins of such hope?

At the convergence of Hebraic hope and Hellenic serenity, we find an unknown Alexandrian Jew writing in the first century B.C.: "The souls of the righteous are in the hand of God, and no torment will ever touch them" (Wisd. of Sol. 3:1, RSV).

Several notions intertwine in this passage. The old Egyptian notion of a judge weighing conscience and the heart in death judgment is present. This weighing up comes at life's end with the balance of righteousness over sin yielding eternal life. To the Hellenic notion of the ubiquity of divine presence, even in death, is added the Hebrew (old West-Asian) notion of the human pilgrim in a death-bound search for the lost soul and eternal life. "Their hope is full of immortality" (Wisd. of Sol. 3:4, rsv).

The first man we meet in the Hebrew Bible is fallen man who searches for lost immortality. "Behold, the man has become like one of us, knowing good and evil; and now, lest he put forth his land and take of the tree of life, and eat, and live forever" (Gen. 3:22, rsv).

We first sense that we might be immortal and that our soul ought to find eternal repose (requiem) in God when we realize our separation and alienation, our distance from our eternal life-giving maker. Fall signals ascent. Death poses a line that we cannot cross. We are mortal and that mortality implies immortality, that finitude, infinity across the horizon. J. S. Bach, as Paul Hindemith's biography pointed out,[2] intuited a perfection beyond the veil of death, a perfection he sought to mimic. But Bach could not penetrate the veil, and even his beatific harmony and melody could never finally rest.

Two Babylonian stories offer parallels in the ancient Near-Eastern belief about life, death, and the gods. In the story of Adapa, the primal and progenerative person had been created and given wisdom by Ea, the god of water and wisdom. Anu, the god of heavens, summoned him for breaking the wing of the South Wind. Ea, the god of sustenance, counseled that he not receive Anu's bread and drink, saying it was the substance of death. Refusing this hospitality, Adapa refused also the bread and water of life and returned to earth mortal.

The meaning of this myth is complex. On the one hand the gods wish to share sustaining gifts of life and their own immortal nature in companionship with earthlings. On the other hand, we see what myth analysts have called "the envy of the gods." Here death is interposed on alienated humanity both to censure refusal of sustenance and companionship and to restore that fellowship by eventual reunion. These stories reflect the struggle of the human soul when confronted with death experienced as judgment and atonement. The wanderings of death avoidance and the mystic yearnings for restored wholeness become the active moral responses of the divided soul.

The search for eternal life is the theme of the archetypal Babylonian story of human destiny—the Gilgamesh epic. This masterpiece of world literature reveals an insight into the human soul matched only by Indian and Asian texts.

> Who, my friend, can ascend (as man) to heaven?
> Only the gods live forever with Shamash.
> As for men, their days are numbered,
> Only Wind remains, whatever they do!
> But already here you live in fear of death—
> What has become of your heroic strength?
> I will go before you, and then you will only need
> To call to me, "Forward! Have no fear!"
> And if I die, I will make a name for myself.
> Then they will say, "Gilgamesh has fallen
> In battle with the terrible Huwawa" . . .
> For truly I will lift up my hand,
> Will cut down the cedar;
> I will make a name for myself that will endure.[3]

Heroism and courage ensure the only imaginable immortality against the gods who carefully guard that gift. The name (implying presence and power) will live on. The frantic incessance of Gilgamesh's search for his lost friend and lost self is questioned:

> Gilgamesh, where are you hurrying to? You will never find that life for which you are looking. When the gods created man they allotted to him death, but life they retained in their own keeping. As for you, Gilgamesh, fill your belly with good things; day and night, night and day, dance and be merry, feast and rejoice. Let your clothes be fresh, bathe yourself in water, cherish the little child that holds your hand, and make your wife happy in your embrace; for this too is the lot of man.[4]

The elusive quest for one's soul and for immortality is discouraged in favor of the mundane pleasures that life here affords and an appreciation for each grace that friendship, family, and love offer. This noble literature towers above most of the frenetic and fantastic projections of immortality quest that will follow not only in Semitic texts but in the Greek, Persian, and other Near Eastern parallels.

The search of Gilgamesh is a testament to the human achievement of a proper sense of human destiny, one transfigured from a prideful quest for personal glory and immortality to one where accepted and sacrificial generosity to others and exultation in the goodness of life displaces wistful longing for some plant of eternal youth. Elysian fields of blessed requiem and return are received (as we will note later when we look at the evangelist Matthew's gathering of this long eschatological and ethical history), not from a deliberate desire to gain eternal reward but as a surprising gratuity in summation of a life seeking to live well. Absorbed in the search for his lost father Odysseus, Menelaus, his son, receives the promise of their 'beautiful isle of somewhere':

> As for your own end, Menelaus, you shall not die in Argos, but the gods will take you to the Elysian plain, which is at the ends of the world. There fair-haired Rhadamanthus reigns, and men lead an easier life than anywhere else in the world, for in Elysium there falls not rain, not hail, nor snow, but Oceanus breathes ever with a west wind that sings softly from the sea and gives fresh life to all men. This will happen to you because you have married Helen, and are Zeus' son-in-law.[5]

Death is our inescapable destiny. Though the quest for immortality is implanted in our soul, incessant obedience to such a quest diverts us from taking proper measure of our days and applying our heart unto wisdom (Ps. 92), which is justice and kindness. We should seek to live as well as we can not as long as we can. The poet Meander lamented that "He whom the gods love dies young," and the psalmist pleaded, "O my God, take me not away/in the midst of my days" (Ps. 102:24). The finality of death calls us to authenticity of life. The end has power to mark a beginning.

The ethical teaching of the Platonic Socrates about death resonates with this earlier Mesopotamian wisdom. He reasoned from this
side of the veil of ignorance that no one could know whether death was
simple and benign annihilation or perhaps "the greatest among all
goods" (*Apology*, 29A). Reflecting the Pythagorean belief on moral
vindication and transmigration of the soul, Socrates spoke:

> The state of being dead is one or the other of two things:
> when a man is dead, he is the same as nothing, not having
> any kind of sensation of anything. Or as is also said, it is
> removal and relocation of the soul from here to another
> place (*Apology*, 40C).

It is a moral confidence and inspiration rather than logic that finally
forms the Socratic view of life's end and the hereafter. His *daimon* or
divine companion convinced him that truthfulness and rectitude in their
own inherent virtue constituted life beyond death.

> He [Socrates] experiences his eternality as the certainty that
> the man who stands firm in his commitment there can be no
> evil either in life or in death. And thus even the masters of
> his destiny and his fate, the gods, cannot allow him to fall
> into death.[6]

"Once to every man and nation comes the moment to decide,"
wrote American poet James Russell Lowell. In Socratic, as in prior
Pythagorean thought, each person is given a moral watch-post in the
world and a moral challenge, throughout experience, in which she or
he must choose life or death. As in Hebrew scripture, the choice is laid
before every person to choose life or death (Deut. 30:19). The worldview that I have sought to offer blends that biblical outlook with a
range of naturalistic and humanistic perspectives. I have contended
that the meaning of the story of nature and history is revealed by the
normative punctuations of those realms by apocalyptic and eschatologic turbulence. In and of themselves, nature and history are amoral,
descriptive realms. In the classic metaphysic, which my position
accepts, the reality of God and the inherent meaning and purpose,
which that reality maintains, is disclosed not only in the overarching

panorama and drama of nature and history but in those special dispensations where spirit breaks into matter in what we call apocalypse and
eternity ruptures time in eschatology.

Suffering, death, and transfiguration is going on in this world. The
drama is enacted by God for whom nature and history display God's
inaugurating kingdom. In this drama, each of us is confronted with the
choice to cling to life and self and die or to live in justice, dying in sacrifice of self and love for others, thereby finding life. Socrates, when
told to shut up and cease corrupting the youth of Athens, continued to
speak and through death he chose life. Jesus' friends, as had Socrates',
begged him to flee, but he chose to live the truth—to die, and live.
Gandhi knew the Salt March to the sea or the subsequent mission to rec-
oncile Hindu and Muslim would kill him; he never wavered. Martin
Luther King Jr. went to the mountaintop, saw the long life that he would
have loved, but also saw death whereunto he stayed the course.

Each of us across our experience of life is confronted with countless decisions where we lose our soul or save it by choosing to life to
self and die to God or die to self and life to God. "No greater love is
there than that we lay down our lives for our friend" (John 15:13, my
paraphrase).

Sometimes the moral message comes back from the dead. It may
take one coming back to us from the dead to convince us of the imperative of righteousness in life as antidote to eternal death. In the twelfth
tablet of the Gilgamesh epic we are told that Enkidu descended into the
underworld to reclaim the goods of Gilgamesh that had fallen there. In
going down into death as Christ did in identification and expiation,
leading captivity captive, Enkidu was trapped in perpetual imprisonment
in the land of the dead. The god Ea pleads for the soul of Enkidu from
Ereshkigal, ruler of the dead. He allows the spirit of Enkidu to escape
up to earth through a hole to warn his master and friend of the order of
heaven and hell.

The New Testament picks up on this motif with the story of Dives,
the rich man, and Lazarus (Luke 16:19–31). Here the messenger comes
back from the dead to warn that eternal destiny depends on the ministries
of care one offers here in the present. Eschatological ethics are the ethics
of warning. Faure makes Lazarus the last text of his Requiem Mass:

May the angels receive thee in paradise; at thy coming may the martyrs receive thee, and bring thee into the Holy City Jerusalem. There may the chorus of angels receive thee and with Lazarus, once a beggar, may thou have eternal rest (requiem).

The sacred future presents us with an ethic of how we should live and how we should die. Indeed, the two acts are of one piece. We should live so that our death completes a picture of our life. From the very earliest texts that interpret what life and death is about, we have passages of messages back from the dead and descriptions of an abode of the dead where departed souls reside either perpetually or in preparation for heaven or hell. From spirits or angels we hear predictions and warnings about our own death or that of theirs. Scrooge is visited that cold winter night by the ghost of Christmas future. All of this ethical teaching from beyond space and time has the effect of waking us out of our own dreaming innocence of immortality with the inevitability of our death. It usually implies a time or place of reckoning where one will be called on to make account for what one has been and has done. Some method of securing righteousness and salvation, either through personal work or the vicarious vindication of life by animal or human sacrifice, is offered.

In sacred future our times and places are also in God's hands. The Lord kills and brings to life; he brings down to Sheol and raises up (1 Sam. 2:6 RSV). Even in life and certainly in sickness, in prison or under persecution, we are already in the hands of death. Yahweh decides if the sick will recover, if captives will be released or the persecuted will be delivered (Pss. 18:4–5; 116:3; Job 30:23). This same apportionment and appointment is found in Homer's *Iliad*:

> But when for the fourth time they were come to the springs,
> lo then the father lifted on high his golden scales, and set
> therein two fates of grievous death, one for Achilles, and one
> for horse-taming Hector; then he grasped the balance by the
> midst and raised it; and down sank the day of doom of Hector, and departed unto Hades; and Phoebes Apollo left him.

While we never know when the unexpected will happen—sickness, accident, war—we do know that our life becomes increasingly fragile and vulnerable as we age. This fact counsels remembrance in youth and preparedness in age:

Remember also your Creator in the days of your youth,
before the evil days come, and the years draw nigh, when
you will say, "I have no pleasure in them"; before the sun
and the light and the moon and the stars are darkened and the
clouds return after the rain; in the day when the keepers of
the house tremble, and the strong men are bent and the grind-
ers cease because they are few, and those that look through
the windows are dimmed, and the doors on the street are
shut; when the sound of the grinding is low, and one rises up
at the voice of a bird, and all the daughters of song are
brought low; they are afraid also of what is high, and terrors
are in the way; the almond tree blossoms, the grasshopper
drags itself along and desire fails; because man goes to his
eternal home, and the mourners go about the streets; before
the silver cord is snapped, or the golden bowl is broken, or
the pitcher is broken at the fountain, or the wheel is broken
at the cistern.

(Eccles. 12:1–6 RSV)

It is the wrath of God that kills. Just as refreshing *Ruach*, the life
wind, inspires cosmos to creation and breath to human beings, wrath
is the dry and exhausting expiration.

The years of our life are threescore and ten,
　　or even by reason of strength fourscore;
yet their span is but toil and trouble;
　　they are soon gone, and we fly away.

(Ps. 90:10 RSV)

Lord, let me know my end,
　　and what is the measure of my days;
　　let me know how fleeting my life is!
Behold, thou hast made my days a few handbreadths,
　　and my lifetime is as nothing in thy sight.
Surely every man stands as a mere breath!
　　Surely man goes about as a shadow!
Surely for nought are they in turmoil;
　　man heaps up, and knows not who will gather!

And now, Lord, for what do I wait?
My hope is in thee.

(Ps. 39:4–7 RSV)

Yet this awful eventuality is tempered by God's good will, which sees us through life's vicissitudes and death's treachery:

As for man, his days are like grass;
  he flourishes like a flower of the field;
for the wind passes over it and it is gone,
  and its place knows it no more.
But the steadfast love of the LORD is from everlasting
    to everlasting
  upon those who fear him,
  and his righteousness to children's children,
to those who keep his covenant
  and remember to do his commandments.

(Ps. 103: 15–18 RSV)

Death, Divine Justice, and Job

The Bible and its counterparts in archaic and classic texts thus sets us up for an agonizing dilemma. Is God the author of life or death or both? Is death a judgment on our sin and salvation beyond death a reward for righteousness? Why then do the good die young and the apparently righteous suffer? Why do the evil prosper?

The Deuteronomic covenant had promised that faith would be rewarded by the blessings of home, health, longevity, and prosperity (Deut. 28:1ff). When Job's tormentors confront him with this traditional theodicy and imply that Job's suffering must be evidence of God's wrath, Job queries: "Why do the wicked live, reach old age, and grow mighty in power" (21:6). Implying never to his rhetorical question, with resentment he laments: "How often is it that the lamp of the wicked is put out?" (21:1).

Empirical evidence suggests that evil prospers, bad guys win out, at least in the short run, and that the corrupt gain power. It is against this felt injustice that we construct our answers of final judgment and Hollywood endings. The first thought to cross the mind of an innocent person who has been falsely charged or convicted is that the truth will eventually or ultimately (in God's sight) come to light. "You'll get yours!" or "God will get you!" are embittered demands for justice.

We often pay the price for the sins of the ancestors. The inhumane economic settlements imposed on the German people at Versailles contributed to the fact that millions would then die under Hitler in the Second World War. The poor and undereducated tend to remain that way for generations. Holiness scripture both acknowledges transgenerational guilt and death yet at the same time repudiates it:

> The fathers used to eat sour grapes, and the children's teeth are set on edge as a result.
>
> (Ezek. 18:2)

> The soul that sins, it shall die. A son shall not bear the guilt of the father, nor a father the guilt of a son. The righteousness of the righteous shall only come upon him, and the ungodliness of the ungodly shall only come upon him . . . Therefore, O house of Israel, I shall judge every one of you according to his own conduct, says the Lord GOD.
>
> (Ezek. 18:20, 30)

These apparent injustices aside, there is a great indiscriminate leveling in death.

> One dies in full prosperity,
>   being wholly at ease and secure,
> his body full of fat
>   and the marrow of his bones moist.
> Another dies in bitterness of soul,
>   never having tasted of good.
> They lie down alike in the dust,
>   and the worms cover them.
>
> (Job 21:23–26 RSV)

Does goodness pay death dividends? Probably not, if that quest has become one's obsession. The sun shines and rain falls on the just and unjust. The ways of God far transcend our poor patterns of justice.

The panorama of nature and the processions of life are wisely and intricately ordered for their own good reason. Humanity should not be so audacious to confront these, constantly in bitterness and "I would do betterness" seeking to transform them or in ingratitude grumble along in perennial resentment. Seize life, *carpe diem*, is the watchword of Job and of the film the Dead Poet's Society.

In the brilliant British film that inspired *Chariots of Fire (The Loneliness of the Long Distance Runner)*, a young wayward lad is sent to Borstal's boys' detention home where he philosophically recounts his life and achieves some aesthetic distance all the while striving for athletic achievement to appease a sports-obsessed governor. In the end he has the chance to win the cross-country race against a public school, bring glory to old Borstal and its vain governor. Well ahead near the finish line, he stops and lets his competitor win.

> Again I saw that under the sun the race is not to the swift, nor the battle to the strong, nor bread to the wise, nor riches to the intelligent, nor favor to the men of skill; but time and chance happen to them all. For man does not know his time. Like fish which are taken in an evil net, and like birds which are caught in a snare, so the sons of men are snared at an evil time, when it suddenly falls upon them.
>
> (Eccles. 9:11–12 RSV)

Hope in the Old Testament and archaic preclassical texts like Job is ultimately silent wonder and trust before the "deep which calls to deep." The preacher of Ecclesiastes accedes to this unfathomable mystery "that which is, far off, and deep, very deep is; who can find it out?" (Eccles. 7:23, 24 RSV). Reverent waiting is counseled; not Wagner and Nietzsche's demand *Götterdämmerung* and apotheosis; "For every appetite desires eternity, deep, deep eternity."[7]

The sacred future in Hebrew and Christian scripture is not merely just one of sobering natural inevitability. It also sends back apocalyptic spontaneity and eschatologic promise. A new vision of death begins to emerge as the people of Israel live in subjection to Babylonian and Persian rule and even after restoration are subjected to the persecutions of the Roman occupation. Enormous new concepts enter the mind. The separability of the soul and body; the breakthrough rescue of a divine mediating messiah; the division of humanity at judgment into the saved and the damned; the promise of resurrection of the body. Under the Selucid occupation, Daniel offers his apocalyptic prophesy of dramatic deliverance from persecution and from the terrors of death.

> At that time shall arise Michael, the great prince who has charge of your people. And there shall be a time of trouble, such as never has been since there was a nation till that time; but at that time your people shall be delivered, every one whose name shall be found written in the book. And many of those who sleep in the dust of the earth shall awake, some to everlasting life, and some to shame and everlasting contempt. And those who are wise shall shine like the brightness of the firmament; and those who turn many to righteousness, like the stars for ever and ever.
>
> (Dan. 12:1–3 RSV)

This apocalyptic rescue of the dead is anticipated in Isaiah 24–27, and Psalms 49 and 132. The rescue is not that of Enoch and Elijah who were delivered *from* death, now the righteous are delivered *out of* death. Now the soul is to be awakened from the sleep of death and a wholly new creation is forthcoming (2 Macc. 7:28, 29; 1 Cor. 15:50; Mark 12:25). Influenced by Persian and Zoroastrian ideas, death becomes a moment of rigorous judgment yielding salvation or damnation.

> When a man has died in Zarathustra's teaching, [6-3d c. AD] his soul appears before its judges and must walk across the infinitely narrow bridge of decision, the famous *CINVATO PERETU*, the good survive the danger and unscathed attain the realm of light, while the evil plunge into the abyss of Ahriman, the spirit of falsehood.[8]

The faith, hope, and morality, which come from this chapter in our ethical system, bear on our thesis in two profound ways. From the side of morality two impulses are injected into culture. Regarding killing, intense prohibition is now found unless it is to purge infidels, convert savages, punish capital crime or pursue war. The spirit of mercy and forgiveness is also intensified. It is this imperative that grounds the alleviation of suffering and the exception ethic for those who will fully enact their own death as during the Roman siege of Masada, or in the case of the seven virgins who committed suicide rather than accept violation. Another very important new element in spiritual and moral consciousness, coming from this religious history is a vivid hope for afterlife and a commensurate disregard for clinging to the life and body. Apocalyptic Judaism like the primitive Christian ethos that it yields, comprehends and encourages laying down life to help one's friends and to be with God.

Christian Hope and Death

It is the Christian scriptures that give to modern western culture and the global Christian community its distinctive ethos concerning death. Several themes characterize this ethos. In Kaiser and Lohse's depiction these are: (1) the power of death; (2) the death and resurrection of Jesus Christ, (3) the victory over death, and (4) the new life in Christ.[9]

Despite the vibrant otherworldly hope of apocalyptic Judaism and primitive Christianity, the somber Homeric and Hebraic realization of inevitable death persists. "It is appointed unto man once to die" (Heb. 9:27). Herodotus recalls the Egyptian practice of carrying a wooden figure in a casket through the revelry of a banquet, reminding all that they must face death. In primitive frenzy burghers would dance in the old European church graveyards, keeping company with the departed and calling dread mortification to oneself, thus tasting life more fully. A sense of judgment added dread to the necessity of death. The mass and requiem mass spoke of sin and death.

> Deliver me, O lord from eternal death in that awful day when heaven and earth shall be moved and when thou shalt come to judge the world by fire . . . from that day of wrath, calamity and misery . . . liberate me

The setting of the cathedral or chapel depicted in stone, tapestry, and glass the judgment—the *dies irae*, the descent of crucified love, the agonal death. Adam, in forsaking God, had called down death on the race and the devout soul identified with Adam.

In Christianity, liturgy was the language of the common life, just as in late antiquity Judaism, Adam's rebellion and plight was the plight of every man. The Syrian Baruch Apocalypse contains this passage:

> If Adam first sinned and brought premature death upon all, yet every single one of those who are descended from him has brought upon himself the future pain, and again every single one of the them has chosen the future glory. . .Thus Adam is solely and exclusively responsible for himself and every one of us has become Adam for himself.[10]

The apostle Paul, steeped in these Hebrew Scriptures and in rabbinic teaching and acquainted, we may assume, with the death eschatology of the classical Greeks and early Roman Stoics, forged what would become the Christian eschatology of death in his fifth chapter of the letter to the Romans. Sin and death, drawn into the creation by the fall of Adam, now has taken hold of the whole creation. But a new Adam has come, has suffered the sin and died the deserved death of all who would ever live. All of us caught up in the inevitable cycle of sin, guilt, and death now die with Christ the death of death. In Christ's conquest of death it becomes apparent what death really is. Sin is enmity with God, an aversion and contempt for God's lordship and ways. The sting, as painful outcome of setting ourselves against the giver of life, is death. That kind of truth only paradox can capture:

> It was a strange conflict,
> When life and death contended;
> Life gained the victory,
> And swallowed up death
>
> —Martin Luther, Easter Hymn

Death and life have been eschatologically redefined in the cross and resurrection of Jesus Christ. Empirically they are the same natural event and process. Life begins with a conception, develops across a life span in which a personality unfolds. Death then ensues and this person is gone forever. Yet in another reality, one hidden from sight and knowledge, but evident to faith and hope, death is terrible aloneness and misery and life is being whole and together with God. Out of this otherness and beyondness, another ethic, an ethic about death takes form.

Christian proclamation claimed that Jesus had to suffer and die to break the reigning power of sin and death, which was the ethic of alienation and animosity. Jesus' death frees humanity from this subservience to self-will and hurtful living. The prisoner has been set free, the slave liberated. Anyone who now trusts in Christ will not be abandoned by God in death. The Judge has come to our side; we have been purchased back from the marketplace. Satisfying sacrificial blood has been shed. Lost sheep have been found. All these metaphors say that the inner meaning of death is not to know who, whose, or where we are. The inner meaning of life is restoration by God of those we were meant to be.

Christ did not return from the dead. He moved through and beyond death to life. The mysterious postresurrection appearances to students and friends and the palpable way Christ has transected persons' lives ever since, are evidence of a new reality and power available from the future and the beyond. It is this eschatological power that is at work renewing the world. A new being and new creation are now being fashioned from premonitions and faithful anticipatory enactments of that kingdom in the here and now. The kingdom or realm is apocalyptic or eschatological. It is a supernal that breaks into nature, an eternal that comes back into time. The kingdom is the striving forward for a state of affairs here, that there is already accomplished. "On earth as in heaven . . ." In the meanwhile, between the dawn of the new age and its consummation, life in this world with God is a co-adventure as Christ puts all enemies under his feet, the last enemy to be vanquished is death (Ps. 110:1; Rom. 5:26).

What are those penultimate enemies to be subdued before the ultimate enemy? Ways of life perdure throughout human affairs and down through history that inflict death in the midst of life. Wars and violence, hatreds and envy, those overt killings we have enumerated in this study: ecocide, disrespect or lack of committed care for the natural world; genocide; writing-off, partitioning off or liquidating those who are different; gendercide; animosity based on insecurity or fear toward the other sex or the homosexual; infanticide in all its banal and grotesque forms where we refuse our obligations and opportunities of tuteledge and generativity; suicide, not the gun to the temple, but the countless ways we fail to live and respect our selves. And so on. Eschatologic ethics of impending kingdom strive against these assaults and insults. In moments of indwelling or inbreaking grace, life intrudes its way into our death and we are made new and alive.

> God will wipe away all tears from their eyes, and death will be no more, nor will there be any suffering or crying or pain, for the old is passed away. And the one who sat upon the throne said, 'Behold! I make all things new'. . . God's dwelling shall be with his people.
>
> (Revelation 21)

The new world is a reality to hope for and work for. Existence under God is the eschatologic act of ameliorating pain and suffering bringing in the homeless into your home—listening to the troubled, brokenhearted, grief-stricken and frightened; gaining amnesty for the tortured and those in jail, a drink of water and a pound coin for Lazarus to get some supper.

> We know that we have passed from death to life, because we love the brethren. Anyone who does not love remains in death.
>
> (1 John 3:14)

> When did we see you hungry, thirsty, or imprisoned. In as much as you did it to the least of these my brethren . . .
>
> (Matt. 25:40ff.)

The end, or better beginning, of Christian existence is concerned and sacrificial love. Love stands up against the belligerent and those who would build up power by oppressing others. Love seeks justice for those who have been victimized by war and political oppression. Love seeks to distribute wealth so that those who have much share with those who barely subsist. Love holds the friend near as she is dying; whether that friend is old and smelly, contorted in a coma, or bruised and crazed with AIDS. Love hangs in through any darkness or desperation, for life has overwhelmed all death.

"I am the resurrection and the life; he who believes in me, though he die, yet shall he live, and whoever lives and believes in me shall never die."

(John 11:25-26 RSV)

The Humanization of Hope

And then the spirit brings hope in the strictest Christian sense, hope which is hoping against hope. For an immediate hope exists in every person; it may be more powerfully alive in one person than in another; but in death every hope of this kind dies and turns into hopelessness. Into this night of hopelessness (it is death that we are describing) comes the life-giving spirit and brings hope, the hope of eternity. It is against hope, for there was no longer any hope for that merely natural hope; this hope is therefore a hope contrary to hope.[11]

Human beings can't live by bread alone. Like it or not they are creatures of spirit. We celebrate the transcendence in reality and in ourselves by the mass and all rituals that acknowledge the history of God in our midst. Our own mass occurs on earth. We do live by bread. To render spiritual truth palpable we humanize and secularize our hope. The ethical life of human beings proceeds principally from these sources in the humanities, arts, and sciences.

I have suggested in the proceeding chapter that science secularizes our hope, translating it into concrete technological endeavors to ameliorate disease and debility and to prolong life with well-being. I then chronicled the death eschatology of our civilization in its long pilgrimage from Gilgamesh to Paul the apostle's resurrection hymn in first Corinthians. Now we need to enact our mass on this earth. We do this not to offer a scientific apotheosis of the vitality of humanity, but to seek a humanistic vision of the future with specific reference to our dying.

The modern soul is torn between a spiritual belief and hope about death and destiny as outlined above and a materialist-mechanist realism. Frantic efforts to prolong life are found from both sides—on the one to avoid or attain judgment toward one or the other everlasting destiny and on the other to get the most from the functional body-machine before its breakdown and extinction. A serenity also pervades both eschatologies. "For me to live is Christ," writes Paul, "to die is gain" (Phil. 1:21 RSV). Like the ancient Egyptians, the secularist can rest in death as reversion to crystalline hardness or as one "stands up after table and goes to rest" (Ernst Bloch). Hans Jonas whose own soul bridges Judaism and Christianity, the scientific and the spiritual, becomes, to our generation, a helpful teacher, forging a humanistic eschatology of dying for our technical world. Schooled with Heideigger and Bultmann, knowledgeable about Gnosticism and biological theory, Jonas has suggested that lives well lived in justice, love, and hope build up an eternal legacy in history and contribute to the future of God. In the crises of decision, when we risk our lives for righteousness against the threats of evil and death, we offer a sacrifice of life that, because it participates in the ultimate, is never lost.

Jonas affirms the truth found in the panvitalism and spiritualism of a primitive and preclassical worldview. The discovery of an entirely nonmundane inwardness is the origin of the sense of self—its glory and indestructiveness, its indomitable strength. This affirmation of the soul and "its incommensurability with anything in nature"[12] undergirds the interhuman imperatives of respect and justice. It also generates the dualism of body and soul and the eventual materialist and spiritualist monisms that plague the modern world.

Take for example, again, the Gulf war. On the one hand it may be nothing more than what the antiwar students call it: "Gulf's [Oil Company] War." Probably it is actually the more basic confrontation of two contending and exaggerated eschatologies of death. One seeking death in the fiery Arabian sand as the assurance of Jihād immortality. The other, assured of technophilic immortality with its computers and lasers exults in precision bombing that can drop a warhead down a chimney from stratospheric heights. Devastation without death might be its motto. Islam, since the moment Muhammad drew his sword against Mecca, has seen frenzied battle against satan and infidel as the very portals of paradise. "Between heaven and us," Muhammad told his troops before the Battle of Bedr, "is nothing but the enemy." For wretched hungry seventeen-year-old boys hunkered down in the sand without water or medicines, covered with lice in constantly bombarded trenches, the promise of the Koran's heaven with succulent fruits, cool oases and breezes, and the virginal embrace of love is irresistible. Similarly the physicalist immortality of the West is satisfied when in just "the few days" of creation, third-world savages can be subdued in the Sinai and Golan Heights, the Falklands, Grenada, Panama, and Iraq. Quenching the daimonic flame rapidly is Rambo eschatology.

Philosophically, Jonas contends our age has seen mechanism and its ontology of death swallow up all theories of life. He argues that responsible maturity in late technological society can only come if we see again that spiritless materialism and matterless spiritism are two mirror images of reality. There cannot be matter without spirit nor spirit without matter. The world in which a future can come from science is such a humane and biunified future.

His writing is ultimately grounded in the living and dying human being.

> The living body that can die, that has world and itself belongs to the world, that feels and itself can be felt, whose outward form is organism and causality, and whose inward form is selfhood and finality: this body is the memento of the still unsolved question of ontology, "what is being?"[13]

Pure consciousness and pure matter are abstractions. Truth is conscience informing matter. "In my body. . .the immediacy of outwardness and inwardness become one."[14] Jonas here proposes a blending of epistemology—especially ontologic epistemology with eschatology, to provide a new framework for humanistic ethics. Technology deals with the mastery of things. Philosophical theology deals with the primacy of the person and the life of love and justice. Technology applied to *mors in homine*, serving only *res extensa* and mechanistic prolongation of vitality, becomes absurd. In death the barrier between matter and spirit is broken and ontology interpenetrates physiology. Here matter and mechanism collapses, consciousness disappears, and only goodness or "godness" lives on.

Modern history is one long, sad tale of how the loss of a sense of eternity and belief in the soul have led to a massive disregard for life. The natural and eventual wreckage and human wastage of the twentieth century could only have been wrought by a generation that had lost the eternal dimension of existence. What Heidegger called existence toward death (*seinzumtod*) has been subliminated into technological mastery over life and economic and political power that exerts mastery over the world and over vulnerable peoples. The world we condescendingly call the "Third World" (Arabia, Africa, Asia, Latin America, and the "third worlds" within our "first worlds"—blacks and hispanics in America, South Africa, Asians in England, Turks in Germany, Muslims in the Eastern Europe, etc., have been subjected to oppression and exploitation so that we the privileged might achieve an affluence and comfort which is our disguised aversion to death.

Bultmann argued against his teacher Heidegger that eschatology called us to exist not toward death but toward the neighbor. Christian faith and hope has shown the connection of love and death. Transforming the power of death into human service robs it of its power over us. We are back to Socrates. In relegating death to memory (sacrament or daimon) or hope we strip it of its terror and in Martin Luther's rough tongue we leave Satan holding only shells in his *Nussknacker*. A travail of love, peace, and justice is now proceeding through the history of nature. In suffering we who have been bound by hope are drawn to defend and help the victims of hate, strife, and injustice even unto death. Transfiguration and reconciliation only comes when control yields to a relinquishing sympathy, compassion, and sacrifice. This is the most fundamental reality in creation. Jesus was and is eternally crucified for the world. What Teilhard de Chardin called the "cross-shaped" curve in the progression of nature is its inner meaning. Nikos Kazantzakis, whose Zorba the Greek is the kind of life-loving, dancing, Christ figure who stands by the woman taken in adultery goes to the heart of this world pathos. Kazantzakis reflects in *Saviors* on that thread of suffering through life that is its redemptive meaning:

> Which is that one force armed all of God's forces which man
> is able to grasp? Only this: we discern a crimson line on this
> earth, a red bloodspattered line which ascends, struggling,
> from matter to plants, from plants to animals, from animals
> to men . . . Difficult, dreadful, unending ascension.[15]

This is not Loren Eiseley's downward swirling whirlpool of destruction that stirs loose on earth with the appearance of man. This is an ascending spiral of grace that lifts suffering and death up into the heart of God where like the turbulent Sea of Galilee that evening in the fishing boat, is calmed by Jesus' word and becomes still. Mahler's songs on the Death of Children *(Kindertotenlieder)* reflect this same serene hope:

> In diesem Wetter, in diesem *Braus*
> nie hatt ich *gesender* dis kinder hinaus,
> man hat sie gerragen linaus
> ich duefte nichts dazu sagen

> In diesem wetter, in diesem *Saus*
> Nie hatt ich *gelassen* die kinder hinaus,
> ich furchtete sie erkrenken;
> das sind nun eitle gedenken.

> In diesem wetter, in diesem *Graus*
> nie hatt ich *gelassen* die kinder hinaus,
> ich sorgtre sie Stirben morgen
> das ist nun nicht zu besorgen

> In diesem wetter, in diesem *Graus*
> nie hatt ich *gesendet* die kinder hinaus,
> man hat sie hinaus gettengen
> ich durfre nicht dazu sagen

> In diesem wetter, in diesem *Saus*
> in diesem *Braus,* sie ruh'as
> sie ruh'n wie in der Mutter Haus.[16]

> Gustaf Mahler, *Kindertotenlieder*, 1905.

The inversion of this serene surrender to the storm of life is our evasion of death that prompts a protectionism of oneself and our possessions and seeks an indefinite prolongation of our own existence. Our desire for physical immortality searches for safeguard in the conquest of disease, development of healthy lifestyles (no smoking, drinking, fasten seat belts, exercise, rest, etc.) and in the removal of noxious and toxic insults to the self (not necessarily others). Hermetically-sealed existence in one's pollution-free apartment, eating only oat bran and yogurt, with aromatic hot tub and sound system in the main living area, the bathroom, wired with direct computer modem and telephone line to one's stock broker—this becomes the ultimate insular existence. Suicide in this lifestyle becomes all that is left since one has evaded every other challenge that offers suffering, commitment, and life. In the play *Whose Life is It Anyway?* the desperate young quadriplegic demands that he be left alone to die. He despises even his own friends, all who would tinker with him, cajole him, shower him with pity to satisfy their puny and needy souls. In the end he has his wish. Everyone leaves. He is left to himself—to die.[17]

Humane death is not alienated death. It is death in community and in solidarity with all others and all that lives. Good death, writes the Marxist philosopher Ernst Bloch, arises in our identification with the liberation of humanity in the world.

> Whenever existing comes near to its core, permanence begins, not petrified but containing Novum without transitoriness, with corruptibility.[18]

In our dying we become connected with all of life that has gone before. We become part of the future of the world both physically and spiritually. More basically, we die and become part of the All, the past and present agony and future hope of the people of the world. Our dying, like our living, ought to be an act of giving. We may die in battle, in accident, in disease. All our deaths are in some sense sacrifices to a world of caprice, to an eschatological world that is not yet complete. "All creation groans in birth pangs until now," wrote the apostle (Rom. 8:23). Our deaths, even in a physical sense, mark the inauguration of a new world. Our sign of death resonates with the first gasp of breath down in labor and delivery. In biblical language we die when our work is done and our succession is ready.

Bloch is most eloquent in describing a humanistic eschatology of death, responsive to both the material and spiritual dimension, where he chronicles and interprets songs of death and requiem. Music is an expression of the soul that intimates ultimate reality: the music of the spheres. Music is an architectonic counterpoint of eternal and temporal, supernal, and natural. Music reminds us of the "corrective primacy of space over time . . . the Kingdomlike over the situational.[19] It may be our finest eschatological instrument—a song from beyond.

The composer Palestrina represents the balance of distant and immediate being. One feels in Palestrina's *Miserere* based on Psalm 51 and his *Missa Aeterna Christi Munera* change modulated into composure, freedom into form. Bach takes the fugue up through the flight of striving, yearning for height, intensity, and complexity down again into resolution. In death music, the outer light is known, therefore the darkness can be explored and fathomed. Orpheus plucks the harp victoriously only in death, in Hades. It is widely reported in home and clinic that the dying person, while sinking away, hears music. In music we are bold to face the beyond and hereafter. The power and grace of music allow us to confront the darkness and the light. Music really does go to face death and intends outwardly and inwardly—in accordance with the context of the biblical saying—"to swallow it in victory" (Isa. 25:8). Bach takes up all the homesickness (*Heimweh*) and fear of death and cries in the cantata "Strike, a longed for home, longed for home, strike."

"Dying," writes Bloch, "has itself developed dark-bright images," Eternity (*ewigkeit*), wrote philosopher of aesthetics Wassily Kandinsky, is blue. In the *Eroica* symphony Beethoven takes the dull C-minor color in the opening and culminates in the bright azure of the oboes in the C-major central movement. Even for people who no longer believe the texts of damnation and deliverance in the mass in general and requiem mass in particular, music still has power to draw into *de profundis*. Mozart, Cherubini, Berlioz, Verdi, and Faure, among others, have composed a requiem mass, more or less taking the ancient text and giving it current musical idiom. Not only Brahms' *Ein Deutsches Requiem*, which seeks to be a national and natural expression, and Bernstein's *Mass* in its gentle and radical mood, but all the classical expressions have the power to captivate and inspire, showing the universal power of death and resurrection. Although Bloch cannot accept the "early period of chiliastic fear and longing," which gave rise to the church texts, the great archetypes and symbols of religion express the morality of "death, contra-death and utopia which is constantly present for music."[20] Brahms builds the *Deutsches Requiem* around simple and worldly texts.

> Here we have no continuing (*bliebende*), city but we seek one to come (*Zukünftige*)

> How amiable are thy tabernacles
> *wie lieblich . . . diene wohnungen*

Precisely for this reason all music of annihilation points towards a robust core which, because it has not yet blossomed, cannot pass away either; it points to a *non omnis confundar*. In the darkness of this music gleam the treasures which will not be corrupted by moth and rust, the lasting treasures in which will and goal, hope and its contents, virtue and happiness could be united as in a world without frustration, as in the highest good;—*the requiem circles the secret landscape of the highest good.*[21]

Requiem sounds into all creation the trumpet theme that there is a somewhere we can hope for, in Beethoven's words that Marzelline sings to Leonora in *Fidelio*, "A rainbow, resting brightly on dark clouds, shines on, and guides my way." The haunting fear of the beyond in old Egypt, Gilgamesh and Israel, becomes "a cry for help, fear of life and dread of death" in early Christianity, then a search for *civitas dei* anticipated in the medieval church. In the modern world it becomes the confident construction of human ability and power. Through it all is the confidence that we are guiding toward that new being and a new world that ever comes back to us from God's future. In death we culminate life and anticipate kingdom. We find out what life is really about. Since eschatological ethics conveys such opportunity we seek therefore to die our own authentic death in search for and in service of that abiding city. The German theologian Karl Rahner has best outlined the meaning of this eschatology for human death. Ending the Orphic escapism of so much religion and the physico-mechanical immortalism of modern scientific and biomedical pride, Rahner would have us achieve a genuinely human death as our rightful worship. One who has lived long years as a priest and survived the war can be trusted to have gained perspective on these matters. I remember meeting Rahner on the street in Munich when he was eighty-two-years-old. He could not visit too long, since he was going to celebrate his mother's birthday, she being close to 100. One still looked after by mother church and natural mother into one's ninth decade can surely be trusted with even these weighty matters.

For Rahner death is a personal event.[22] Persons in their freedom are not forced by death into some final choice to opt for or against God. We have been pilgrims toward this event all of our lives. We must live our own death, will and receive our own death, not concede to any extraneous authority—technical, human, or political. The fundamental moral commitment we have made throughout life is not now confirmed definite and final by death.[23]

> The end of man as a spiritual person is an active consummation from within, a bringing of himself to completion, a growth that preserves the issue of his life; it is his total entry into possession of himself, the state of having produced himself, the fullness of the being he has become by all his free acts.[24]

Two themes begin to emerge as eschatological ethics impinge on our dying. Freedom and responsibility are the human qualities that come to the fore when faced with the finality of death. Human beings are free and mature partners with God in the ongoing work of redeeming the creation in love. Our death is an act that confirms our commitments of trust in God's overarching purposes of redemption and our concerns to love the world forward toward its renewal. Christian eschatology has a public and personal dimension. We exist in time to redeem the time. We exist as personal selves with responsibility to fulfill the gifts potential in those selves. Our death is the act where we decide what we *mean* the world to be. It is the person's coming into final maturity.[25] Death is the act where, in Christ, we lay down our life for the life of the world. Of course death is usually a moment of extreme fear and powerlessness. Modern death in hospitals, on machines, is an event radically at the mercy of others. Yet this vulnerability itself is our unique offering to a world that is incomplete and suffering, but one that is being made whole. When we accept death we affirm to the world "I shall not die," and to those who keep company with us, "You shall not die." As with our life, our death is an act of "witness" (literally, martyr). To die one's death in witness and service, death must be free and voluntary.

I think now on the dying and living of David Greenstone, a beloved teacher of history at the University of Chicago. He struggled against a persistent head-neck tumor with resolute purpose, never losing those values that marked his life of concern for family, friends, and his beloved college. He lived with a passion for justice in the world around him. His concentration was always upon the needs and the life-challenges faced by other people. While still a young man in his forties, he was stricken with this frightening and potentially life-consuming disease. He took it into himself as some part of the pain of life he could absorb from the broader hurt abroad in the world. He did not let it interrupt his ministry to others as scholar, teacher, husband, colleague, and friend. When he became critical, he grappled with the ethical choices of struggling on, trying last-ditch heroic therapies and eventually the question of life-supports and resuscitation. Here *in extremis*, he died as he had lived, in a tough realism, a gentle smile at the ironic and tragic in life and an abiding sense of faith and justice. His death confirmed his life, the world and humanity to which he was committed and the future for which he hoped.

A disturbing thought, almost messianic in its arrogance, but can we say of our dying, "I die that you might live"? Our death is not relieving the world of a mouth to feed or a family of a burden of care. Our death is the supreme culminating event when we are invited to enter God's judgment and God's future. The "I am-who will be," (Ex. 3:14) now makes us part of that preserve of service that is drawing toward completion. Death is not loss. It is the confirmation both to the world we leave and to the community of whom we have been a part, of who we are and who we have been. That gift can never be lost. Our death is vindication of the value we have embodied. It is contribution to cumulative moral wealth that life builds up in God.

In sum, eschatologic ethics puts a capstone on our vision of the moral meaning of mortality. It gathers all finite and penultimate perspectives into a final design when one comes up against one's own death, when one superintends the death of another or when one holds life and death of another in one's hands. The moral soul drives towards this finality, this "science of ends." Here history and philosophy fail, as does science and psychology. Indeed all opaque vision slides away. Now we see through a glass darkly—then face to face. Now we know in part—then fully (1 Cor. 13:12).

Epilogue

We have sought to provide a moral framework for an ethic of prolonging and ending life which is naturalistically, humanistically and theistically valid. Consulting the various sources of ethical insight we have discovered and developed a multifaceted moral suasion that efforts of life-sustenance and prolongation must be reciprocated by appropriate measures to allow and perhaps in exceptional cases, facilitate death. The comprehensive ethical system we have outlined generates both imperatives and cautions. Philosophic autonomy is balanced by theological sacredness doctrine. Natural tendencies to eliminate and recycle life are checked by historical and societal precautions and protections. Scientific enthusiasm is chastened by eschatological hope. The interplay of imperative and prohibitive within such a comparative and comprehensive ethical framework assures our personal and communal life of moral wisdom as it protects us against the excesses and exaggerations which threaten ethical civility.

Voluntary and Deliberate Death

Human maturity aided by cultural and technological development has brought us to the point where we can participate more knowingly and humanely in the concluding events of our own lives. We can also cooperate in the gentle and careful support of others as they face their deaths. We are coming into a period of history when we will be invited to make decisions—medical, legal, religious—about how, where, and when we will die. Advance intentions and directions, lively participation in all discussions affecting our own living and dying and social and ecclesial provision and covenants will be more commonplace in

189

the *ars moriendi* at the end of this millennium. The awkward and noteworthy parade of cases over the last thirty years where dying has not gone well will prompt us into corrective actions to universalize the custom of dying well and finding good death. Personal action, constitutional structures and public policy should make it possible for us to live long and well but not too long. The traditions of rational suicide and incessant biomedical life-prolongation should slowly temper each other into a *via media* where the living and dying, which we personally wish, comes to coincide with what scientific medicine can achieve and what global society's resources can allow. Doctors are now being asked in our own state university hospital to ascertain of every patient whether advance directives for terminal care have been made. This is a step in the right direction.

Passive/Active Euthanasia

I expect that in the years ahead moral sobriety and responsible participation in patient and community concerns will not only open up a broad practice of passive euthanasia but will allow active euthanasia in some cases. Persons will see, in concert with their physicians, families and pastors, that withholding and withdrawing medical therapies is often the right and sensible thing to do. There will be many life-prolonging measures available to us that simply will not make sense in terms of our own desires or society's capacities. This will include machines such as respirators, artificial hearts, dialyzers, all of which have good use in carrying us through crisis and in some cases offering permanent life-assistance. Selective nontreatment will also include antibiotics as well as nutrition and hydration support.

The next moral challenge our society will face will be to accept active euthanasia as a companion action to passive acts where we choose to withdraw life supports. The experience, now in cautious beginnings, with patients with Lou Gehrig's disease and cystic fibrosis, may set the ethical and legal precedents we need. When respirators are withdrawn and medication is given to ease the withdrawal and hasten death, we see the horizon of new ethical possibility. The case of Sidney Greenspan teaches us another level of moral response in cases involving withdrawal of feeding. Mr. Greenspan, in vegetative state for seven years, was finally allowed by court, family, physician, and guardian to have the feeding mechanisms withdraw. Rather than accompany this decision with instructions to carefully guide him into death with analgesia, the judge left the situation hanging. He even posed the absurd option of trying to feed him orally, perhaps precipitating an aspiration pneumonia death, a final expression of our moral paralysis. We should not only allow but help our Sidney Greenspans and Baby Does to die. To stop heroic life support then plead bad conscience so that we can only "let nature take its course," is not morally worthy of humanistically and theistically mature people.

We have exerted vigorous efforts to forestall death and prolong life. Much of the effort has been salutary, granting significant measure of longer and better living to some people. Some of the effort has been futile, even harmful. In the care of dying patients, a moral category since Hippocrates that we have now abandoned, we often tie a complicated knot tethering the patient down to a miserable and prolonged dying. We need to find the moral courage in these days to disentangle that knot so that the cord of life can be broken and the person be set free.

Helping Death Along?

Even from the conservative side of our moral heritage, as we have seen in theological and eschatological purview, receiving impending death, not delaying or resisting the angel of death, dying one's own death, can be seen as virtue not violation of divine prerogative. Can we gently nudge this conviction one step further and allow the hastening of a disease course? Three therapeutic modes of response are possible when confronted with terminal diseases. We can resist with all force and seek to stop or exorcise the morbid process. Sometimes this is good, and it works; often it fails. We can also back off and allow a disease to "run its course." Sometimes "the course" is swift and sure, other times it can become gruesome and agonizing. Sometimes it can stall and leave one severely debilitated but still alive. The third course would be to facilitate and ease the way for death along a given vector.

Ethics is clear in its emphasis that conceding to disease is not killing. What about helping along the mortal elements in malignancy, Alzheimer's disease, lung and liver disease, kidney failure, coronary and vascular disease, infection? Clearly there are a range of morbid and mortal potentialities in every disease condition. It may well be a therapeutically sound and morally licit choice to guide the trajectory of disease in one way rather than another. Specific decisions will be matters of precise clinical judgment and detailed dialogue between clinician and patient. In general, choosing the specific path of one's death may be every bit as responsible as faithfully waiting for whatever life brings. Either posture finds moral grounding as it affirms duty toward self and others and God.

Dying in the Midst of One's People

Throughout this work I have offered the suggestion of a different setting for one's dying. Must one meet his or her end alone, in a clinical labyrinth or surrounded by the intrusion of attorneys and bureaucrats? We do need a supportive community for personally bearable death and society needs representation to insure against mischief and evil. The presence of community in this supportive and monitoring function can best come from one's own moral or faith community. Can we marshal the enormous potential in these voluntary communities to shepherd ourselves into better deaths. In our homes or in hospices built into our temples, churches, synagogues, or mosques, the community of faith can gather around us as we prepare to die. Ritual and sacrament, prayer and fellowship can revive the historic meanings of religious ministry and meet the person's special need at the moment for deep understanding, a context of meaning and a theater to exert one's final ministry to others.

Coming to the end of a book like this may be in some small way an experience like the subject it has explored. One feels empty and beat, yet strangely grateful and hopeful. You hope your publisher will like it and that your readers will find it helpful. If Aristotle is right in saying that no one should attempt philosophy until he is fifty, perhaps even one that old should never be foolish enough to attempt discourse on the mystery of death. The reader will decide whether this was an exercise in edification or futility. I can only thank my teachers, especially those who have gone out into that valley of shadow where one finds a companion in whom death will be no more.

Notes

Introduction

1. W. S. Gilbert, *Plays and Poems* (New York: Random House, 1932), 469.

2. Kenneth Vaux, *Birth Ethics: Religious and Cultural Values and the Genesis of Life* (New York: Crossroad, 1989).

3. *Cruzan vs. Director,* Missouri Department of Health, United States Supreme Court, June 25, 1990.

4. Lisa Belkin, "Hospital to Seek an End to Woman's Life Support," *New York Times* (11 June 1991):1A, 3.

5. Kenneth Vaux, "Medicide: A Matter of Life and Death," *Chicago Tribune* (11 November 1991), sec. 1, p. 15.

1. The Philosophical Ethics of Suicide

1. John M. Cooper, "Greek Philosophers on Euthanasia and Suicide," in Baruch A. Brody, ed., *Suicide and Euthanasia* (Dordrecht: Kluwer, 1988), 12.

2. Ibid., 10ff.

3. Ibid., 12ff.

4. Cicero, *de finibus* III 60, 61. Quoted in John M. Cooper, "Greek Philosophers," 27.

5. David Hume, "Of Suicide," in *Essays: Moral, Political and Literary* (Oxford: Oxford University Press, 1963) and "On Suicide" in J. Lenz, ed., *On the Standards of Taste and Other Essays* (Indianapolis: Bobbs-Merrill, 1975), 11.

6. The great English jurist, Sir William Blackstone (1723–80),

called suicide a cowardly act and crime against self, the King [depriving him of a subject], and God himself [for rushing into his presence uncalled for].

7. Albert Camus, *The Myth of Sisyphus* (London: Penguin Press, 1975), 11.

8. Martin Heidegger, *Being and Time* (London: Kroft, 1962), 22.

9. Robert J. Lifton, *The Nazi Doctors* (New York: Basic Books, 1986).

10. Henk Rigter, "Euthanasia in the Netherlands: Distinguishing Facts from Fiction," *Hastings Center Report* (January/February 1989 Special Supplement): 31.

11. "Level of Care Determination in Acute Care Patients and How It Relates to a Terminal Patient with a 'No Code Status,' " *Field Instruction Notice 5-81* to Field Office Administrators Medical Consultants and HCSN. From Stephen Harrison, Asst. Chief, Field Services Section (6 February 1981).

12. Daniel Callahan, "Editorial," *Hastings Center Report* (January/February 1989 Special Supplement): 28.

13. Lonnie D. Kliever, *"Dax's Case": Essays in Medical Ethics and Human Meaning* (Dallas: SMU Press, 1989).

14. Andrew H. Malcom, "To Suffer A Prolonged Illness or Elect to Die," *New York Times* (6 December 1984): 1, 18.

15. Jean Jaques Rousseau, *Julie, Ou la Nouvelle Heloise* (New York: French & European Pubns, Inc., 1963).

2. Theological Ethics and Euthanasia

1. Margaret Mead, *Blackberry Winter* (New York: Simon and Schuster, 1972), 283.

2. Baruch A. Brody, "A Historical Introduction to Jewish Casuistry on Suicide and Euthanasia" in Brody, ed., *Suicide and Euthanasia* (Dordrecht: Kluwer, 1989), 39.

3. Immanuel Jacobovits, *Jewish Medical Ethics*, 2nd ed. (New York: Bloch, 1975), 276.

4. Brody, "Historical Introduction," 73, 74.

5. *The Journals of Søren Kirkegaard*, ed. Alexander Dru (Oxford: Oxford University Press, 1938), 603.

6. Jane Mellow, "Report on the 8th World Congress of the

World Federation of Right to Die Societies," *Ethics and Medicine* (Autumn 1990): 43.

7. John Donne, *Biathanatos*, M. Ruddice and M.P. Battin, eds. (New York: Garland, 1982), i.

8. Hesiod, *The Poems and Fragments*, trans. A. W. Mair (Oxford: Clarendon Press, 1908): 110–20.

9. *New York Times* (21 October 1984): 1.

10. A Deadly Serious Dilemma: Evaluating the Right to Die," *Insight* (26 January 1987): 12ff.

11. Francis Bacon, *The Advancement of Learning (1605)* and *Novum Organum (1620)*.

12. Suetonius Tranquillus, *The Lives of the Twelve Caesars*, trans. Alexander Thomas (New York: R. Worthington, 1983), 164–65.

13. Jerry B. Wilson, *Death by Decision: The Medical, Moral, and Legal Dilemmas of Euthanasia* (Philadelphia: Westminster Press, 1975), 25.

14. Ibid., 36, 37.

15. Ibid., 37, 38.

16. Ivan Illich, *Medical Nemesis* (New York: Pantheon, 1978), 175–76.

3. Biology, Ethics, and Letting Nature Take Its Course

1. Michael Ruse, *Taking Darwin Seriously* (Oxford: Basil Blackwell, 1986), 72.

2. W. B. Yeats, "Death," in *Collected Poems*, Definitive Edition (New York: Macmillan, 1956), 322.

3. See Ludwig Edelstein, *The Meaning of Stoicism* (Cambridge: Harvard University Press, 1966).

4. Theodosious Dobzhansky, "An Essay on Religion, Death and Evolutionary Adaptation," *Zygon* 1, no. 4 (December 1966): 320–24.

5. Charles Darwin, *The Descent of Man*, vol. 1 (London: John Murray, 1871), 168.

6. Samuel Hartlib, *Chymical Addresses*, 1655 Appendix. Quoted in Charles Webster, *The Great Instauration* (New York: Holmes and Meier, 1975), 246, 247.

7. S. J. Olshansky, et al., "In Search of Methuselah: Estimating

the Upper Limits to Human Longevity," *Science* 250 (2 November 1990): 634.

8. Alastair McIntyre, "Seven Traits for the Future," *Hastings Center Report* 9 (February 1979): 5–7.

9. Herbert Spencer, "A Theory of Population," *Westminster Review* n.s. 1:468–501.

10. Peter Singer, *Practical Ethics* (Cambridge: Cambridge University Press, 1978).

11. C. S. Lewis, *The Problem of Pain* (London: Centenary Press, 1940).

12. Edward O. Wilson, *Sociobiology: The New Synthesis* (Cambridge: Harvard University Press, 1975), 128, 129

13. Kenneth Vaux, *Will to Live/Will to Die: Ethics and the Search for Good Death* (Minneapolis: Augsburg Publishing House, 1978).

14. Elizabeth Kübler-Ross, *On Death and Dying* (London: Tavistock), 1970.

15. See Robert Williams, *Textbook of Endocrinology,* ed. Jean S. Wilson and Daniel W. Foster (Philadelphia: W.B. Saunders, 1981), 1, 2.

16. Geoffrey Gorer, *Death, Grief and Mourning* (New York: Doubleday, 1967).

17. Augustine, *Confessions,* ed. E. B. Pusey (Oxford: Parker, 1843), 48ff.

18. In this section I have been aided by David Smail, *Illusion and Healing: The Meanings of Anxiety* (London: J.M. Dent and Sons, 1984).

19. Granger E. Westberg, *Good Grief* (Philadelphia: Fortress Press, 1962).

20. C. S. Lewis, *A Grief Observed* (London: Faber and Faber, 1961), 23, 24.

21. James F. Fries, "Aging and Natural Death and the Compression of Morbidity," *New England Journal of Medicine* 303 (17 July 1980): 130–35.

22. Edward J. Schneider, et al., "Aging, Natural Death and the Compression of Morbidity: Another View," *New England Journal of Medicine* 309 (6 October 1983): 854–55.

23. Olshansky, "In Search of Methuselah," 634ff.

24. Ibid., 639.

25. Sidney H. Wanzer, et al., "The Physician's Responsibility

toward Hopelessly Ill Patients,'' *New England Journal of Medicine* 320 (30 March 1989): 844–49.

26. ''Assisted Death,'' Institute of Medical Ethics Working Party on the Ethics of Prolonging Life and Assisting Death, *The Lancet* 336 (8 September 1990): 610–13.

27. Wanzer, ''Physician's Responsibility,'' 844.

28. Ibid., 848.

29. ''Assisted Death,'' 610.

30. Ibid, 612.

31. Ibid., 613.

4. The Ecological Background of Mortality and Ethics

1. Homer, *Iliad*, trans. Richard Lattimore (Chicago: University of Chicago Press, 1951), 146.

2. Paul W. Taylor, *Respect for Nature* (Princeton: Princeton University Press, 1986).

3. Henry David Thoreau, quoted in Bill McKibben, *The End of Nature* (London: Viking, 1990), 196.

4. Walter Brueggemann, ''Land, Fertility, and Justice,'' in *Theology of the Land*, ed. Leonard Weber et al. (Collegeville, Minn: The Liturgical Press, 1987).

5. Wendell Berry, *Recollected Essays 1965–80* (San Francisco: North Point Press, 1981), 215.

6. Ibid., 191.

7. Brueggemann, ''Land, Fertility, and Justice,'' 42.

8. Lynn White, Jr., ''The Historical Roots of Our Ecological Crisis,'' *Science* 155 (1967): 1203–1207.

9. Tanhuma Berakha, sec. 7.

10. Ibid., sec. 8.

11. Gerhard von Rad, *God at Work in Israel* (Nashville: Abingdon, 1980), 90ff.

12. Anthony Kenny, *The Logic of Deterrence* (London: Firethorn Press, 1985), 3.

13. Lewis Thomas, ''Foreward,'' in Paul R. Erlich, et al., *The Nuclear Winter* (London: Sidgwick and Jackson, 1984), xxi.

14. Ibid.

15. An excellent study of this aspect of responsibility, nuclear danger, and ecocide is Jonathan Schell, *The Fate of the Earth* (London: Jonathan Cape, 1982).

16. Bill McKibben, *The End of Nature* (London: Viking Press, 1990).

17. Ibid., 42.

18. John Milton, *Paradise Lost*, Book VIII, vss. 100ff.

19. Schell, *Fate,* 127.

20. Hans Morgenthau, "Death in the Nuclear Age," *Commentary* (September 1961).

21. Daniel Callahan, *Setting Limits: Medical Goals in an Aging Society* (New York: Simon and Schuster, 1987).

22. Rene Dubos, *So Human an Animal* (New York: Scribner, 1984).

23. Derek Humphrey, "The Right to Die," *Rochester Democrat and Chronicle* (27 August 1985; 8 September 1985).

5. Historic Ethics and Genocide

1. Arno J. Mayer, *Why Did the Heavens Not Darken? The Final Solution in History* (New York: Pantheon Books, 1989), ii.

2. Raphael Lemkin, *Axis Rule in Occupied Europe* (Washington: Carnegie Endowment for World Peace, 1944), 79.

3. Leo Kuper, *The Prevention of Genocide* (New Haven: Yale University Press, 1985).

4. Leipzig: F. Meinser, 1920. Further reference on this concept and program is developed in Ernst Klee, "Euthanasia," in N.S. Stodt, *Die Vernichtung Lebensunwerten Lebens,"* (Frankfurt: M.S. Fisher, 1983).

5. Quoted in Robert J. Lifton, *The Nazi Doctors: Medical Killing and the Psychology of Genocide* (New York: Basic Books, 1986).

6. *Time* Magazine (10 November 1986): 79.

7. Ivan Illich, *Medical Nemesis* (London: Marion Boyars, 1976), 185, 186.

8. Earl Shelp and Ron Sunderland, "AIDS and the Church," *Christian Century* (11-18 September 1986). Kenneth Vaux, "AIDS as Crisis and Opportunity," *Christian Century* (16 October 1985): 910–11. John Godges, "Meeting the AIDS Challenge in San Francisco," *Christian Century* (10–17 September, 1986): 771.

9. Elie Wiesel, "Foreword," *Jews and Christians after the Holocaust,* Abraham J. Peck, ed. (Philadelphia: Fortress Press, 1982), xi.

10. Letter to Earl of Hertford, May 1544, M. St. Clare-Byrne, *Elizabethian Life in Town and Country* (London: Methuen, 1901), 346.

11. Sir Robert Wilson, "A Medico-Literary Causerie Euthanasia," *Practictioner* 56 (1896): 631–35.

6. Legalistic Ethics and the Lingering Doubt about Withdrawing Life Supports

1. In the Supreme Court, the State of California and for the County of Riverside, *Elizabeth Bouvia v. County of Riverside, et al.,* No. 159780, V. 9, 1238–1250. Reporter's transcript.

2. Quoted in Irving S. Sloan, *The Right to Die: Legal and Ethical Problems* (London: Oceana Publications, 1988), 5.

3. Richard Epstein, "Voluntary Euthanasia," *The Law School Record* 35 (Spring 1989): 10.

4. Ibid., 11.

5. Ibid.

6. Ibid.

7. Paul Ramsey, *Ethics at the Edges of Life* (New Haven: Yale University Press, 1978), 317.

8. For a full discussion of *Cruzan,* see "Cruzan: Clear and Convincing?" *Hastings Center Report* 20 (September-October 1990): 5ff.

9. "Euthanasia in the Netherlands," *Hippocrates* (September/October, 1989): 60.

10. "Thatcher Rule Made Wealthy More Healthy," *London Times* (2 January 1991): 18.

7. The Ethics of Secular Eschatology: Death and the Scientific Future

1. See Charles Webster, *The Great Instauration* (New York: Holmes and Meier, 1975), 250.

2. Hastings Center, *Guidelines on the Termination of Life-Sustaining Treatment and the Care of the Dying* (New York: Hastings-on-Hudson, 1987).

3. "Ethical and Moral Guidelines for the Initiation, Continua-

tion and Withdrawal of Intensive Care,'' *Chest* 97:4 (April 1990): 949–58.

4. Susan Sontag, *AIDS and Its Metaphors* (London: Penguin, 1988).

5. Ibid., 14.

6. Arnold Toynbee and Daisaker Ikeda, *Choose Life: A Dialogue* (Oxford: Oxford University Press), 29.

7. Ibid., 100.

8. Death and the Sacred Future: Eschatological Ethics

1. Richard Rubenstein, "Thomas Altizer's Apocalypse," in John B. Cobb, Jr., ed., *The Theology of Altizer: Critique and Response* (Philadelphia: Westminster Press, 1970), 133.

2. *Johann Sebastian Bach: Heritage and Obligation* (New Haven: Yale University Press, 1952).

3. *The Epic of Gilgamesh*, trans. Nancy Sandars (New York: Penguin, 1960), 5ff.

4. Ibid., 99.

5. *Odyssey* IV.

6. Otto Kaiser and Edward Lohse, *Death and Life*, trans. by John E. Steely (Nashville: Abingdon, 1981), 32.

7. Friedrich Nietzsche, quoted in Kaiser and Lohse, *Death and Life*, 74.

8. Kaiser and Lohse, *Death and Life*, 88, 89.

9. Ibid., 94ff.

10. Rabbi Ammi, *Babylonian Talmud* Sabbath 550, AD 300. Quoted in W. Harnisch, *Verhängnis and Verheitsung der Geschichte* (Göttingen, 1969).

11. Søren Kierkegaard, *For Self-Examination* (Princeton: Princeton University Press, 1944).

12. Hans Jonas, *The Phenomenon of Life* (Chicago: University of Chicago Press, 1966), 14.

13. Ibid., 19.

14. Ibid., 24.

15. Nikos Kazantzakis, *The Saviors of God*, trans. Kimon Friar (New York: Simon and Schuster, 1960), 93.

16. In the shower, rain or thunderstorm of life we reluctantly send

the children out. Yet we finally send them, and we ourselves go out not into storm but into the arms of our true home.

17. This is my own summary of the play.

18. Ernst Bloch, *The Principle of Hope* (Oxford: Basil Blackwell, 1986), 182.

19. Ibid., 1096.

20. Ibid., 1100.

21. Ibid., 1101.

22. Karl Rahner, *On the Theology of Death* (New York: Herder and Herder, 1965).

23. Ibid., 27.

24. Karl Rahner and Herbert Vongrimer, *Theological Dictionary* (New York: Herder and Herder, 1965), 117.

25. Karl Rahner, *Theological Investigations*, vol. 4 (New York: Crossroad), 348.

Index of Biblical References

Index of Names and Subjects